MS. MARVEL
CIVIL

WRITER: *BRIAN REED*
PENCILS: *ROBERTO DE LA TORRE & MIKE WIERINGO*
INKS: *JON SIBAL & WADE VON GRAWBADGER*
COLORS: *CHRIS SOTOMAYOR*
LETTERS: *DAVE SHARPE*
COVER ART: *DAVID MACK & MIKE WIERINGO*

MS. MARVEL SPECIAL
WRITER: *BRIAN REED*
PENCILS: *GIUSEPPE CAMUNCOLI*
INKS: *LORENZO RUGGIERO*
COLORS: *CHRIS SOTOMAYOR*
LETTERS: *DAVE SHARPE*
COVER ART: *GIUSEPPE CAMUNCOLI*

ASSISTANT EDITOR: *DANIEL KETCHUM*
EDITOR: *ANDY SCHMIDT*

COLLECTION EDITOR: *JENNIFER GRÜNWALD*
ASSISTANT EDITORS: *CORY LEVINE & MICHAEL SHORT*
ASSOCIATE EDITOR: *MARK D. BEAZLEY*
SENIOR EDITOR, SPECIAL PROJECTS: *JEFF YOUNGQUIST*
SENIOR VICE PRESIDENT OF SALES: *DAVID GABRIEL*
PRODUCTION: *JERRON QUALITY COLOR*
CREATIVE DIRECTOR: *TOM MARVELLI*

EDITOR IN CHIEF: *JOE QUESADA*
PUBLISHER: *DAN BUCKLEY*

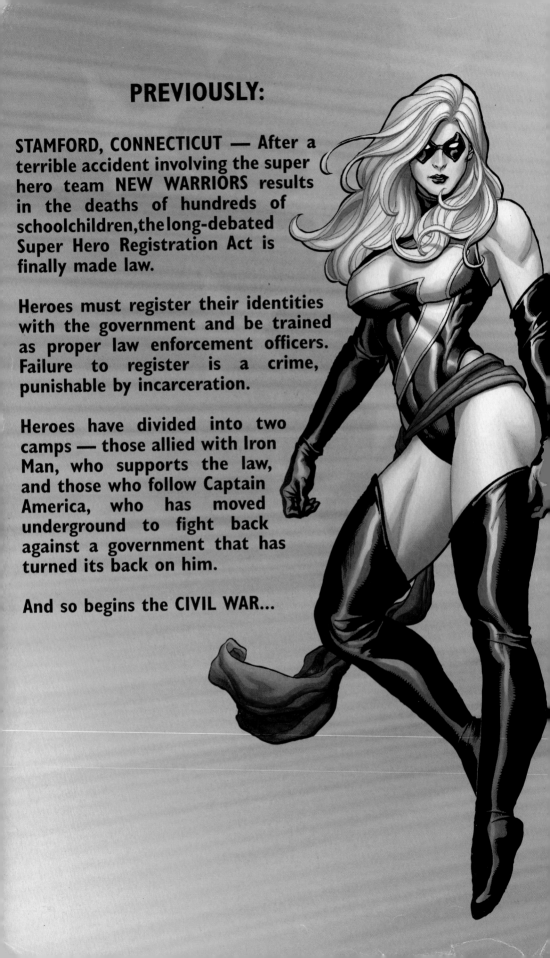

PREVIOUSLY:

STAMFORD, CONNECTICUT — After a terrible accident involving the super hero team NEW WARRIORS results in the deaths of hundreds of schoolchildren, the long-debated Super Hero Registration Act is finally made law.

Heroes must register their identities with the government and be trained as proper law enforcement officers. Failure to register is a crime, punishable by incarceration.

Heroes have divided into two camps — those allied with Iron Man, who supports the law, and those who follow Captain America, who has moved underground to fight back against a government that has turned its back on him.

And so begins the CIVIL WAR...

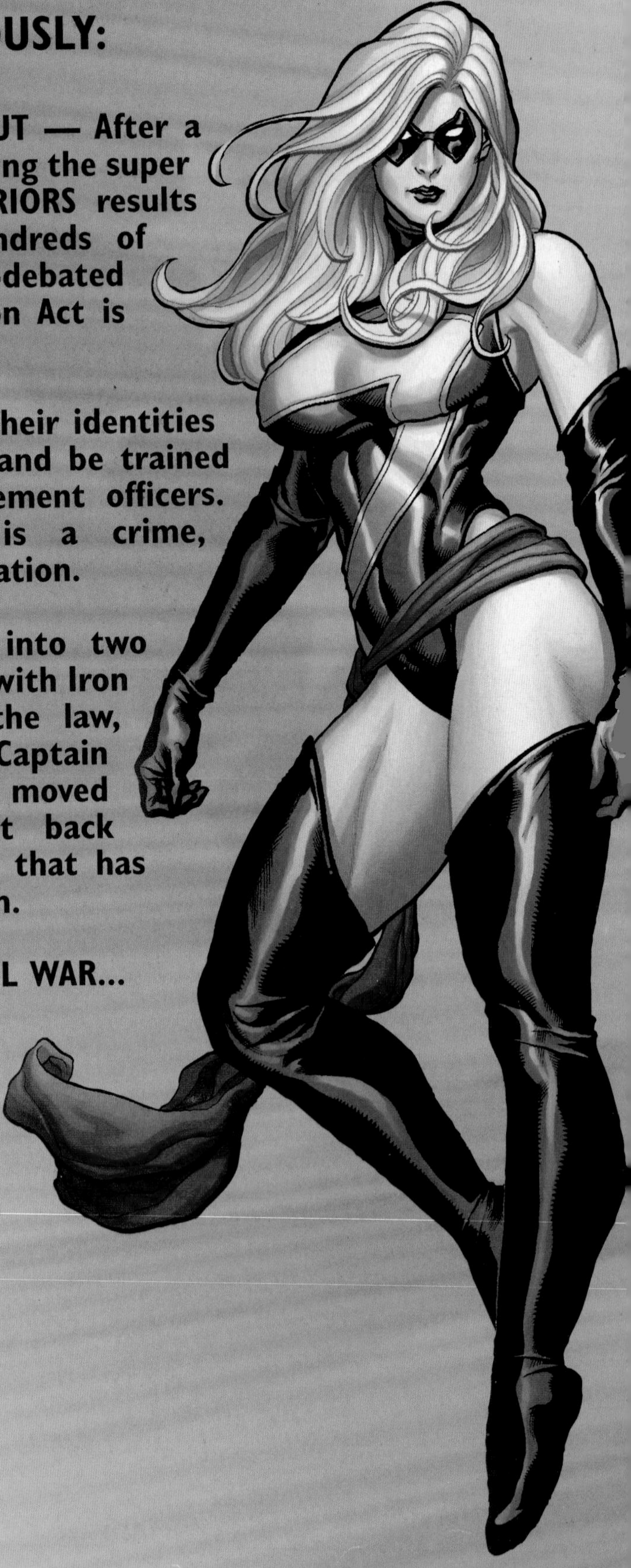

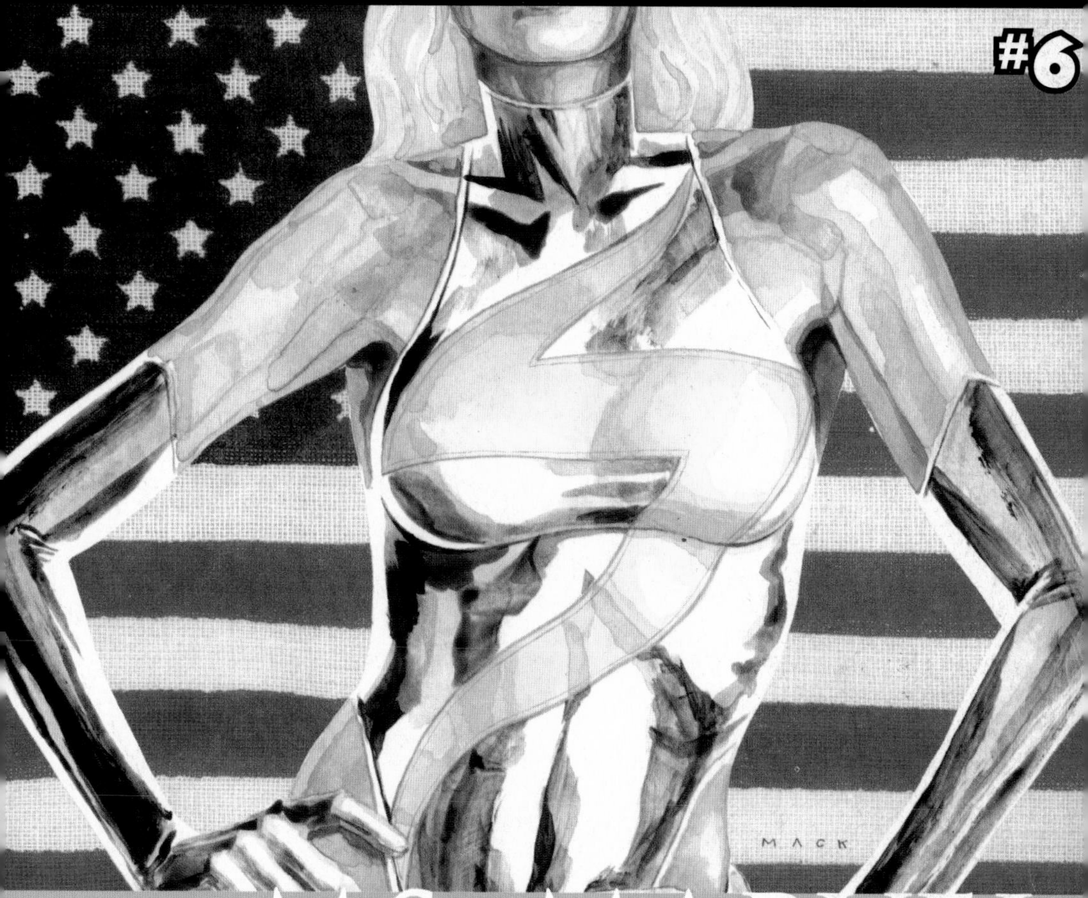
#6
MACK

MS. MARVEL

A MARVEL COMICS EVENT

CIVIL WAR

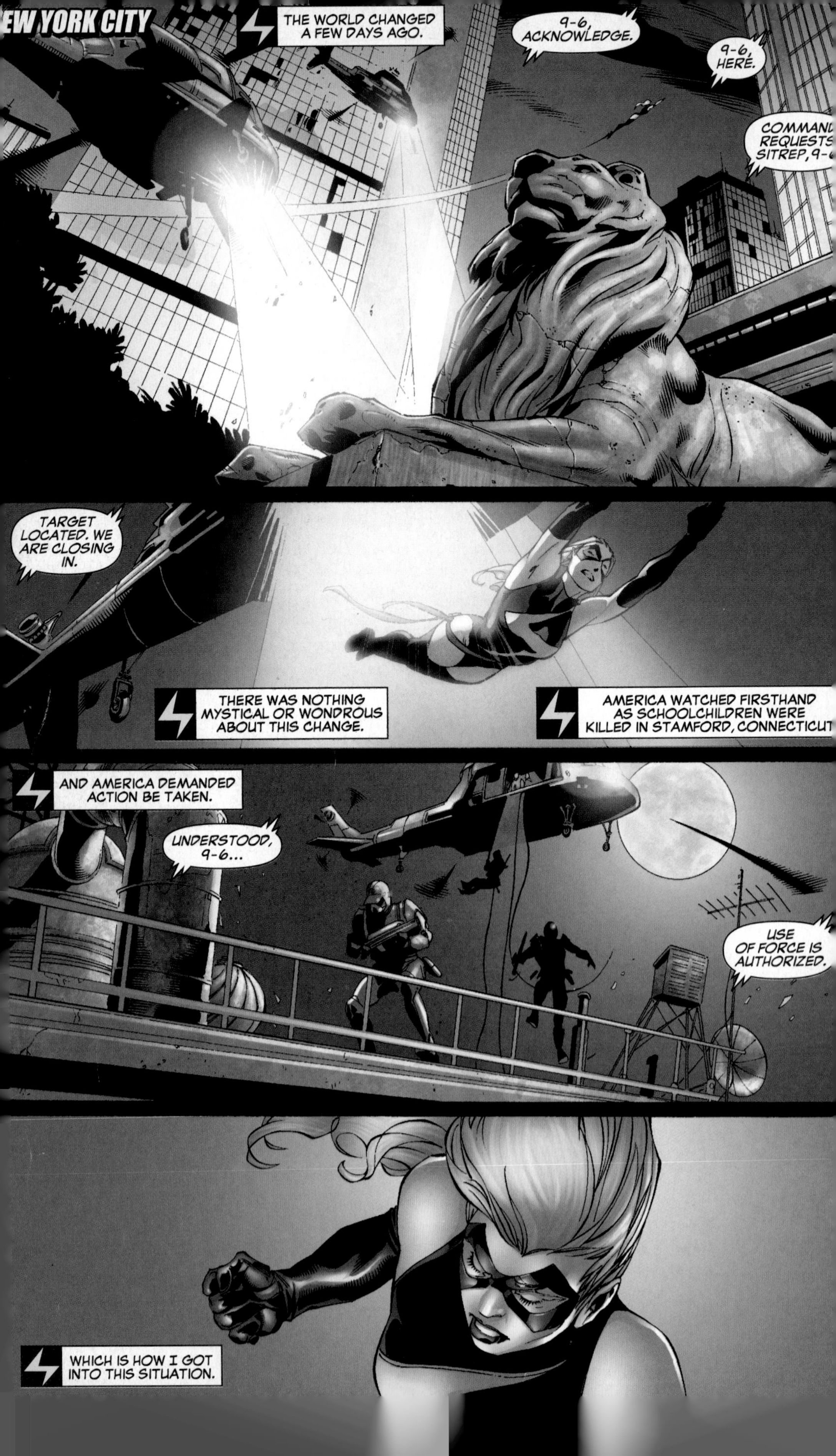
EW YORK CITY
THE WORLD CHANGED A FEW DAYS AGO.
9-6, ACKNOWLEDGE.
9-6, HERE.
COMMAND REQUESTS SITREP, 9-6
TARGET LOCATED. WE ARE CLOSING IN.
THERE WAS NOTHING MYSTICAL OR WONDROUS ABOUT THIS CHANGE.
AMERICA WATCHED FIRSTHAND AS SCHOOLCHILDREN WERE KILLED IN STAMFORD, CONNECTICUT
AND AMERICA DEMANDED ACTION BE TAKEN.
UNDERSTOOD, 9-6...
USE OF FORCE IS AUTHORIZED.
WHICH IS HOW I GOT INTO THIS SITUATION.

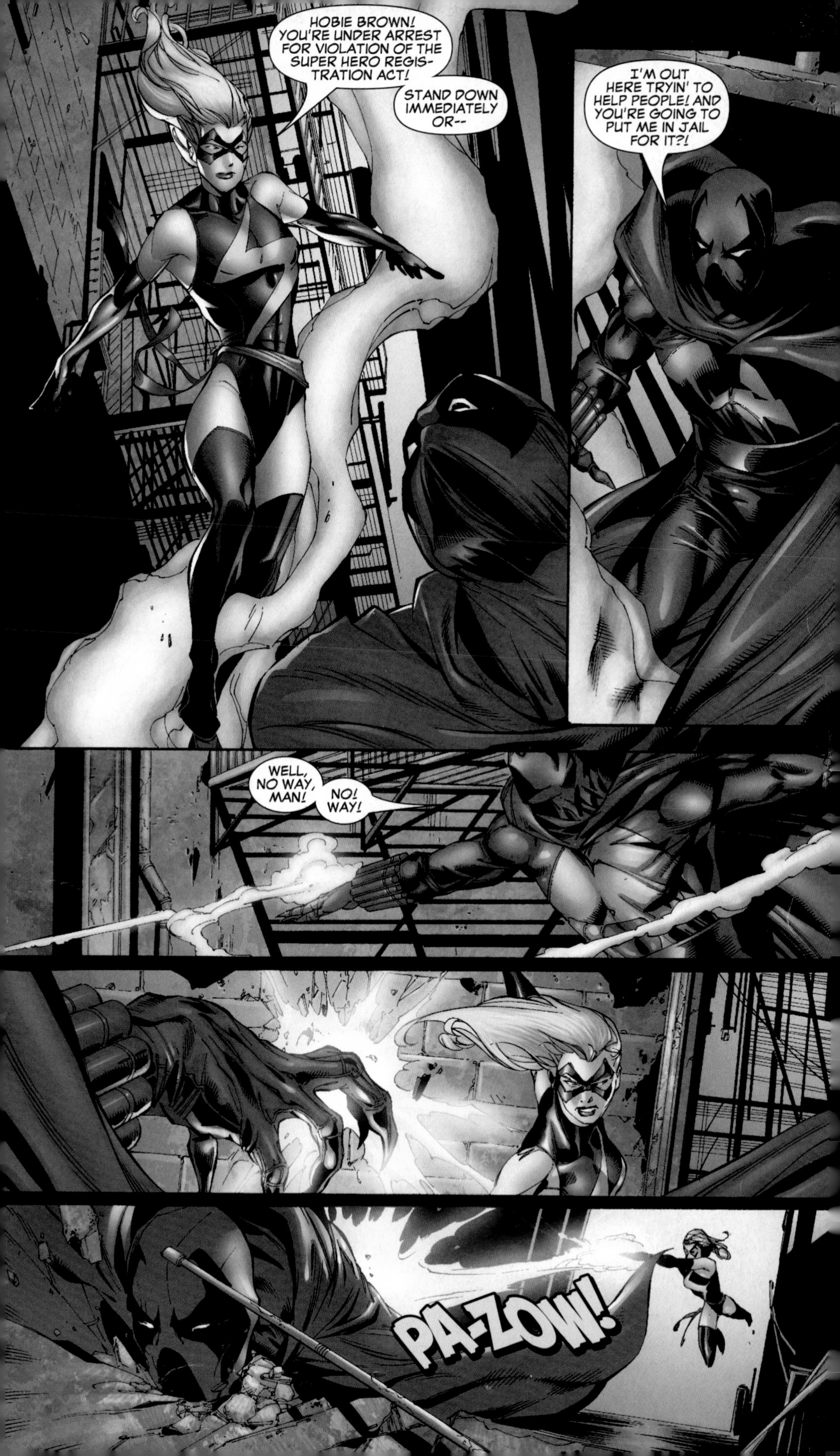
HOBIE BROWN! YOU'RE UNDER ARREST FOR VIOLATION OF THE SUPER HERO REGIS-TRATION ACT!
STAND DOWN IMMEDIATELY OR--
I'M OUT HERE TRYIN' TO HELP PEOPLE! AND YOU'RE GOING TO PUT ME IN JAIL FOR IT?!
WELL, NO WAY, MAN!
NO! WAY!
PA-ZOW!

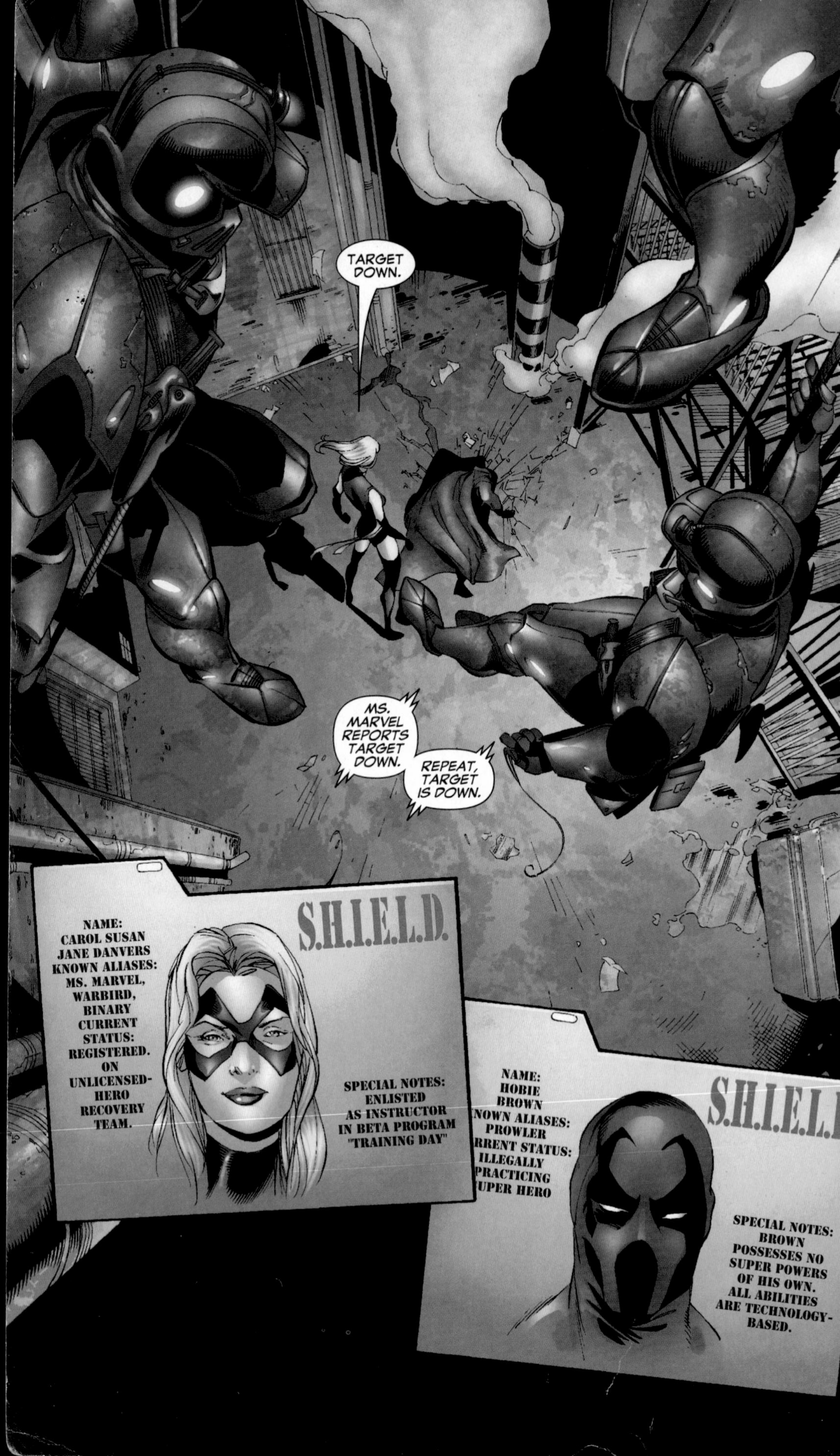

TARGET DOWN.
MS. MARVEL REPORTS TARGET DOWN.
REPEAT, TARGET IS DOWN.
S.H.I.E.L.D.
NAME: CAROL SUSAN JANE DANVERS
KNOWN ALIASES: MS. MARVEL, WARBIRD, BINARY
CURRENT STATUS: REGISTERED. ON UNLICENSED-HERO RECOVERY TEAM.
SPECIAL NOTES: ENLISTED AS INSTRUCTOR IN BETA PROGRAM "TRAINING DAY"
S.H.I.E.L.
NAME: HOBIE BROWN
NOWN ALIASES: PROWLER
RRENT STATUS: ILLEGALLY PRACTICING UPER HERO
SPECIAL NOTES: BROWN POSSESSES NO SUPER POWERS OF HIS OWN. ALL ABILITIES ARE TECHNOLOGY-BASED.

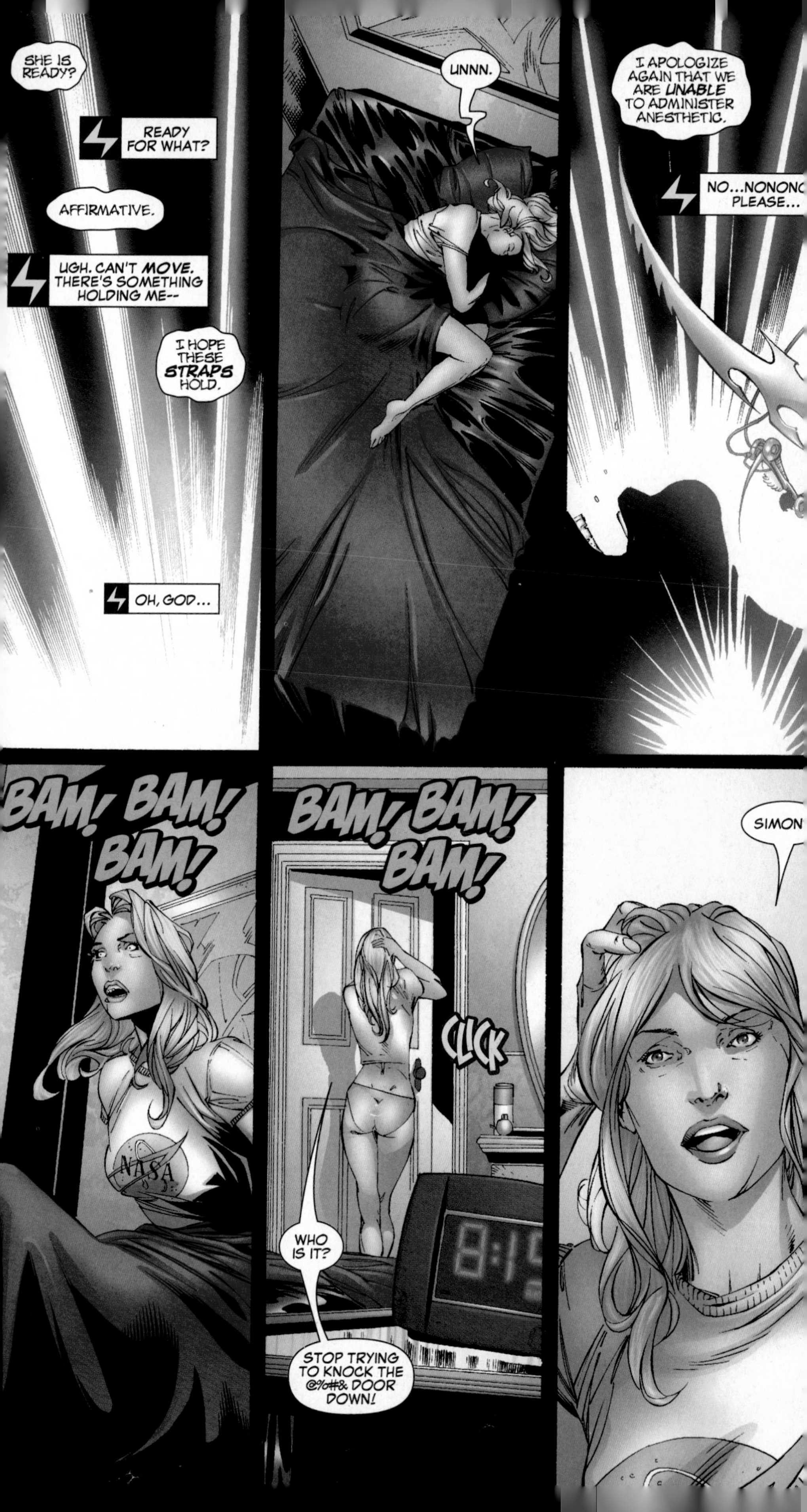
SHE IS READY?
READY FOR WHAT?
AFFIRMATIVE.
UGH. CAN'T MOVE. THERE'S SOMETHING HOLDING ME--
I HOPE THESE STRAPS HOLD.
OH, GOD...
UNNN.
I APOLOGIZE AGAIN THAT WE ARE UNABLE TO ADMINISTER ANESTHETIC.
NO...NONONO PLEASE...
BAM! BAM! BAM!
NASA
BAM! BAM! BAM!
CLICK
WHO IS IT?
STOP TRYING TO KNOCK THE @%#& DOOR DOWN!
SIMON

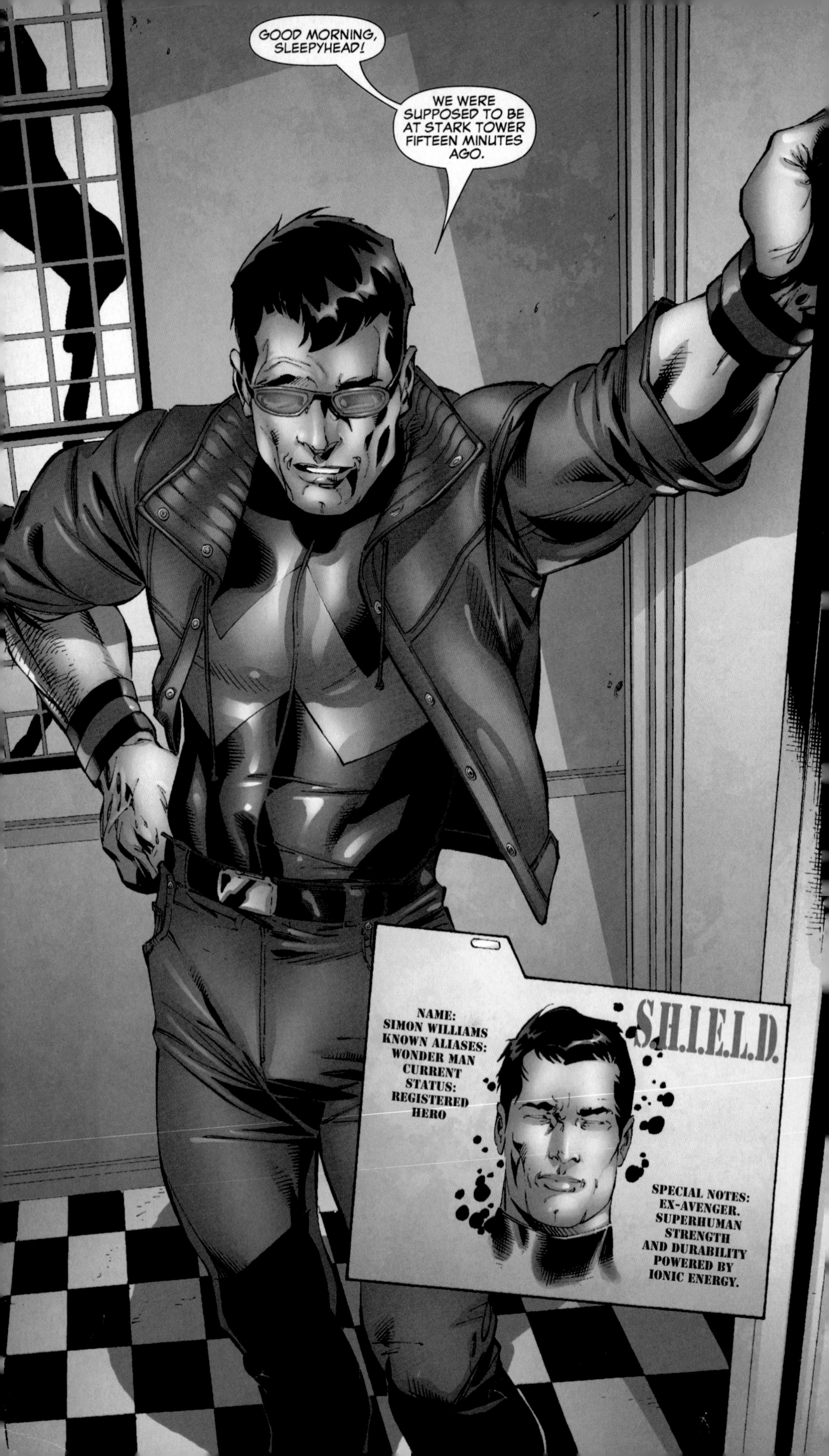
GOOD MORNING, SLEEPYHEAD!
WE WERE SUPPOSED TO BE AT STARK TOWER FIFTEEN MINUTES AGO.
S.H.I.E.L.D.
NAME: SIMON WILLIAMS KNOWN ALIASES: WONDER MAN CURRENT STATUS: REGISTERED HERO
SPECIAL NOTES: EX-AVENGER. SUPERHUMAN STRENGTH AND DURABILITY POWERED BY IONIC ENERGY.

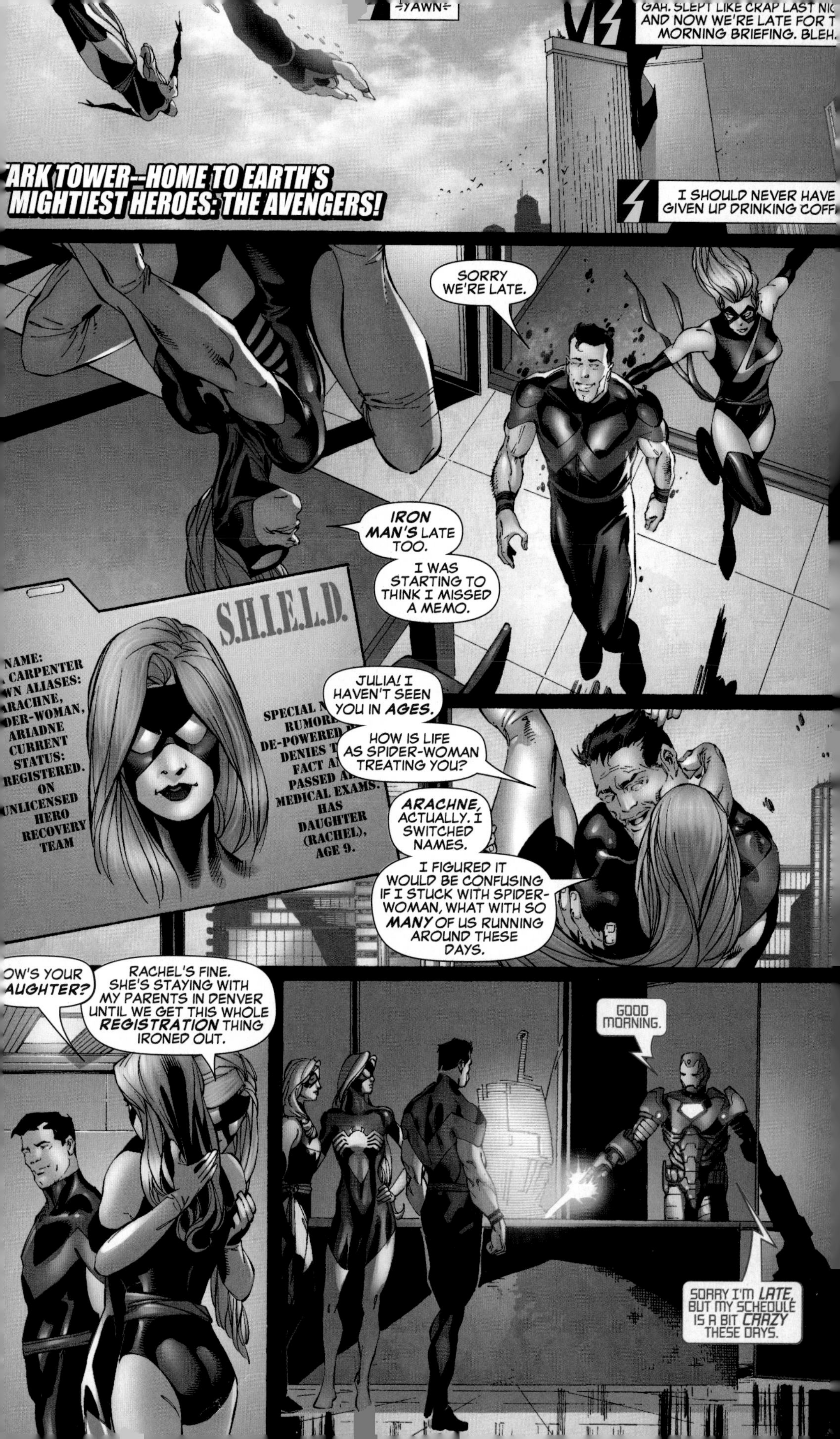

=YAWN=
GAH. SLEPT LIKE CRAP LAST NIG AND NOW WE'RE LATE FOR T MORNING BRIEFING. BLEH.
ARK TOWER--HOME TO EARTH'S MIGHTIEST HEROES: THE AVENGERS!
I SHOULD NEVER HAVE GIVEN UP DRINKING COFF
SORRY WE'RE LATE.
IRON MAN'S LATE TOO.
I WAS STARTING TO THINK I MISSED A MEMO.
S.H.I.E.L.D.
NAME: CARPENTER
WN ALIASES: ARACHNE, DER-WOMAN, ARIADNE
CURRENT STATUS: REGISTERED. ON UNLICENSED HERO RECOVERY TEAM
SPECIAL N RUMORE DE-POWERED DENIES T FACT A PASSED A MEDICAL EXAMS. HAS DAUGHTER (RACHEL), AGE 9.
JULIA! I HAVEN'T SEEN YOU IN AGES.
HOW IS LIFE AS SPIDER-WOMAN TREATING YOU?
ARACHNE, ACTUALLY. I SWITCHED NAMES.
I FIGURED IT WOULD BE CONFUSING IF I STUCK WITH SPIDER-WOMAN, WHAT WITH SO MANY OF US RUNNING AROUND THESE DAYS.
OW'S YOUR AUGHTER?
RACHEL'S FINE. SHE'S STAYING WITH MY PARENTS IN DENVER UNTIL WE GET THIS WHOLE REGISTRATION THING IRONED OUT.
GOOD MORNING.
SORRY I'M LATE, BUT MY SCHEDULE IS A BIT CRAZY THESE DAYS.

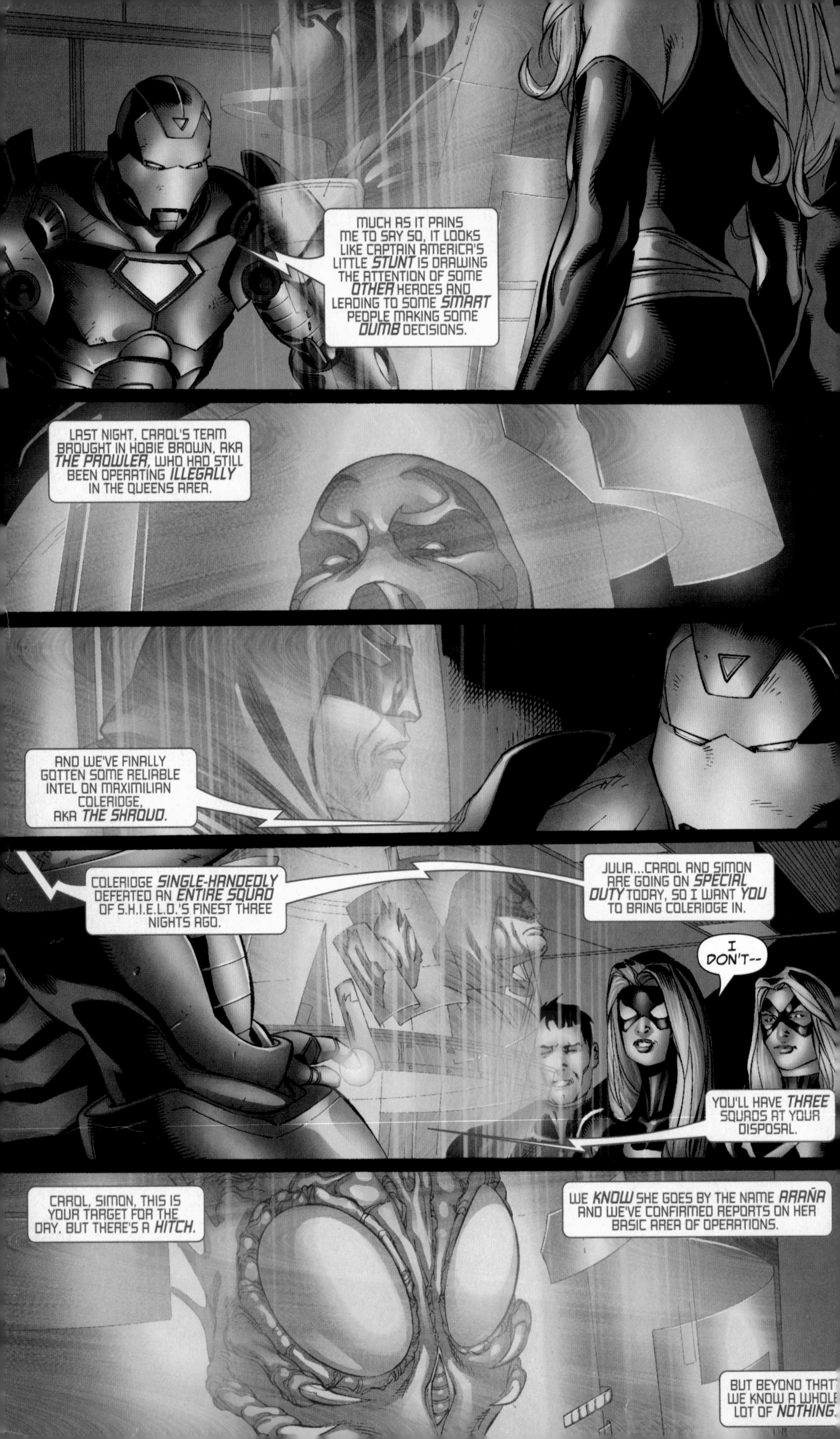
MUCH AS IT PAINS ME TO SAY SO, IT LOOKS LIKE CAPTAIN AMERICA'S LITTLE STUNT IS DRAWING THE ATTENTION OF SOME OTHER HEROES AND LEADING TO SOME SMART PEOPLE MAKING SOME DUMB DECISIONS.
LAST NIGHT, CAROL'S TEAM BROUGHT IN HOBIE BROWN, AKA THE PROWLER, WHO HAD STILL BEEN OPERATING ILLEGALLY IN THE QUEENS AREA.
AND WE'VE FINALLY GOTTEN SOME RELIABLE INTEL ON MAXIMILIAN COLERIDGE, AKA THE SHROUD.
COLERIDGE SINGLE-HANDEDLY DEFEATED AN ENTIRE SQUAD OF S.H.I.E.L.D.'S FINEST THREE NIGHTS AGO.
JULIA...CAROL AND SIMON ARE GOING ON SPECIAL DUTY TODAY, SO I WANT YOU TO BRING COLERIDGE IN.
I DON'T--
YOU'LL HAVE THREE SQUADS AT YOUR DISPOSAL.
CAROL, SIMON, THIS IS YOUR TARGET FOR THE DAY. BUT THERE'S A HITCH.
WE KNOW SHE GOES BY THE NAME ARAÑA AND WE'VE CONFIRMED REPORTS ON HER BASIC AREA OF OPERATIONS.
BUT BEYOND THAT WE KNOW A WHOLE LOT OF NOTHING.

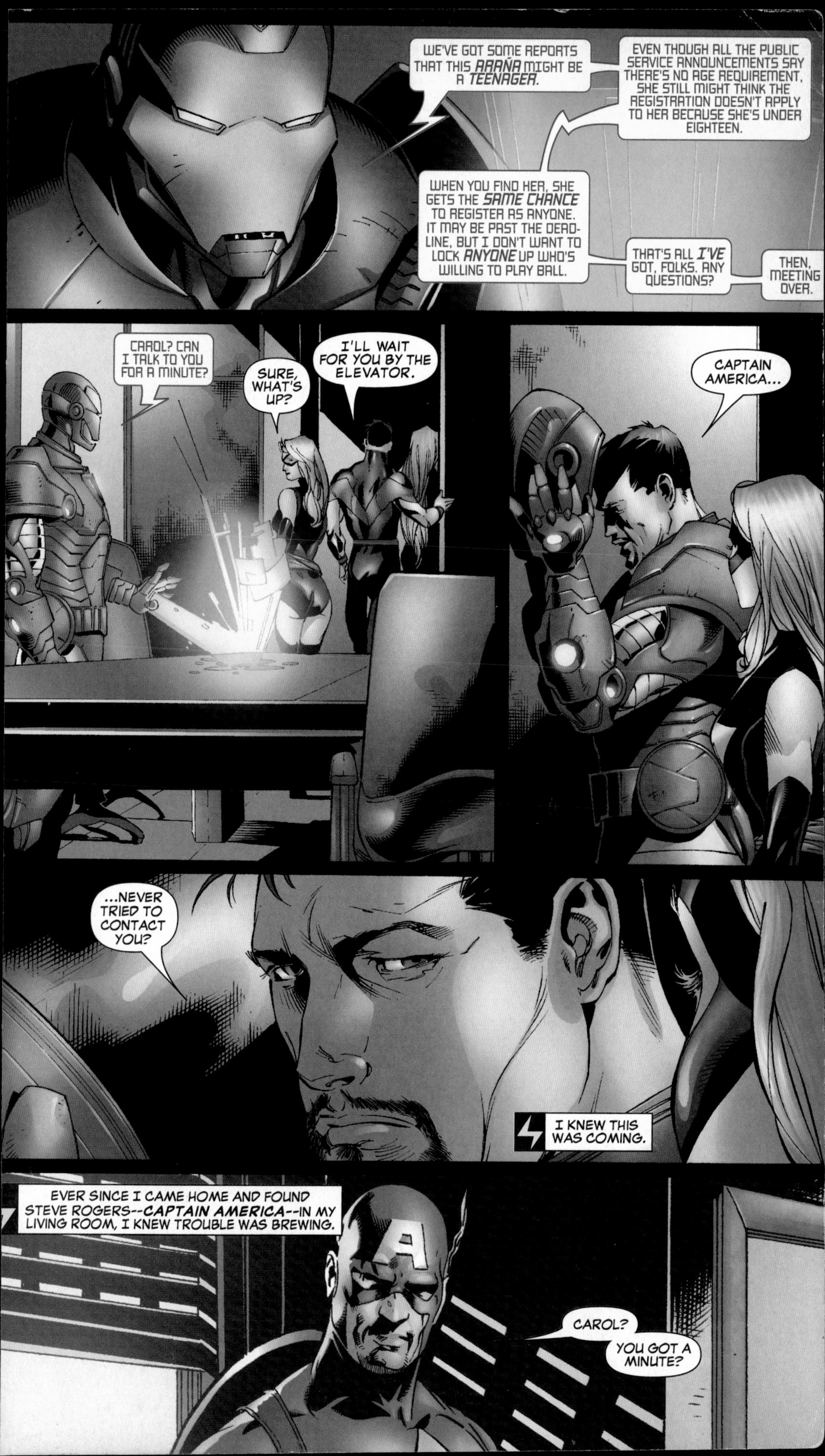

WE'VE GOT SOME REPORTS THAT THIS ARAÑA MIGHT BE A TEENAGER.
EVEN THOUGH ALL THE PUBLIC SERVICE ANNOUNCEMENTS SAY THERE'S NO AGE REQUIREMENT, SHE STILL MIGHT THINK THE REGISTRATION DOESN'T APPLY TO HER BECAUSE SHE'S UNDER EIGHTEEN.
WHEN YOU FIND HER, SHE GETS THE SAME CHANCE TO REGISTER AS ANYONE. IT MAY BE PAST THE DEAD-LINE, BUT I DON'T WANT TO LOCK ANYONE UP WHO'S WILLING TO PLAY BALL.
THAT'S ALL I'VE GOT, FOLKS. ANY QUESTIONS?
THEN, MEETING OVER.
CAROL? CAN I TALK TO YOU FOR A MINUTE?
SURE, WHAT'S UP?
I'LL WAIT FOR YOU BY THE ELEVATOR.
CAPTAIN AMERICA...
...NEVER TRIED TO CONTACT YOU?
I KNEW THIS WAS COMING.
EVER SINCE I CAME HOME AND FOUND STEVE ROGERS--CAPTAIN AMERICA--IN MY LIVING ROOM, I KNEW TROUBLE WAS BREWING.
CAROL?
YOU GOT A MINUTE?

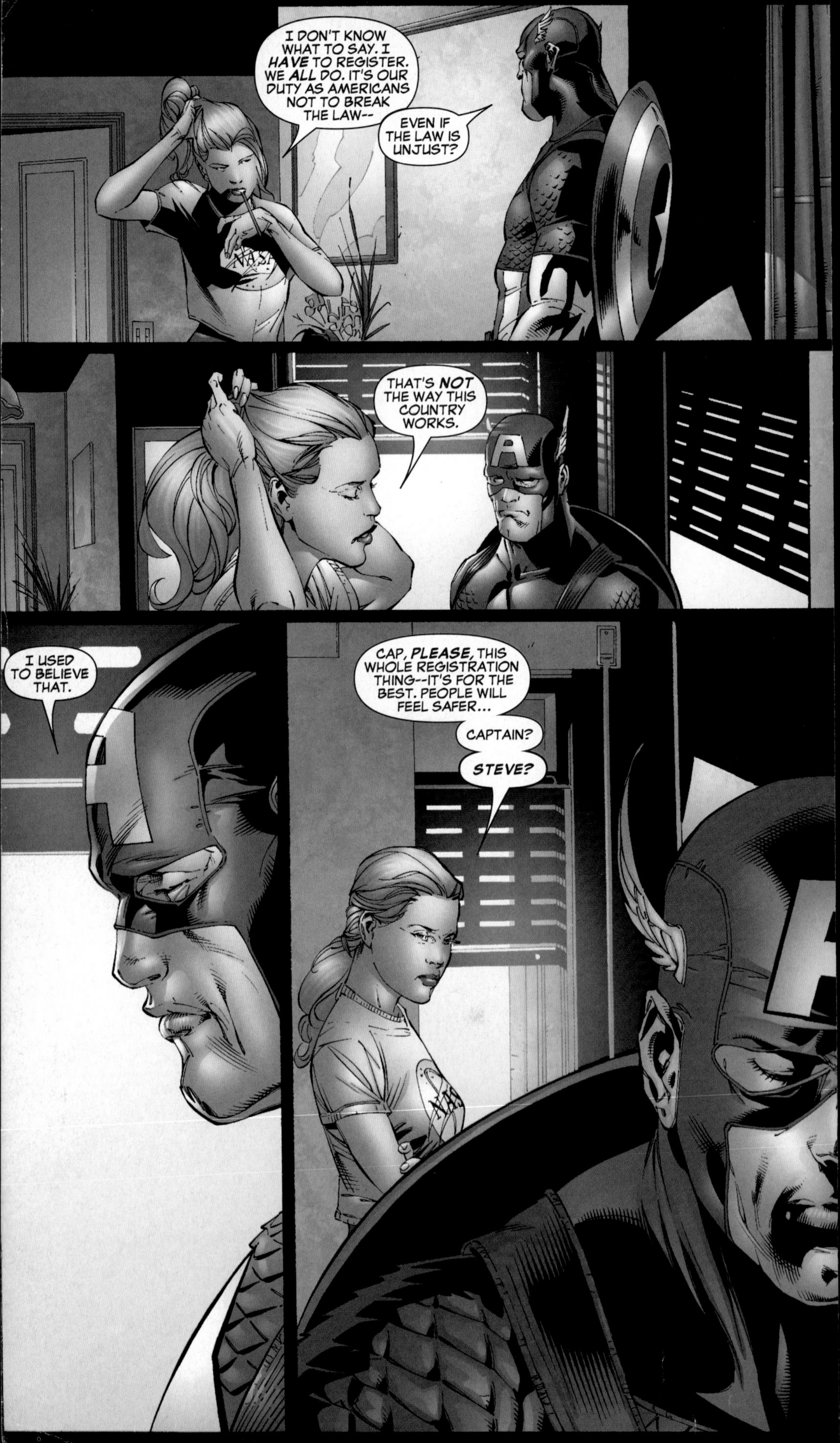
I DON'T KNOW WHAT TO SAY. I *HAVE* TO REGISTER. WE *ALL* DO. IT'S OUR DUTY AS AMERICANS NOT TO BREAK THE LAW--
EVEN IF THE LAW IS UNJUST?
THAT'S *NOT* THE WAY THIS COUNTRY WORKS.
I USED TO BELIEVE THAT.
CAP, *PLEASE*, THIS WHOLE REGISTRATION THING--IT'S FOR THE BEST. PEOPLE WILL FEEL SAFER...
CAPTAIN?
STEVE?

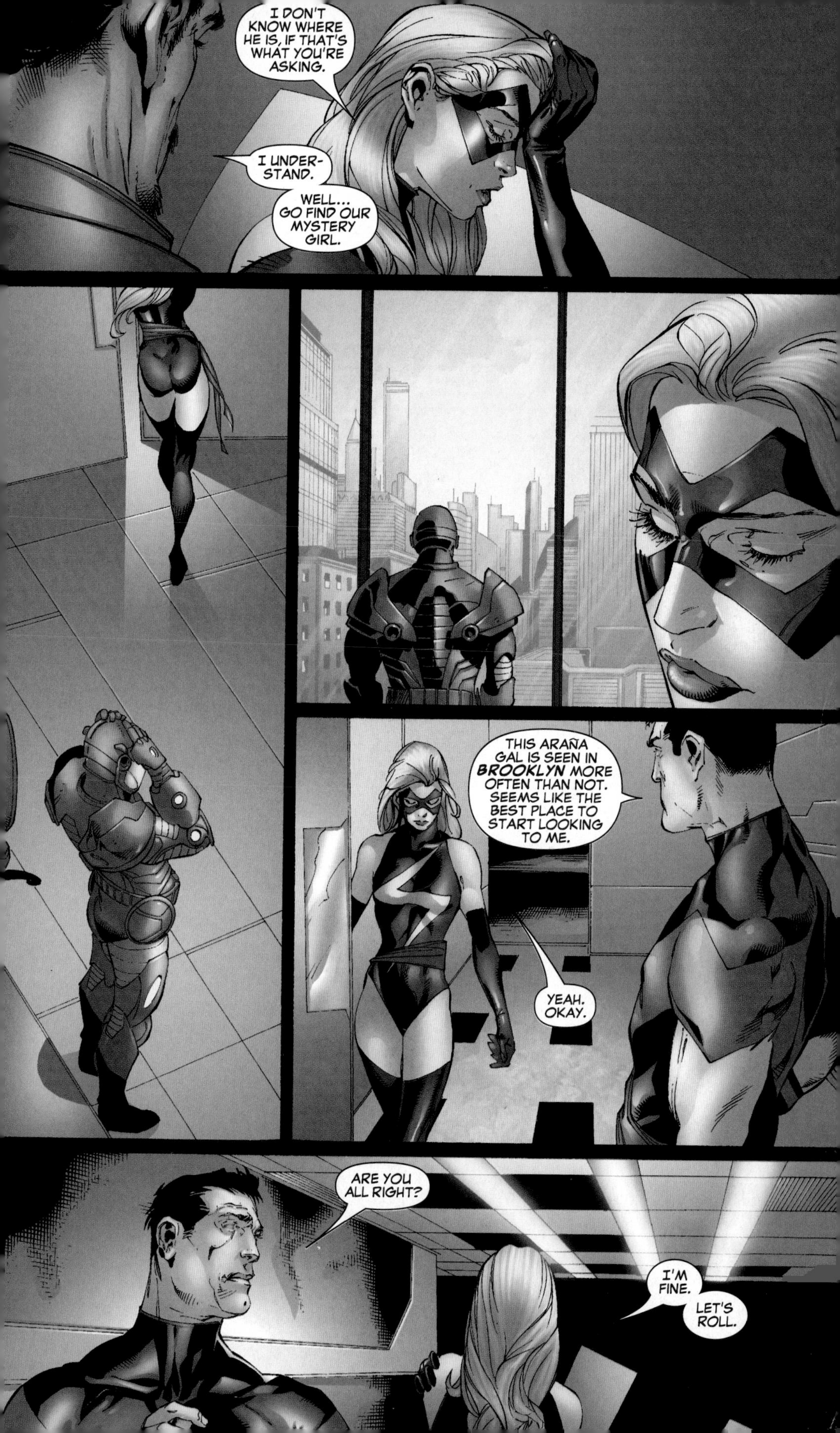
I DON'T KNOW WHERE HE IS, IF THAT'S WHAT YOU'RE ASKING.
I UNDER-STAND.
WELL... GO FIND OUR MYSTERY GIRL.
THIS ARAÑA GAL IS SEEN IN BROOKLYN MORE OFTEN THAN NOT. SEEMS LIKE THE BEST PLACE TO START LOOKING TO ME.
YEAH. OKAY.
ARE YOU ALL RIGHT?
I'M FINE.
LET'S ROLL.

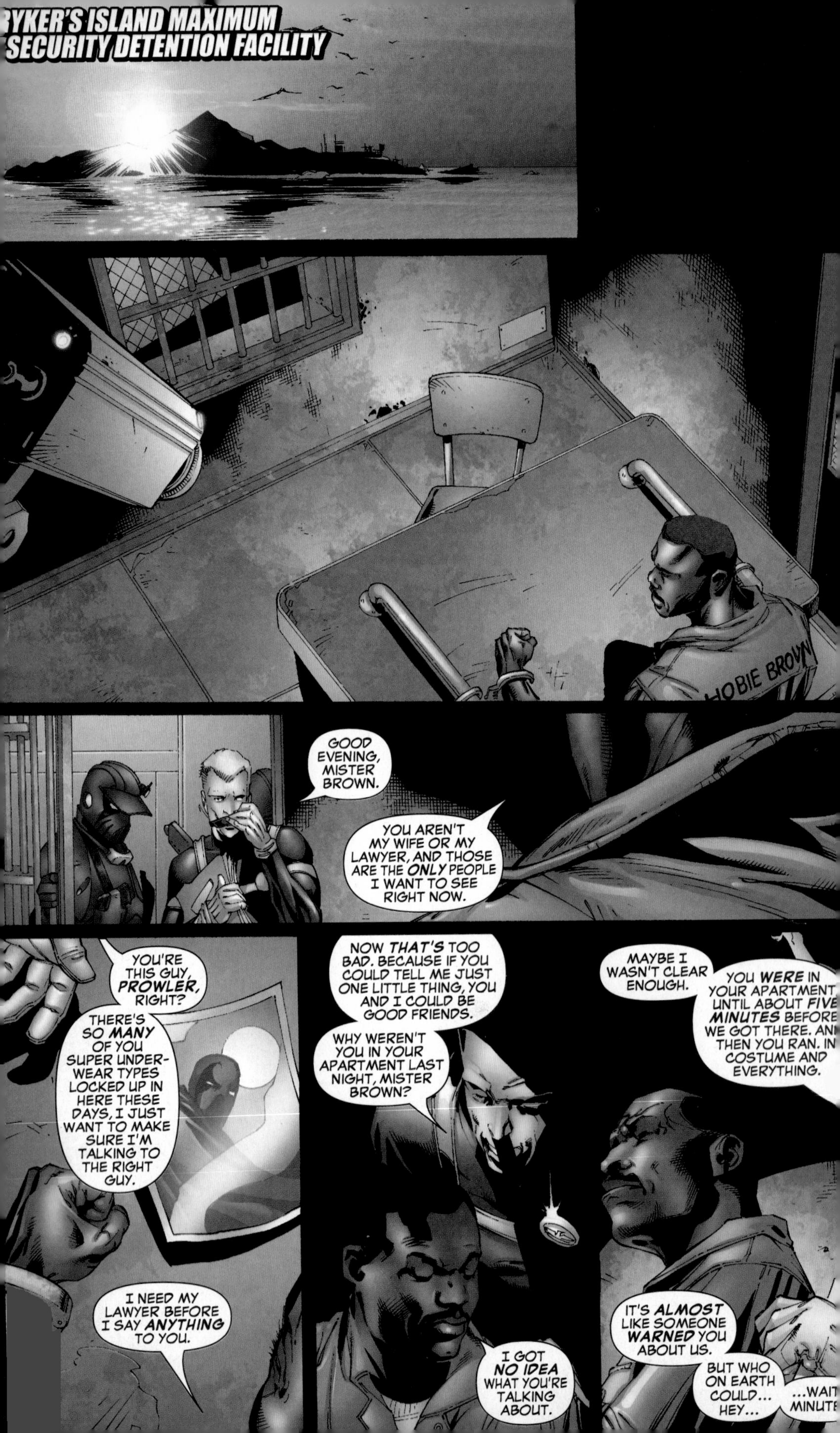
RYKER'S ISLAND MAXIMUM SECURITY DETENTION FACILITY
HOBIE BROWN
GOOD EVENING, MISTER BROWN.
YOU AREN'T MY WIFE OR MY LAWYER, AND THOSE ARE THE ONLY PEOPLE I WANT TO SEE RIGHT NOW.
YOU'RE THIS GUY, PROWLER, RIGHT?
THERE'S SO MANY OF YOU SUPER UNDER-WEAR TYPES LOCKED UP IN HERE THESE DAYS, I JUST WANT TO MAKE SURE I'M TALKING TO THE RIGHT GUY.
I NEED MY LAWYER BEFORE I SAY ANYTHING TO YOU.
NOW THAT'S TOO BAD. BECAUSE IF YOU COULD TELL ME JUST ONE LITTLE THING, YOU AND I COULD BE GOOD FRIENDS.
WHY WEREN'T YOU IN YOUR APARTMENT LAST NIGHT, MISTER BROWN?
I GOT NO IDEA WHAT YOU'RE TALKING ABOUT.
MAYBE I WASN'T CLEAR ENOUGH.
YOU WERE IN YOUR APARTMENT UNTIL ABOUT FIVE MINUTES BEFORE WE GOT THERE. AND THEN YOU RAN. IN COSTUME AND EVERYTHING.
IT'S ALMOST LIKE SOMEONE WARNED YOU ABOUT US.
BUT WHO ON EARTH COULD... HEY...
...WAIT A MINUTE

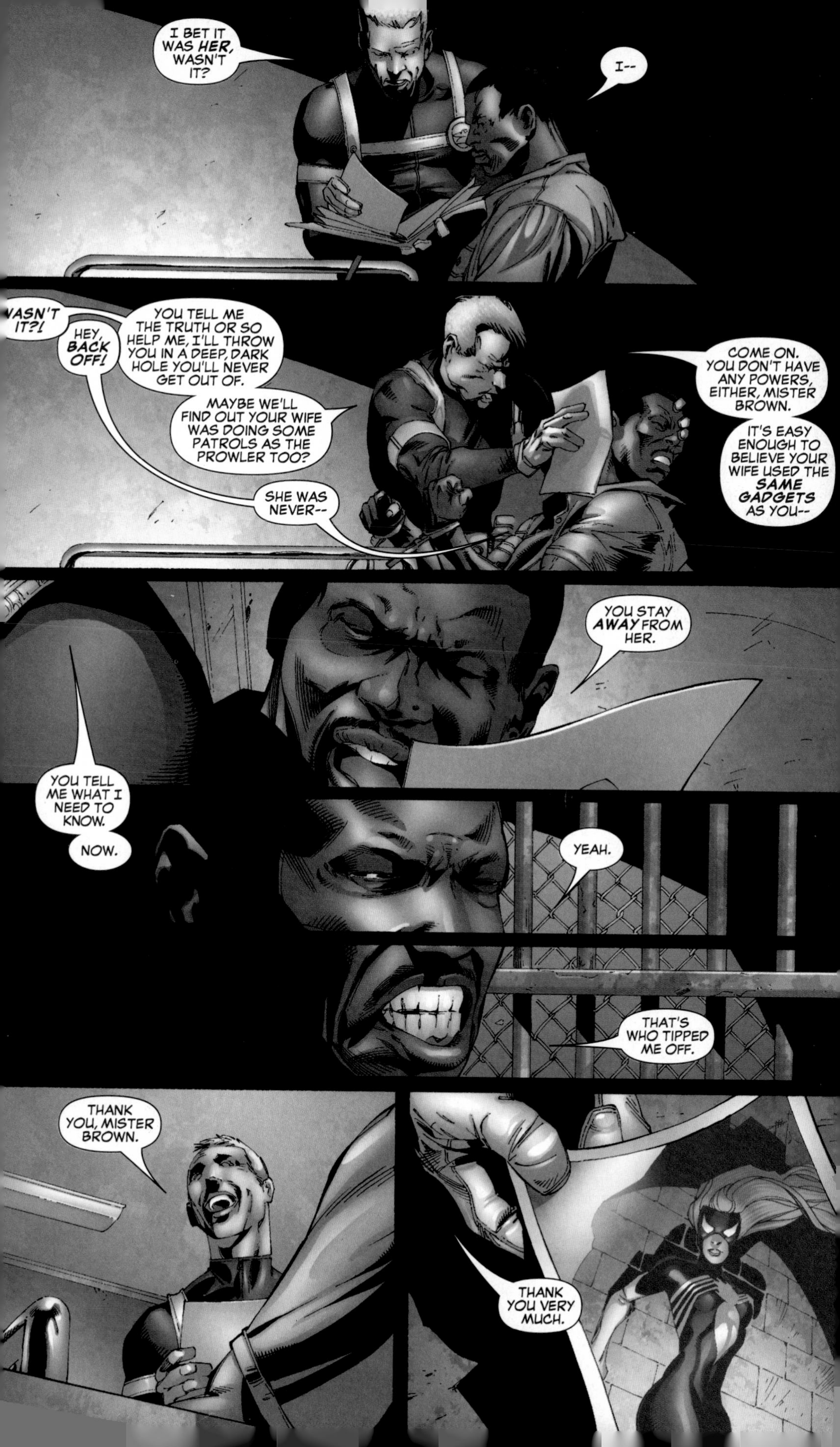
I BET IT WAS HER, WASN'T IT?
I--
WASN'T IT?!
YOU TELL ME THE TRUTH OR SO HELP ME, I'LL THROW YOU IN A DEEP, DARK HOLE YOU'LL NEVER GET OUT OF.
HEY, BACK OFF!
MAYBE WE'LL FIND OUT YOUR WIFE WAS DOING SOME PATROLS AS THE PROWLER TOO?
SHE WAS NEVER--
COME ON. YOU DON'T HAVE ANY POWERS, EITHER, MISTER BROWN.
IT'S EASY ENOUGH TO BELIEVE YOUR WIFE USED THE SAME GADGETS AS YOU--
YOU STAY AWAY FROM HER.
YOU TELL ME WHAT I NEED TO KNOW.
NOW.
YEAH.
THAT'S WHO TIPPED ME OFF.
THANK YOU, MISTER BROWN.
THANK YOU VERY MUCH.

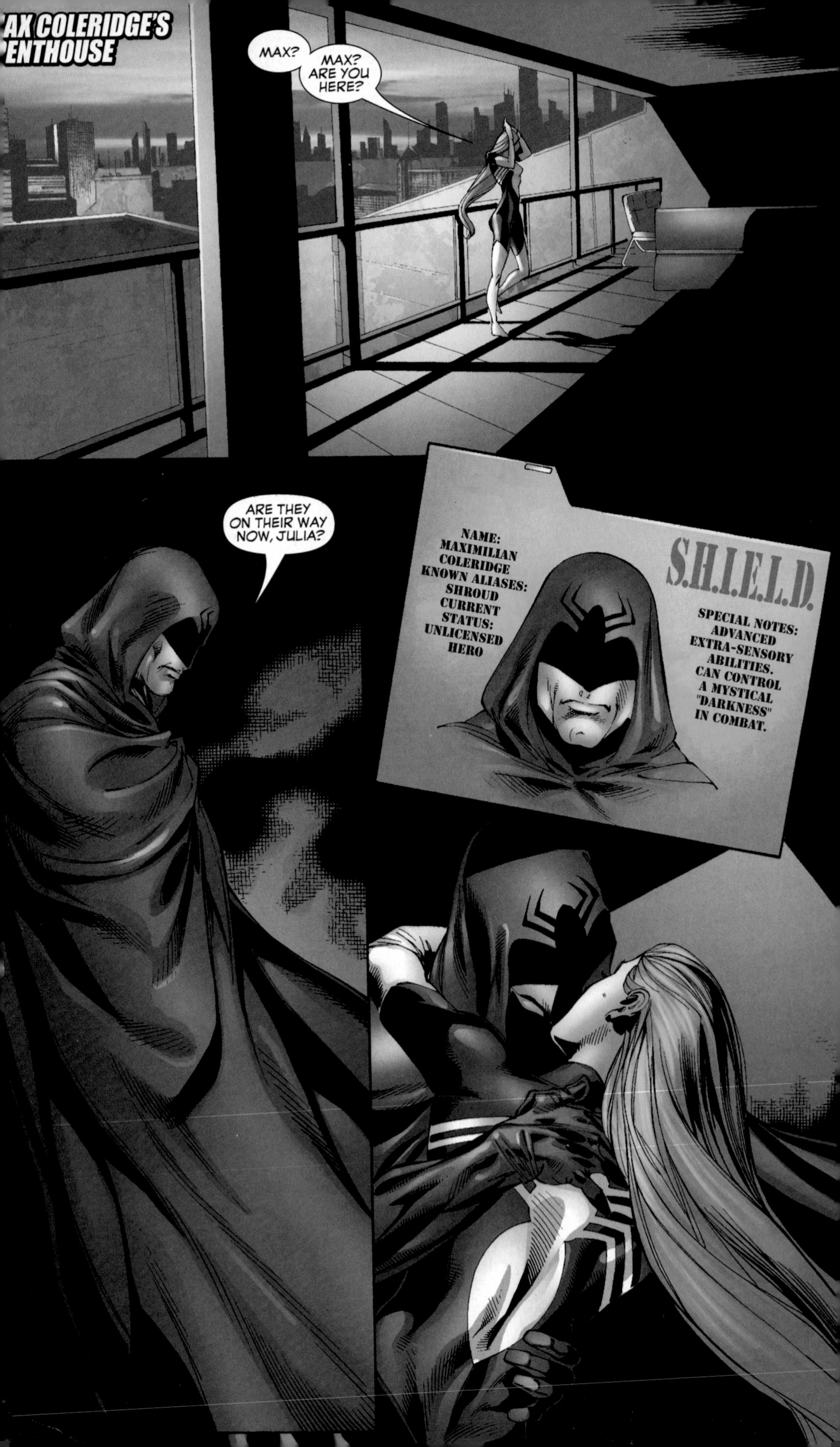
AX COLERIDGE'S ENTHOUSE
MAX?
MAX? ARE YOU HERE?
ARE THEY ON THEIR WAY NOW, JULIA?
NAME: MAXIMILIAN COLERIDGE KNOWN ALIASES: SHROUD CURRENT STATUS: UNLICENSED HERO
S.H.I.E.L.D.
SPECIAL NOTES: ADVANCED EXTRA-SENSORY ABILITIES. CAN CONTROL A MYSTICAL "DARKNESS" IN COMBAT.

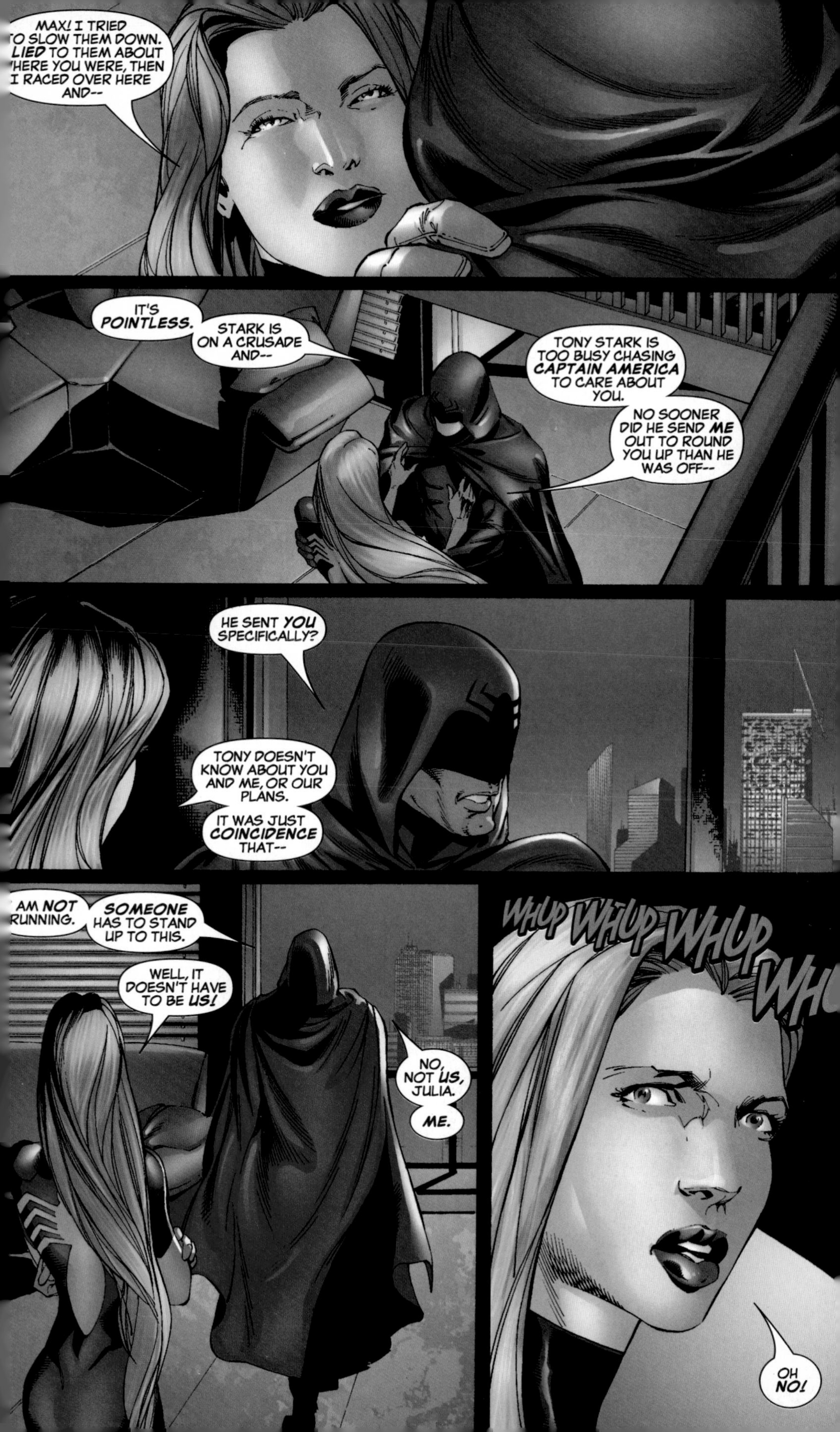

MAX! I TRIED TO SLOW THEM DOWN. LIED TO THEM ABOUT WHERE YOU WERE, THEN I RACED OVER HERE AND--
IT'S POINTLESS.
STARK IS ON A CRUSADE AND--
TONY STARK IS TOO BUSY CHASING CAPTAIN AMERICA TO CARE ABOUT YOU.
NO SOONER DID HE SEND ME OUT TO ROUND YOU UP THAN HE WAS OFF--
HE SENT YOU SPECIFICALLY?
TONY DOESN'T KNOW ABOUT YOU AND ME, OR OUR PLANS.
IT WAS JUST COINCIDENCE THAT--
AM NOT RUNNING.
SOMEONE HAS TO STAND UP TO THIS.
WELL, IT DOESN'T HAVE TO BE US!
NO, NOT US, JULIA.
ME.
WHUP WHUP WHUP
OH NO!

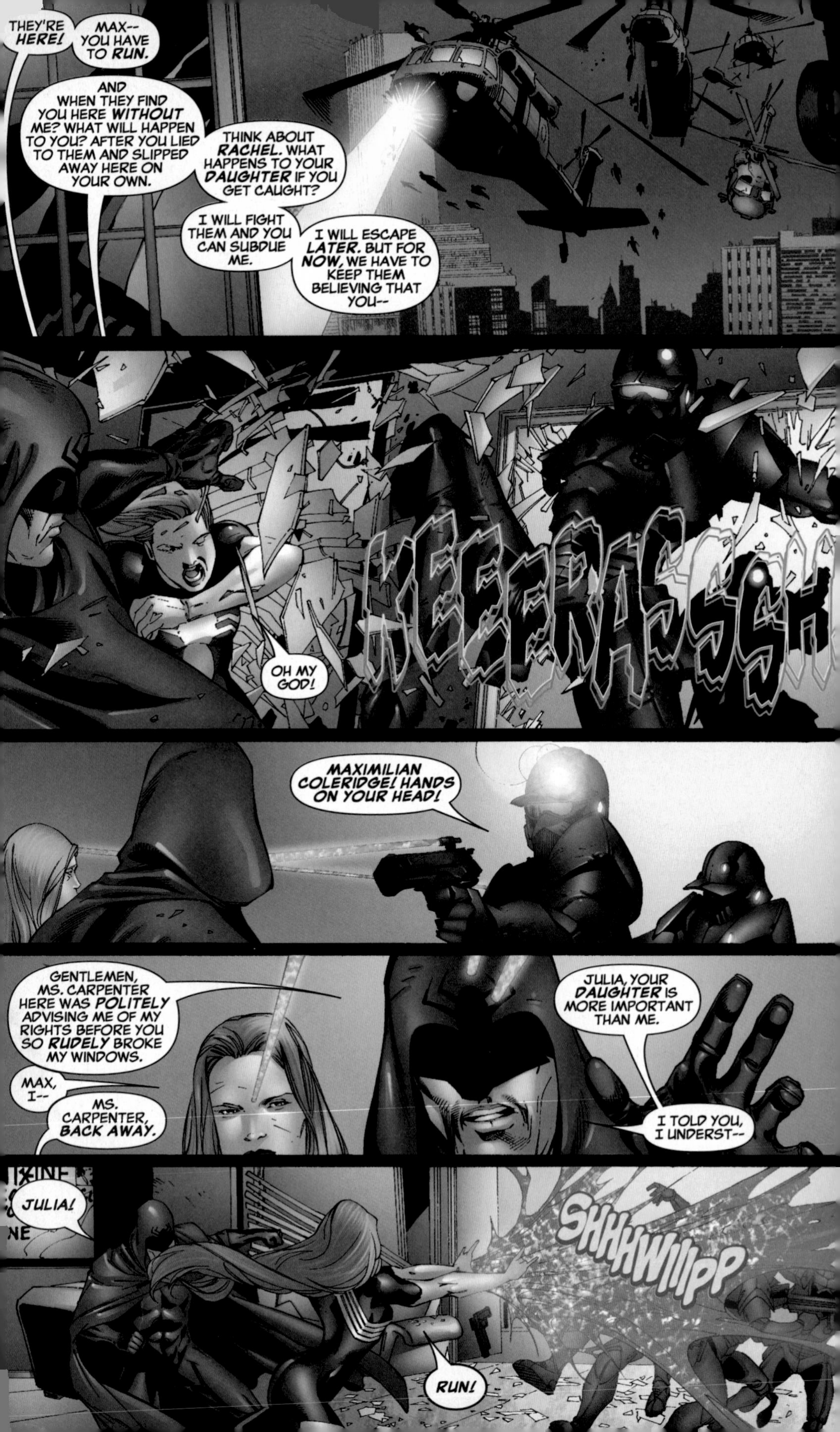
THEY'RE HERE!
MAX-- YOU HAVE TO RUN.
AND WHEN THEY FIND YOU HERE WITHOUT ME? WHAT WILL HAPPEN TO YOU? AFTER YOU LIED TO THEM AND SLIPPED AWAY HERE ON YOUR OWN.
THINK ABOUT RACHEL. WHAT HAPPENS TO YOUR DAUGHTER IF YOU GET CAUGHT?
I WILL FIGHT THEM AND YOU CAN SUBDUE ME.
I WILL ESCAPE LATER. BUT FOR NOW, WE HAVE TO KEEP THEM BELIEVING THAT YOU--
KKEERASSGH
OH MY GOD!
MAXIMILIAN COLERIDGE! HANDS ON YOUR HEAD!
GENTLEMEN, MS. CARPENTER HERE WAS POLITELY ADVISING ME OF MY RIGHTS BEFORE YOU SO RUDELY BROKE MY WINDOWS.
JULIA, YOUR DAUGHTER IS MORE IMPORTANT THAN ME.
MAX, I--
MS. CARPENTER, BACK AWAY.
I TOLD YOU, I UNDERST--
JULIA!
SHHHWIIIPP
RUN!

S.H.I.E.L.D.

NAME:
JULIA CARPENTER
KNOWN ALIASES:
ARACHNE,
SPIDER-WOMAN,
ARIADNE
CURRENT
STATUS:
FUGITIVE.

SPECIAL NOTES:
RUMORED
DE-POWERED BUT
DENIES THIS
FACT AND
PASSED ALL
MEDICAL EXAMS.
HAS
DAUGHTER
(RACHEL),
AGE 9.

FUGITIVE

S.H.I.E.L.D.

NAME:
MAXIMILIAN
COLERIDGE
KNOWN ALIASES:
SHROUD
CURRENT
STATUS:
FUGITIVE.

SPECIAL NOTES:
ADVANCED
EXTRA-SENSORY
ABILITIES.
CAN CONTROL
A MYSTICAL
"DARKNESS"
COMBAT.

FUGITIVE

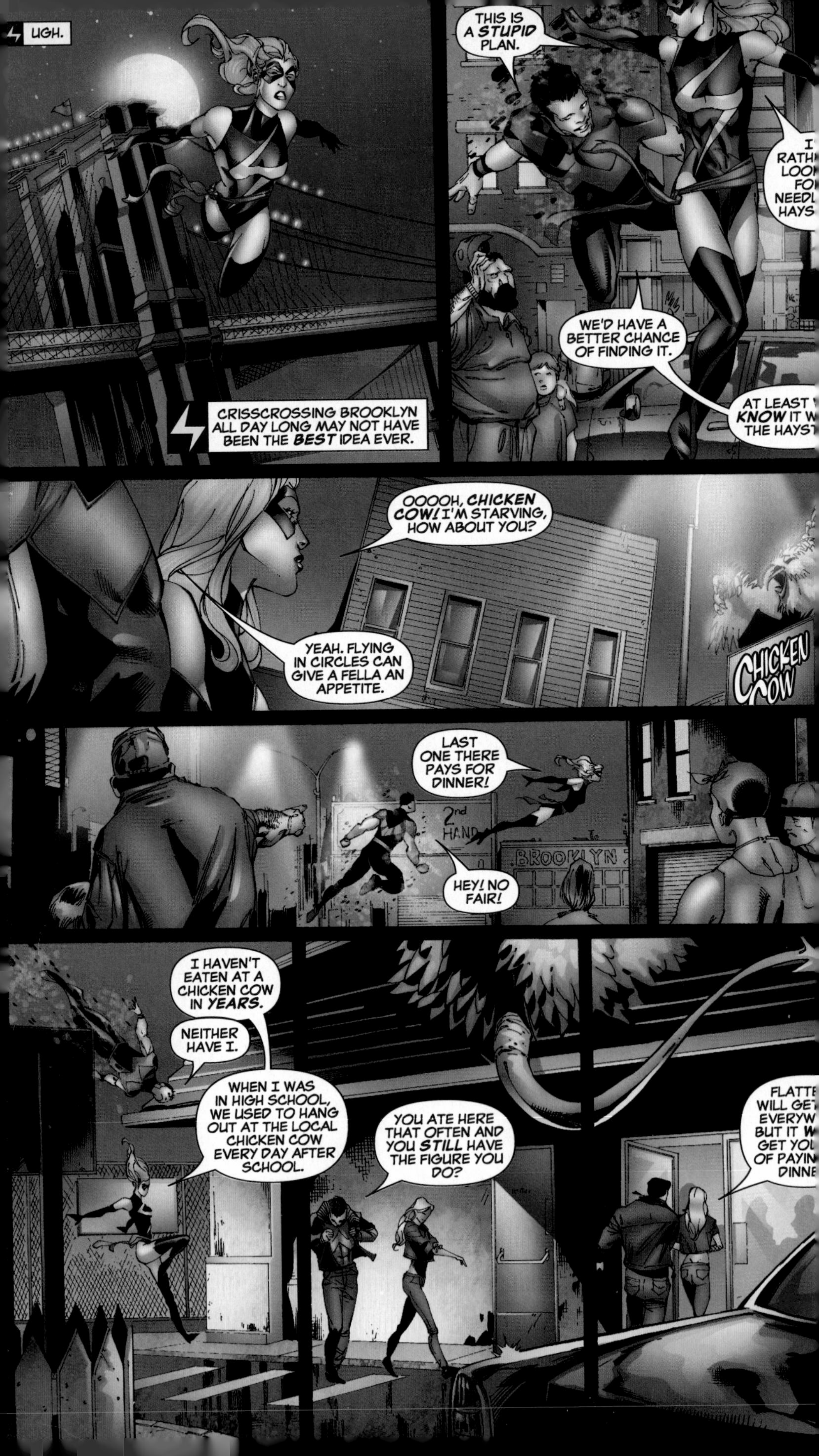
UGH.
CRISSCROSSING BROOKLYN ALL DAY LONG MAY NOT HAVE BEEN THE BEST IDEA EVER.
THIS IS A STUPID PLAN.
WE'D HAVE A BETTER CHANCE OF FINDING IT.
OOOOH, CHICKEN COW! I'M STARVING, HOW ABOUT YOU?
YEAH. FLYING IN CIRCLES CAN GIVE A FELLA AN APPETITE.
CHICKEN COW
LAST ONE THERE PAYS FOR DINNER!
2nd HAND
BROOKLYN
HEY! NO FAIR!
I HAVEN'T EATEN AT A CHICKEN COW IN YEARS.
NEITHER HAVE I.
WHEN I WAS IN HIGH SCHOOL, WE USED TO HANG OUT AT THE LOCAL CHICKEN COW EVERY DAY AFTER SCHOOL.
YOU ATE HERE THAT OFTEN AND YOU STILL HAVE THE FIGURE YOU DO?

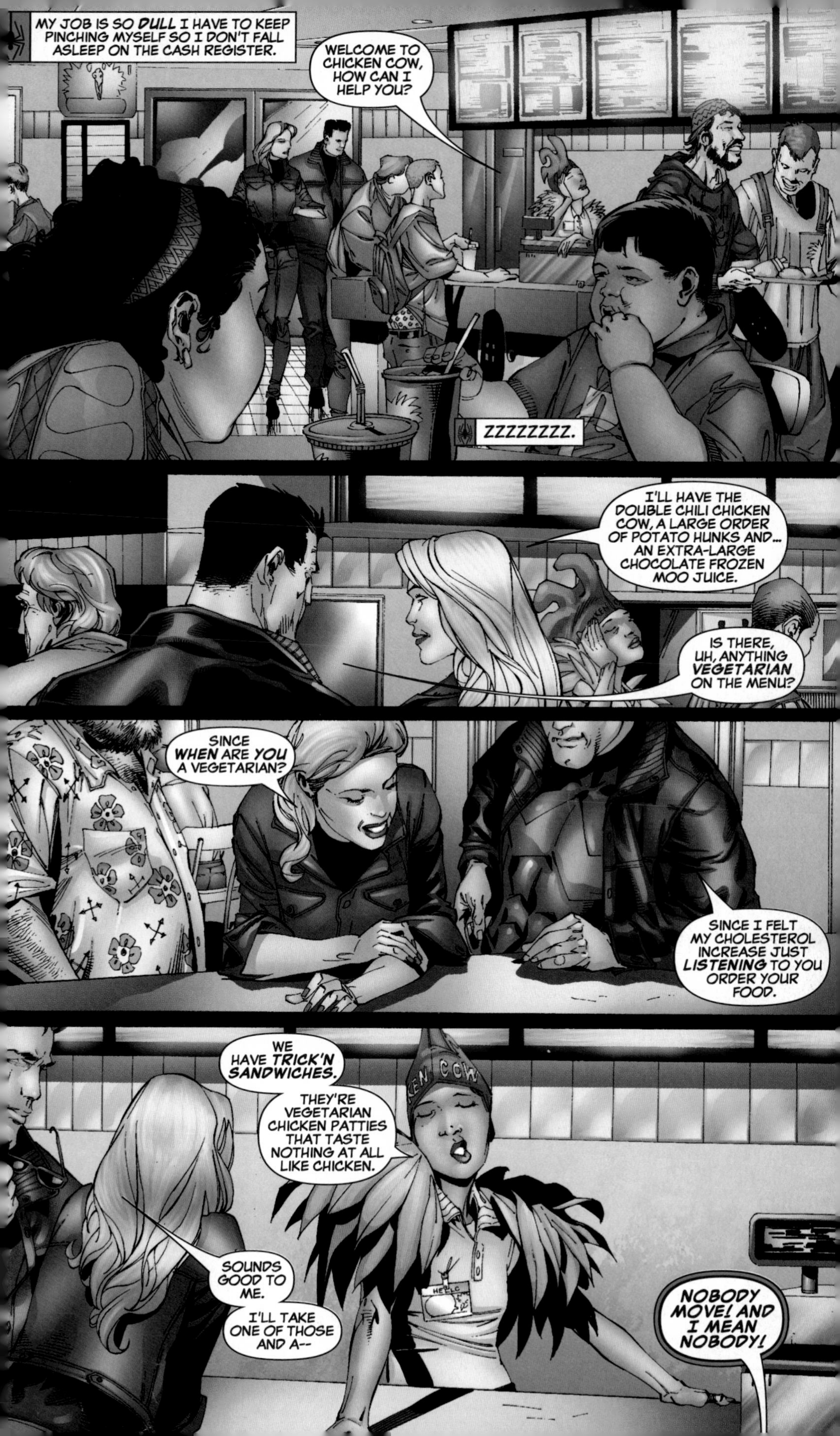
MY JOB IS SO DULL I HAVE TO KEEP PINCHING MYSELF SO I DON'T FALL ASLEEP ON THE CASH REGISTER.
WELCOME TO CHICKEN COW, HOW CAN I HELP YOU?
ZZZZZZZZ.
I'LL HAVE THE DOUBLE CHILI CHICKEN COW, A LARGE ORDER OF POTATO HUNKS AND... AN EXTRA-LARGE CHOCOLATE FROZEN MOO JUICE.
IS THERE, UH, ANYTHING VEGETARIAN ON THE MENU?
SINCE WHEN ARE YOU A VEGETARIAN?
SINCE I FELT MY CHOLESTEROL INCREASE JUST LISTENING TO YOU ORDER YOUR FOOD.
WE HAVE TRICK'N SANDWICHES.
THEY'RE VEGETARIAN CHICKEN PATTIES THAT TASTE NOTHING AT ALL LIKE CHICKEN.
SOUNDS GOOD TO ME.
I'LL TAKE ONE OF THOSE AND A--
NOBODY MOVE! AND I MEAN NOBODY!

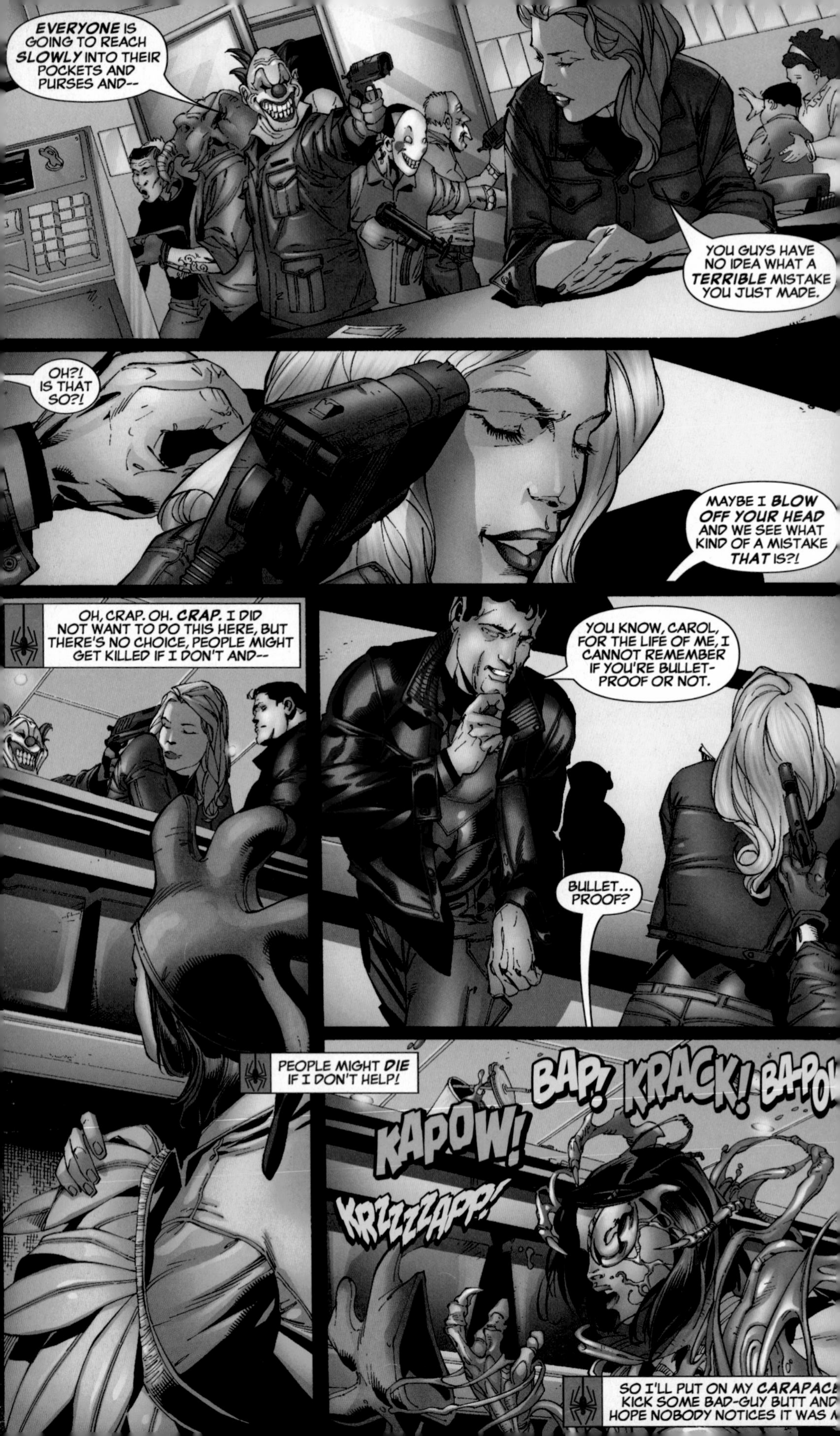
EVERYONE IS GOING TO REACH SLOWLY INTO THEIR POCKETS AND PURSES AND--
YOU GUYS HAVE NO IDEA WHAT A TERRIBLE MISTAKE YOU JUST MADE.
OH?! IS THAT SO?!
MAYBE I BLOW OFF YOUR HEAD AND WE SEE WHAT KIND OF A MISTAKE THAT IS?!
OH, CRAP. OH. CRAP. I DID NOT WANT TO DO THIS HERE, BUT THERE'S NO CHOICE, PEOPLE MIGHT GET KILLED IF I DON'T AND--
YOU KNOW, CAROL, FOR THE LIFE OF ME, I CANNOT REMEMBER IF YOU'RE BULLET-PROOF OR NOT.
BULLET... PROOF?
PEOPLE MIGHT DIE IF I DON'T HELP!
BAP! KRACK! BA-PO
KAPOW!
KRZZZZAPP!
SO I'LL PUT ON MY CARAPAC KICK SOME BAD-GUY BUTT AND HOPE NOBODY NOTICES IT WAS M

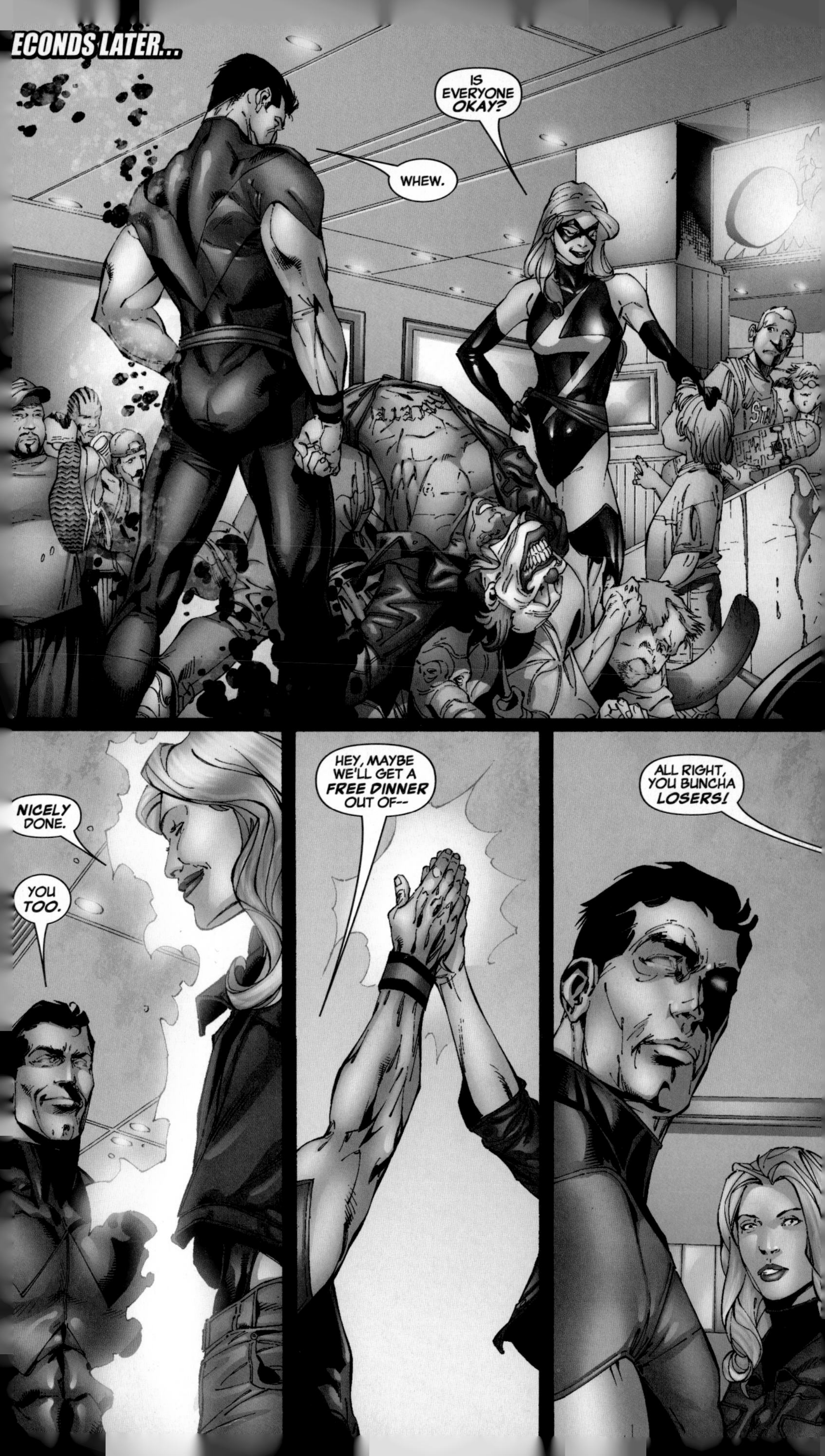
ECONDS LATER...
IS EVERYONE OKAY?
WHEW.
NICELY DONE.
YOU TOO.
HEY, MAYBE WE'LL GET A FREE DINNER OUT OF--
ALL RIGHT, YOU BUNCHA LOSERS!

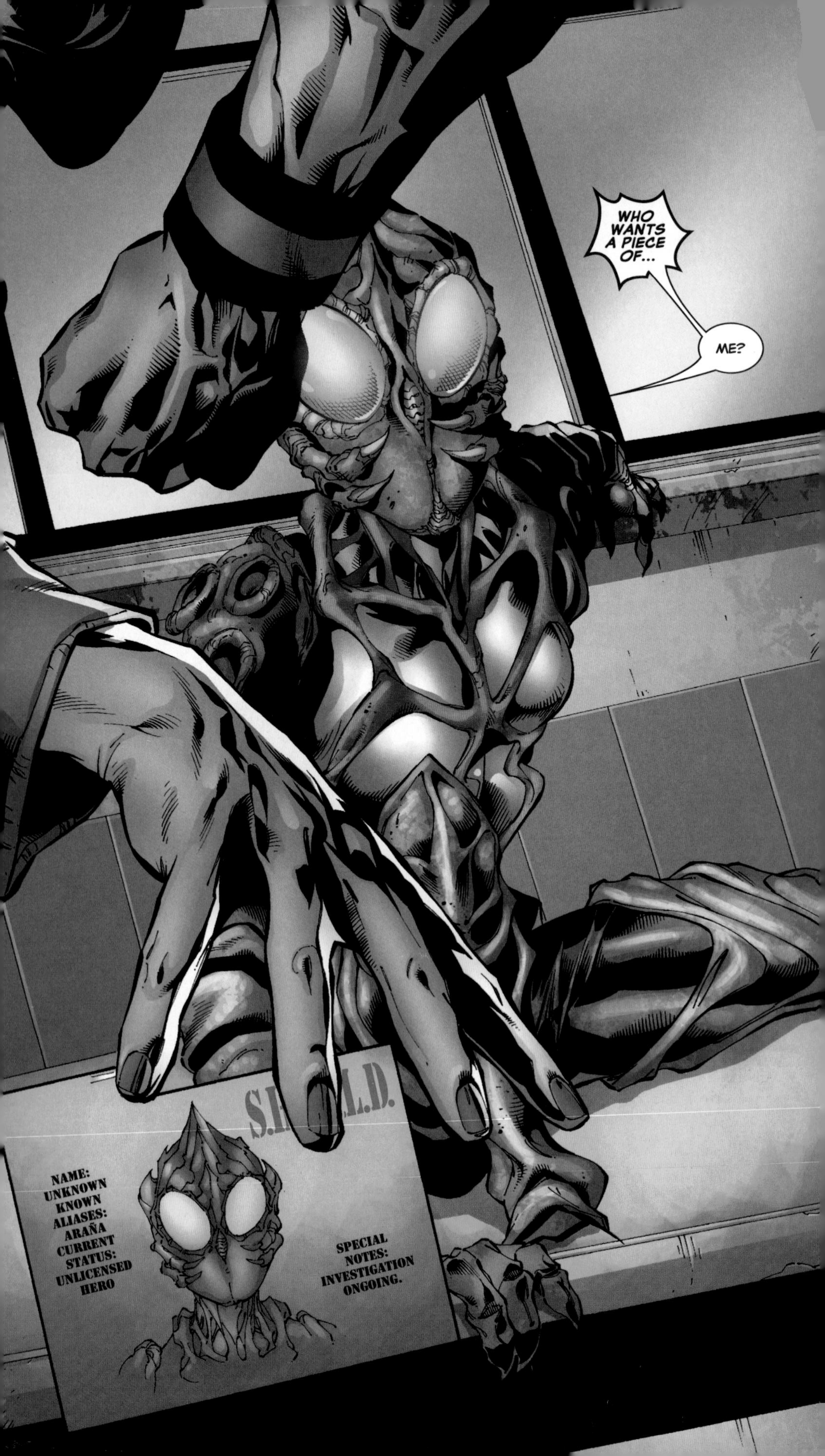
WHO WANTS A PIECE OF...
ME?
S.H.I.E.L.D.
NAME: UNKNOWN
KNOWN ALIASES: ARAÑA
CURRENT STATUS: UNLICENSED HERO
SPECIAL NOTES: INVESTIGATION ONGOING.

MS. MARVEL
A MARVEL COMICS EVENT

CIVIL
WAR

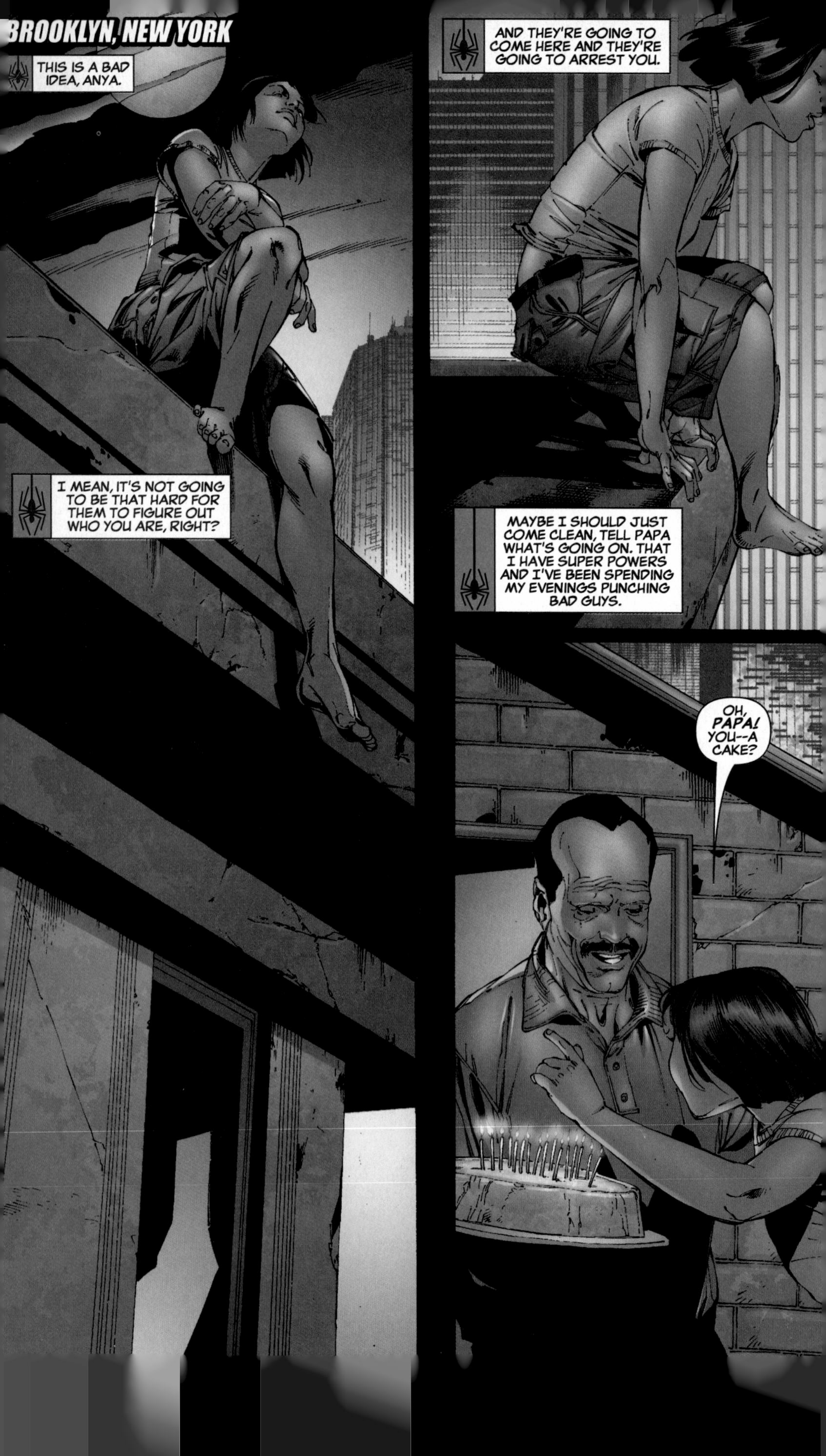
BROOKLYN, NEW YORK
THIS IS A BAD IDEA, ANYA.
I MEAN, IT'S NOT GOING TO BE THAT HARD FOR THEM TO FIGURE OUT WHO YOU ARE, RIGHT?
AND THEY'RE GOING TO COME HERE AND THEY'RE GOING TO ARREST YOU.
MAYBE I SHOULD JUST COME CLEAN, TELL PAPA WHAT'S GOING ON. THAT I HAVE SUPER POWERS AND I'VE BEEN SPENDING MY EVENINGS PUNCHING BAD GUYS.
OH, PAPA! YOU--A CAKE?

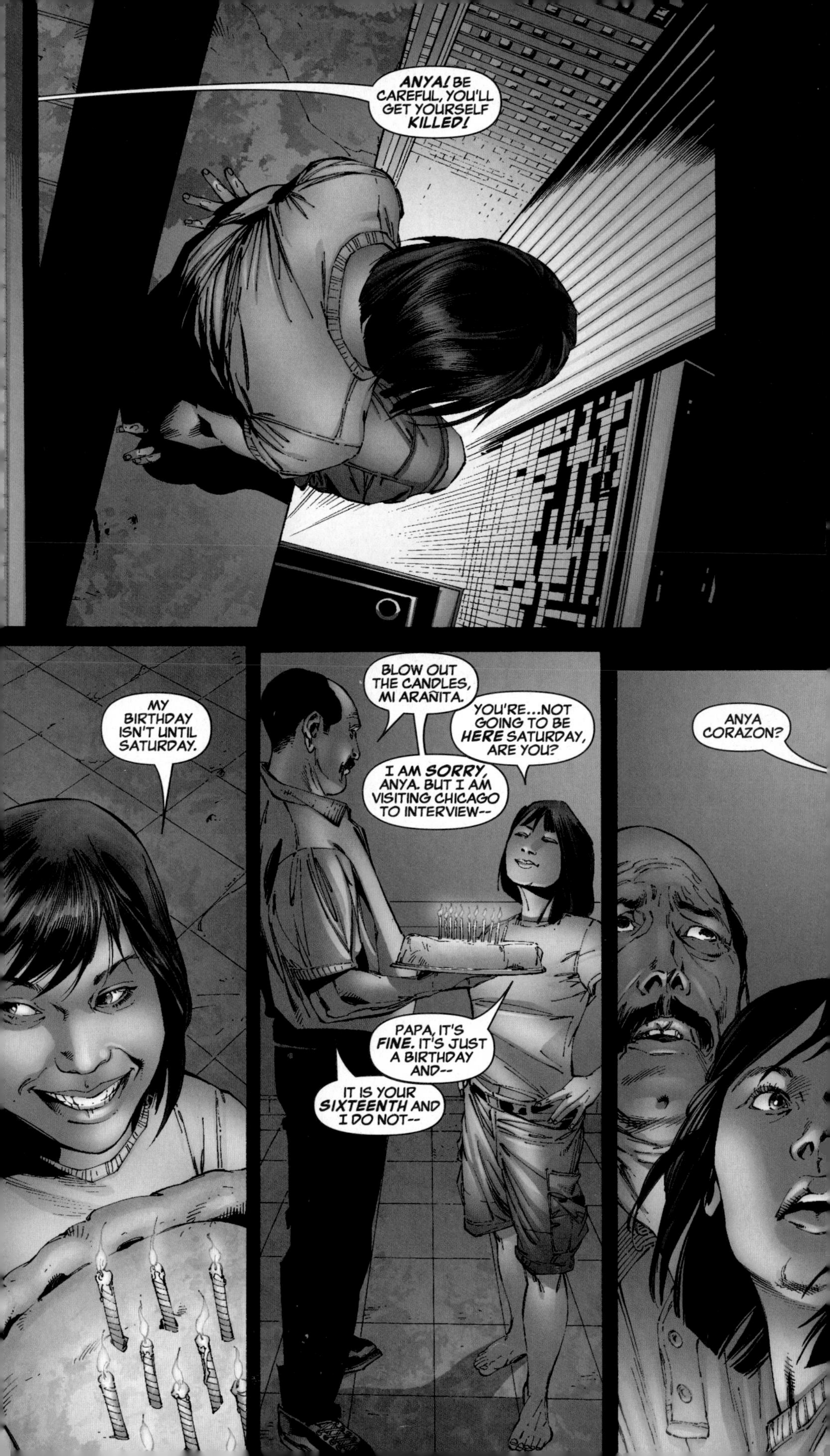
ANYA! BE CAREFUL, YOU'LL GET YOURSELF KILLED!
MY BIRTHDAY ISN'T UNTIL SATURDAY.
BLOW OUT THE CANDLES, MI ARAÑITA.
YOU'RE...NOT GOING TO BE HERE SATURDAY, ARE YOU?
I AM SORRY, ANYA. BUT I AM VISITING CHICAGO TO INTERVIEW--
PAPA, IT'S FINE. IT'S JUST A BIRTHDAY AND--
IT IS YOUR SIXTEENTH AND I DO NOT--
ANYA CORAZON?

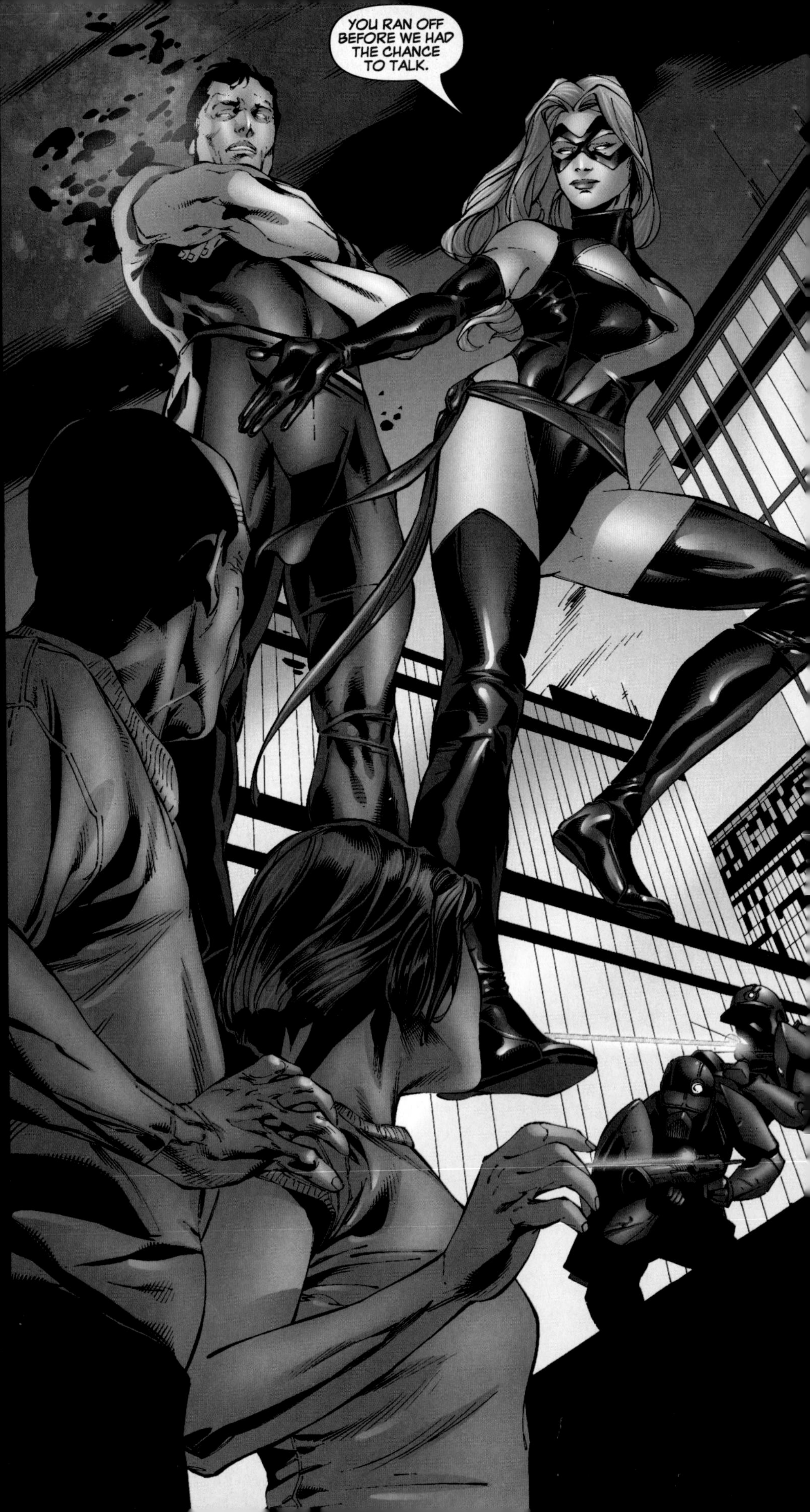
YOU RAN OFF BEFORE WE HAD THE CHANCE TO TALK.

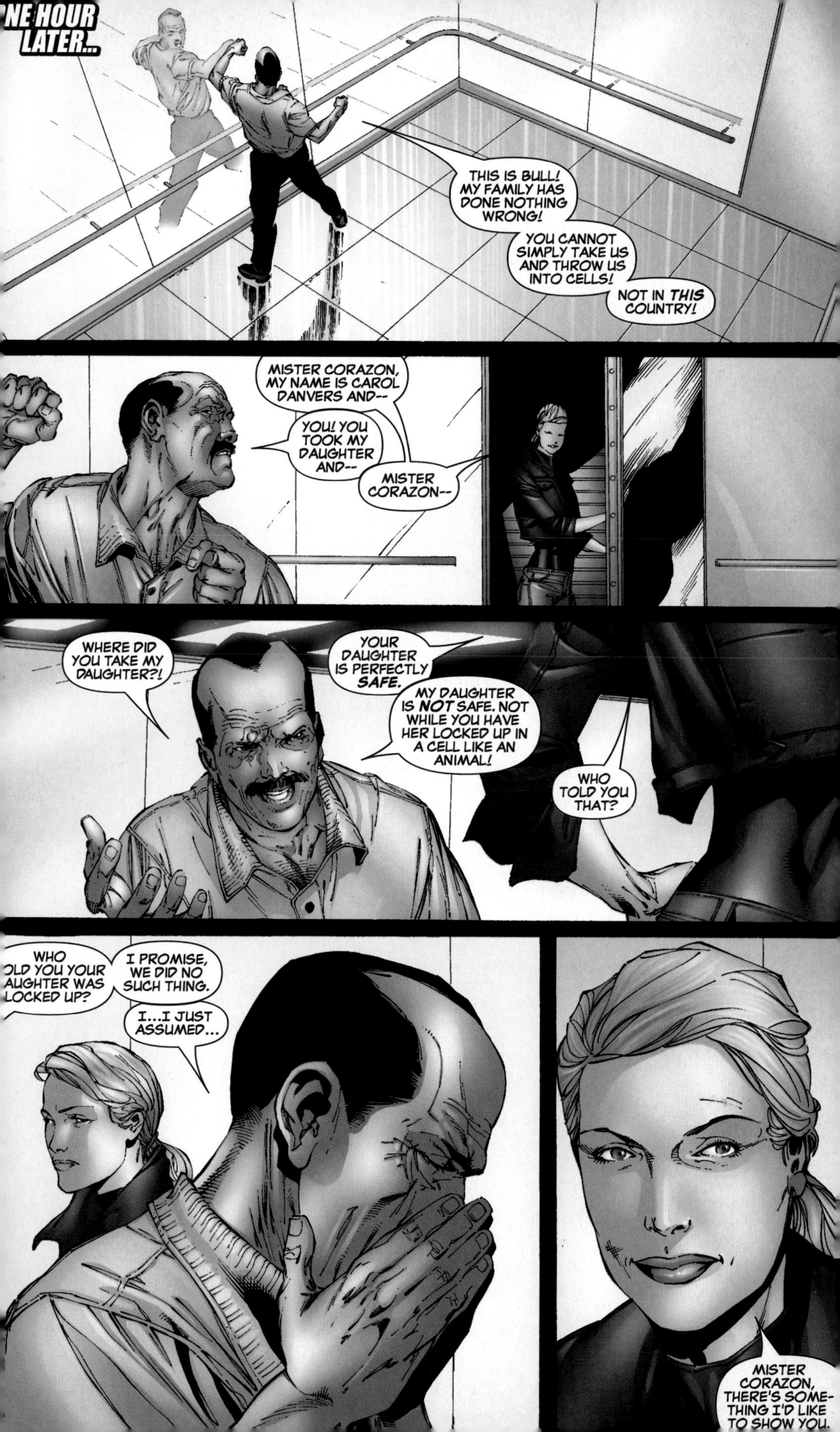
NE HOUR LATER...
THIS IS BULL! MY FAMILY HAS DONE NOTHING WRONG!
YOU CANNOT SIMPLY TAKE US AND THROW US INTO CELLS!
NOT IN THIS COUNTRY!
MISTER CORAZON, MY NAME IS CAROL DANVERS AND--
YOU! YOU TOOK MY DAUGHTER AND--
MISTER CORAZON--
WHERE DID YOU TAKE MY DAUGHTER?!
YOUR DAUGHTER IS PERFECTLY SAFE.
MY DAUGHTER IS NOT SAFE. NOT WHILE YOU HAVE HER LOCKED UP IN A CELL LIKE AN ANIMAL!
WHO TOLD YOU THAT?
WHO OLD YOU YOUR AUGHTER WAS LOCKED UP?
I PROMISE, WE DID NO SUCH THING.
I...I JUST ASSUMED...
MISTER CORAZON, THERE'S SOME-THING I'D LIKE TO SHOW YOU.

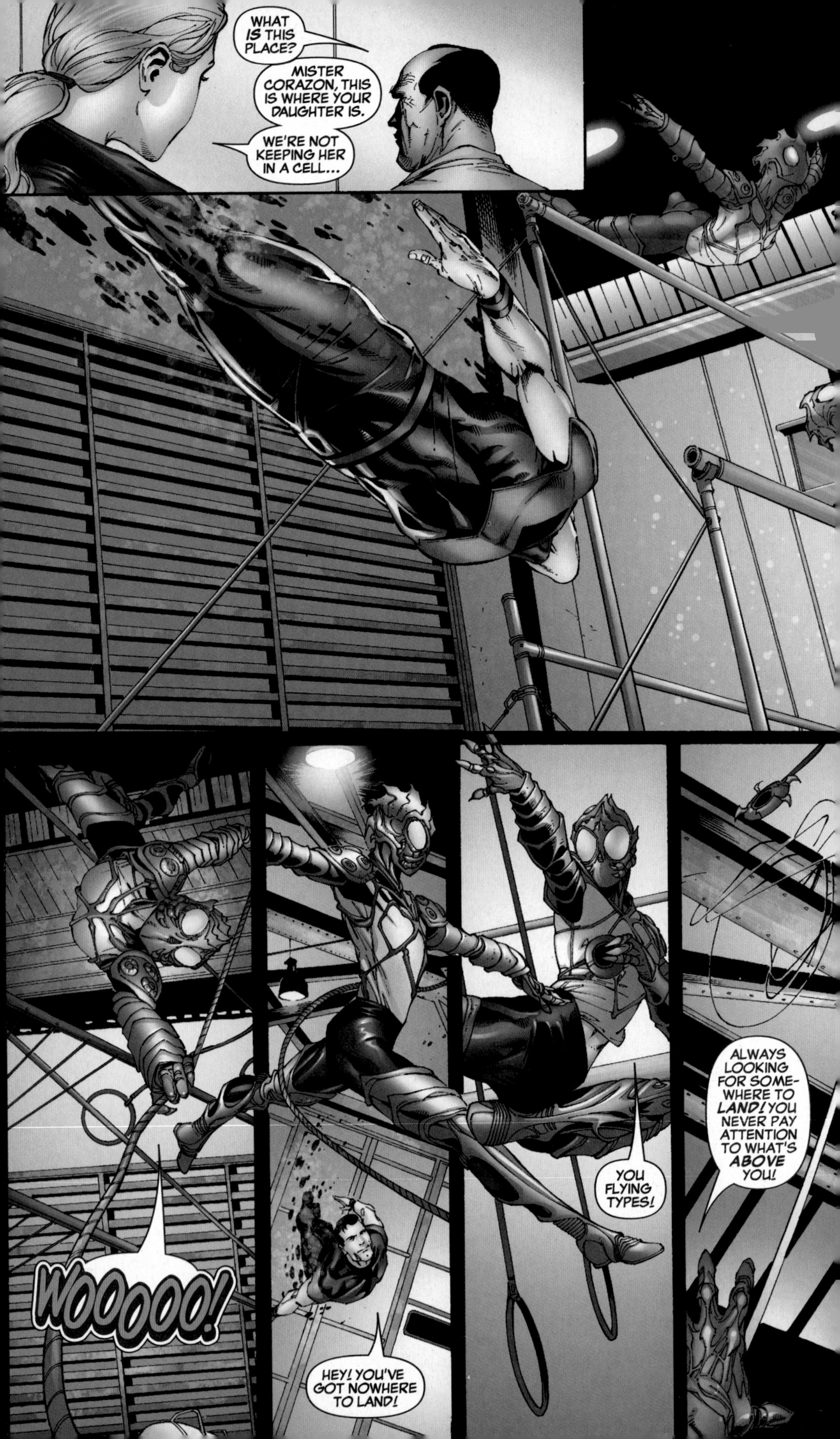
WHAT IS THIS PLACE?
MISTER CORAZON, THIS IS WHERE YOUR DAUGHTER IS.
WE'RE NOT KEEPING HER IN A CELL...
WOOOOO!
HEY! YOU'VE GOT NOWHERE TO LAND!
YOU FLYING TYPES!
ALWAYS LOOKING FOR SOME-WHERE TO LAND! YOU NEVER PAY ATTENTION TO WHAT'S ABOVE YOU!

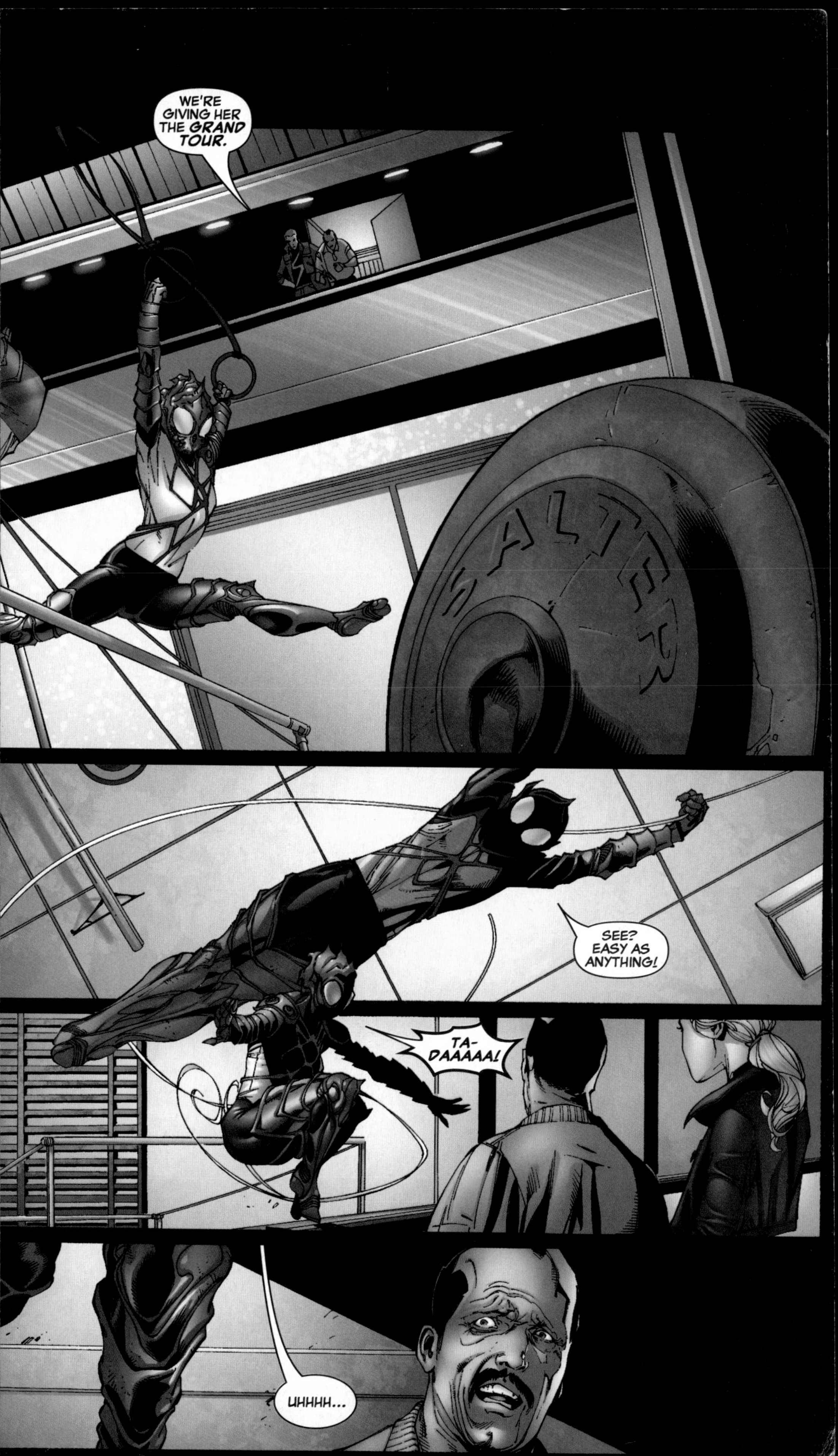
WE'RE GIVING HER THE GRAND TOUR.
SALTER
SEE? EASY AS ANYTHING!
TA-DAAAAA!
UHHHH...

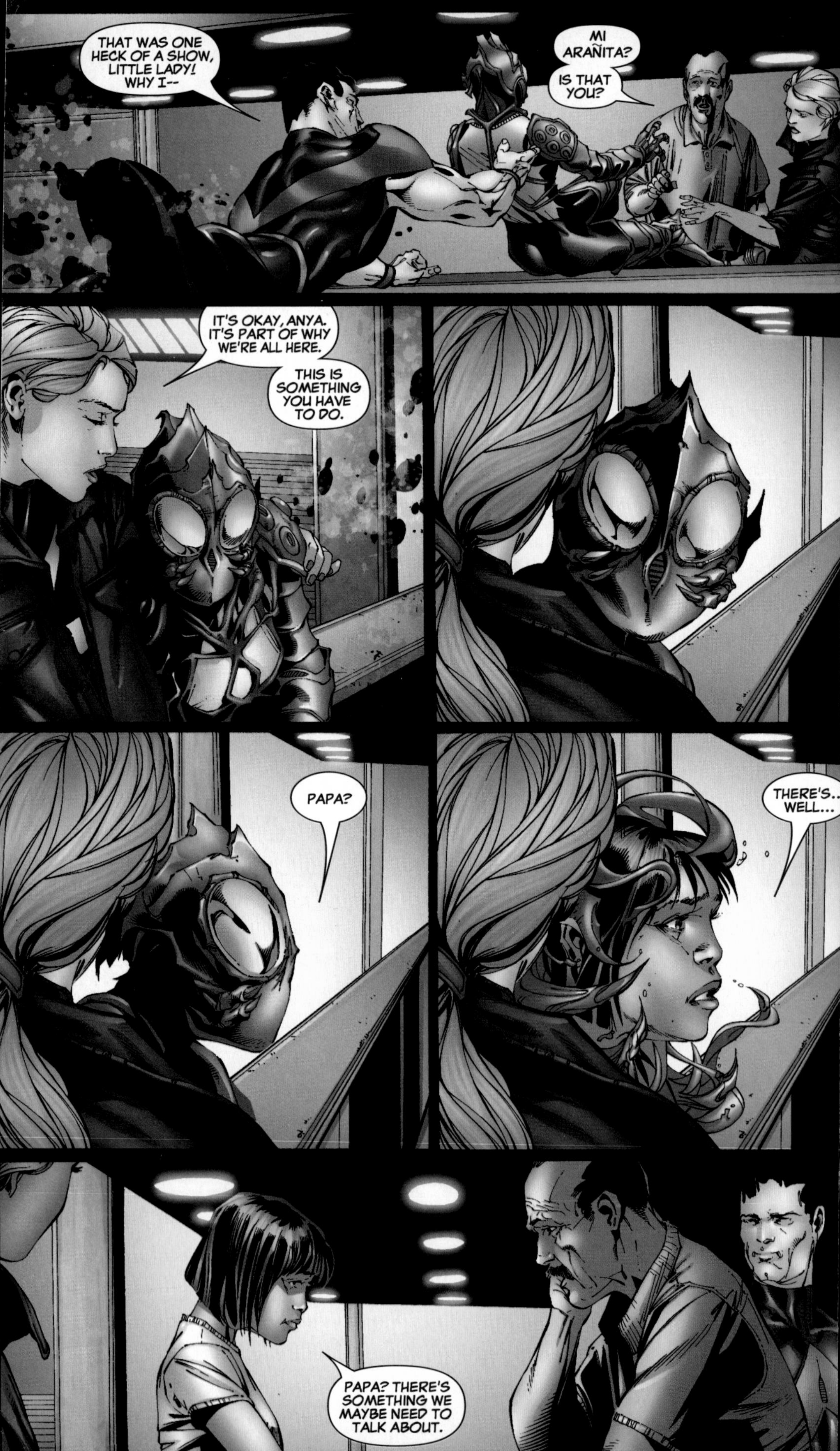
THAT WAS ONE HECK OF A SHOW, LITTLE LADY! WHY I--
MI ARAÑITA?
IS THAT YOU?
IT'S OKAY, ANYA. IT'S PART OF WHY WE'RE ALL HERE.
THIS IS SOMETHING YOU HAVE TO DO.
PAPA?
THERE'S.. WELL...
PAPA? THERE'S SOMETHING WE MAYBE NEED TO TALK ABOUT.

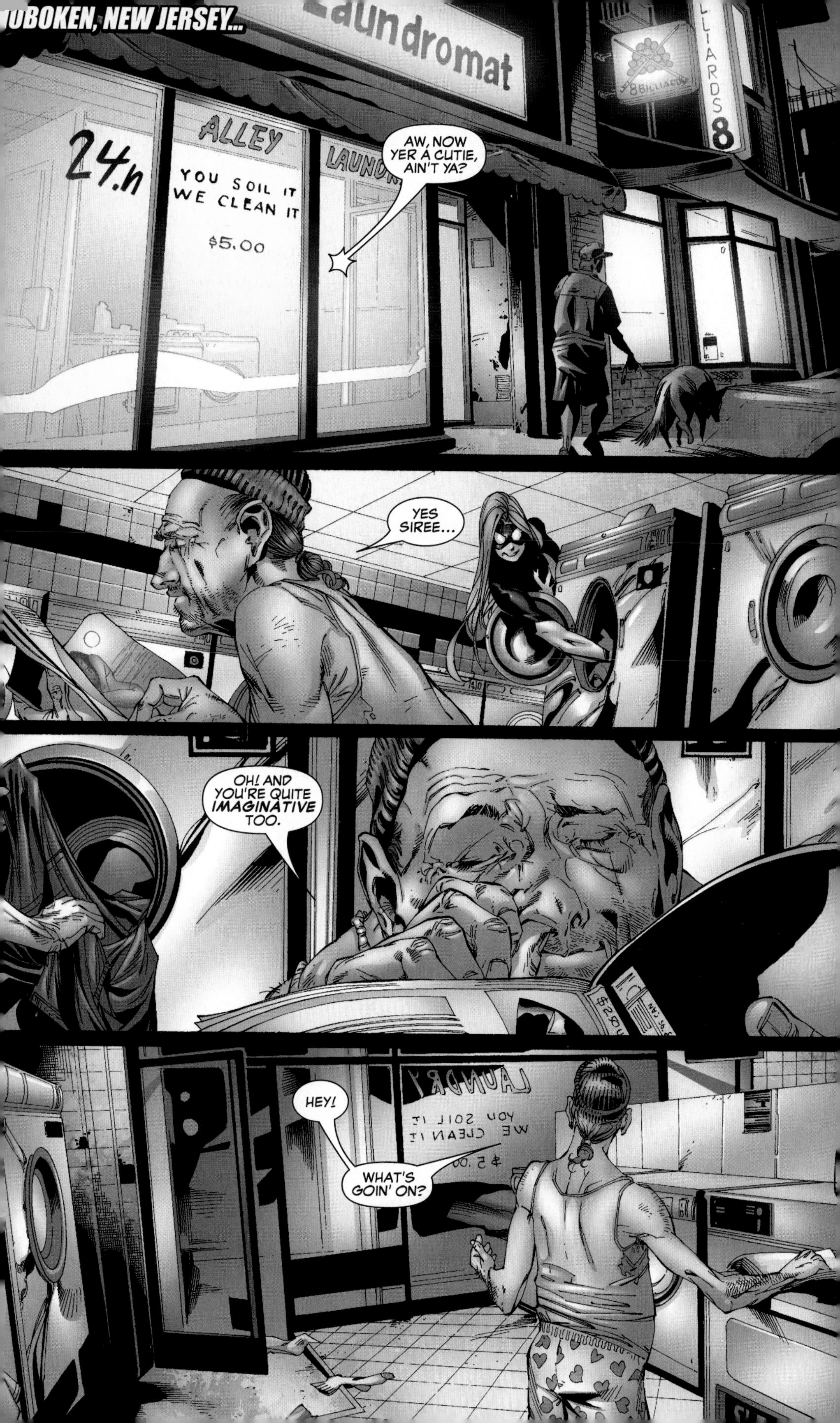

UBOKEN, NEW JERSEY...
Laundromat
ALLEY
LAUNDR
24.h
YOU SOIL IT
WE CLEAN IT
$5.00
8 BILLIARDS
LLIARDS 8
AW, NOW YER A CUTIE, AIN'T YA?
YES SIREE...
OH! AND YOU'RE QUITE *IMAGINATIVE* TOO.
HEY!
WHAT'S GOIN' ON?

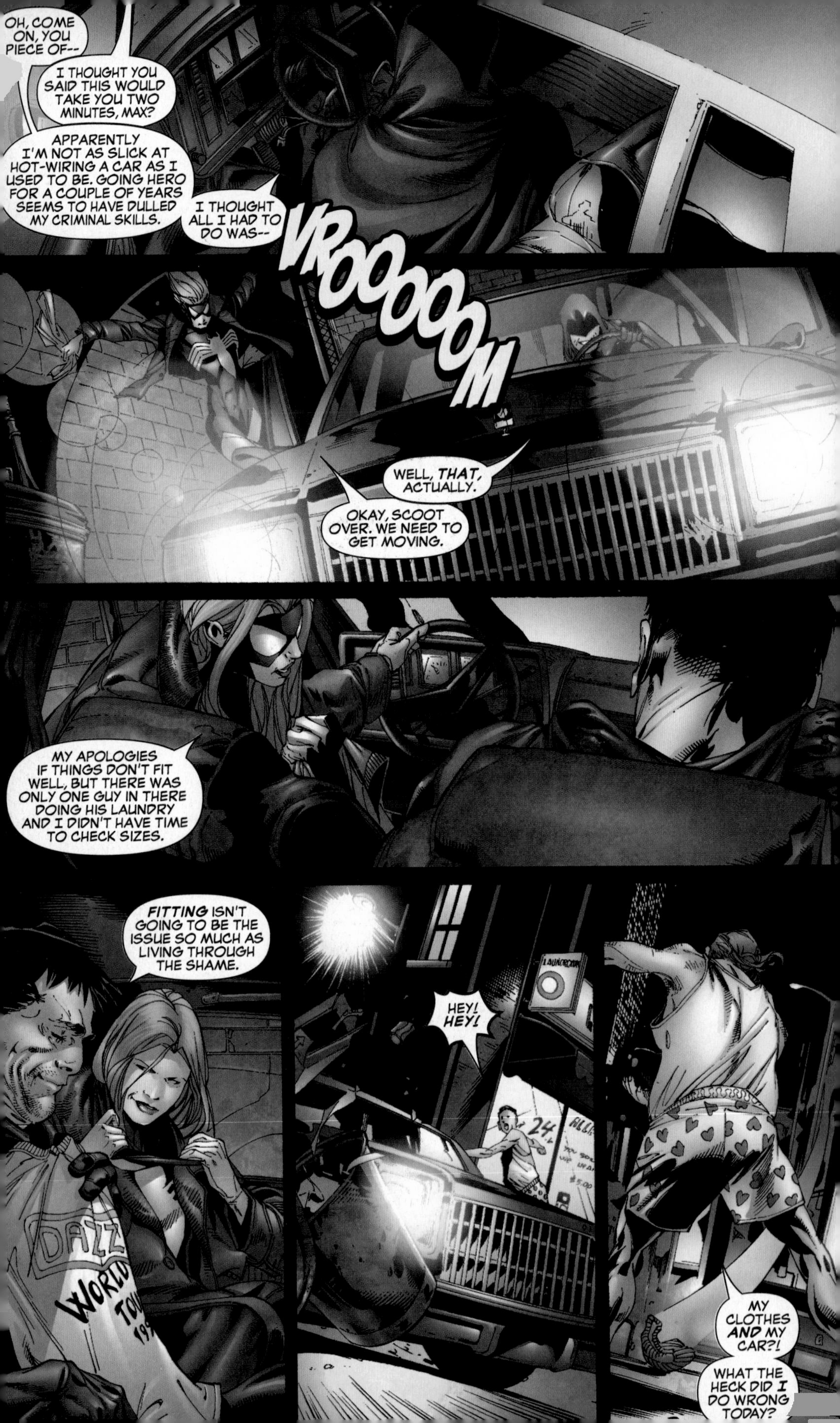
OH, COME ON, YOU PIECE OF--
I THOUGHT YOU SAID THIS WOULD TAKE YOU TWO MINUTES, MAX?
APPARENTLY I'M NOT AS SLICK AT HOT-WIRING A CAR AS I USED TO BE. GOING HERO FOR A COUPLE OF YEARS SEEMS TO HAVE DULLED MY CRIMINAL SKILLS.
I THOUGHT ALL I HAD TO DO WAS--
VROOOOOM
WELL, *THAT*, ACTUALLY.
OKAY, SCOOT OVER. WE NEED TO GET MOVING.
MY APOLOGIES IF THINGS DON'T FIT WELL, BUT THERE WAS ONLY ONE GUY IN THERE DOING HIS LAUNDRY AND I DIDN'T HAVE TIME TO CHECK SIZES.
FITTING ISN'T GOING TO BE THE ISSUE SO MUCH AS LIVING THROUGH THE SHAME.
HEY! *HEY!*
MY CLOTHES *AND* MY CAR?!
WHAT THE HECK DID *I* DO WRONG TODAY?

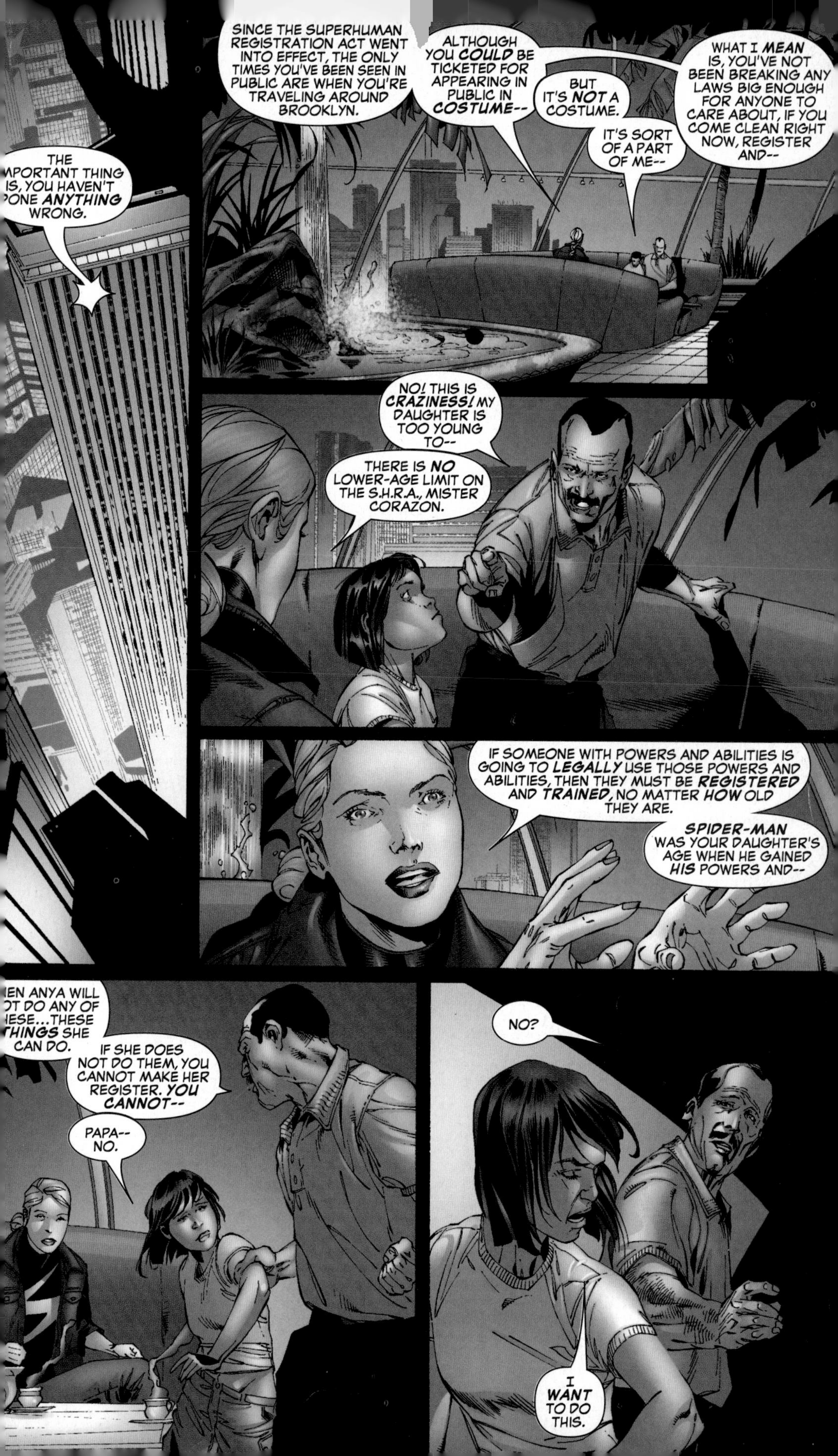
THE IMPORTANT THING IS, YOU HAVEN'T DONE ANYTHING WRONG.
SINCE THE SUPERHUMAN REGISTRATION ACT WENT INTO EFFECT, THE ONLY TIMES YOU'VE BEEN SEEN IN PUBLIC ARE WHEN YOU'RE TRAVELING AROUND BROOKLYN.
ALTHOUGH YOU COULD BE TICKETED FOR APPEARING IN PUBLIC IN COSTUME--
BUT IT'S NOT A COSTUME.
IT'S SORT OF A PART OF ME--
WHAT I MEAN IS, YOU'VE NOT BEEN BREAKING ANY LAWS BIG ENOUGH FOR ANYONE TO CARE ABOUT, IF YOU COME CLEAN RIGHT NOW, REGISTER AND--
NO! THIS IS CRAZINESS! MY DAUGHTER IS TOO YOUNG TO--
THERE IS NO LOWER-AGE LIMIT ON THE S.H.R.A., MISTER CORAZON.
IF SOMEONE WITH POWERS AND ABILITIES IS GOING TO LEGALLY USE THOSE POWERS AND ABILITIES, THEN THEY MUST BE REGISTERED AND TRAINED, NO MATTER HOW OLD THEY ARE.
SPIDER-MAN WAS YOUR DAUGHTER'S AGE WHEN HE GAINED HIS POWERS AND--
HEN ANYA WILL OT DO ANY OF HESE...THESE THINGS SHE CAN DO.
IF SHE DOES NOT DO THEM, YOU CANNOT MAKE HER REGISTER. YOU CANNOT--
PAPA-- NO.
NO?
I WANT TO DO THIS.

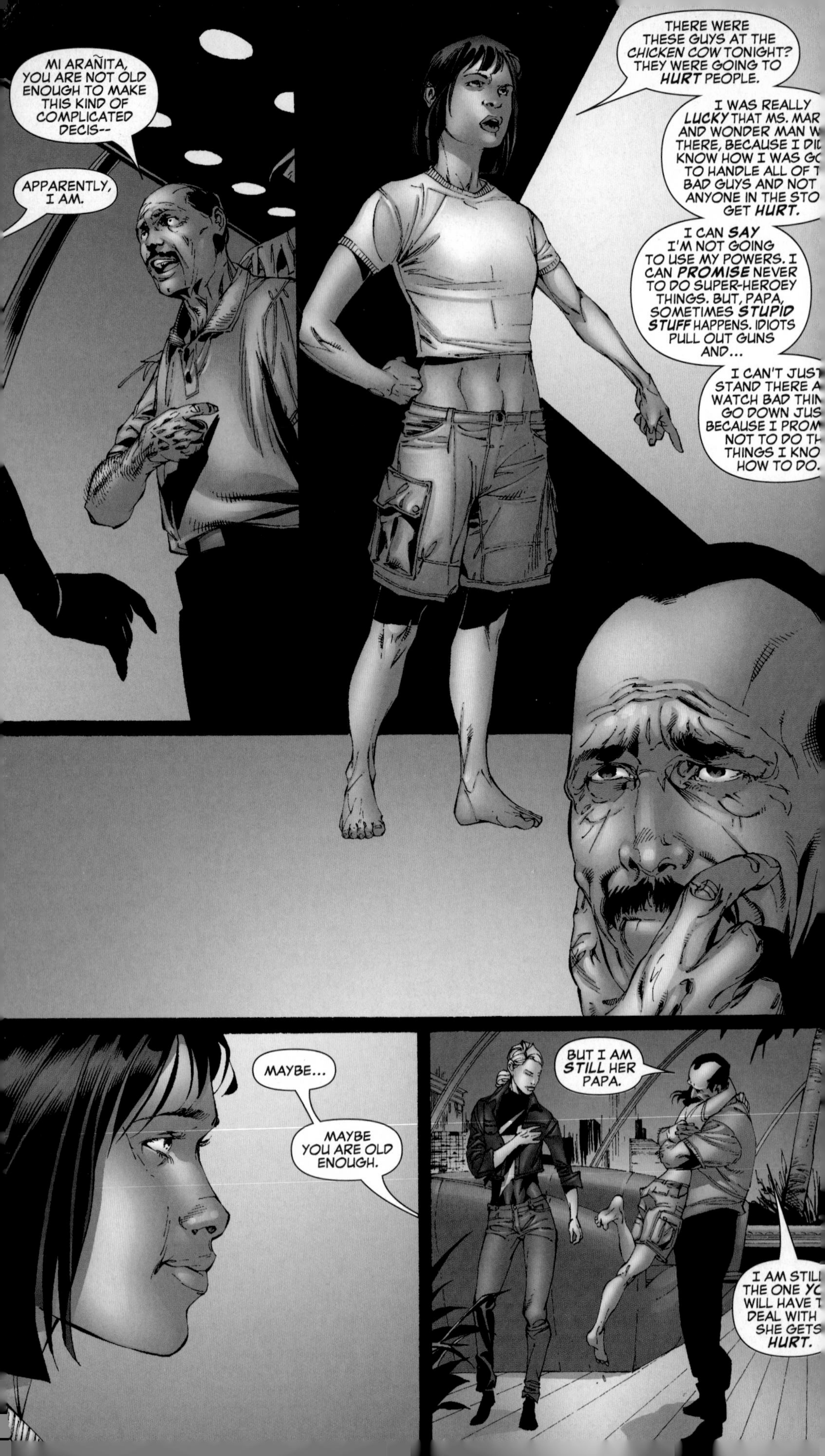

MI ARAÑITA, YOU ARE NOT OLD ENOUGH TO MAKE THIS KIND OF COMPLICATED DECIS--
APPARENTLY, I AM.
THERE WERE THESE GUYS AT THE CHICKEN COW TONIGHT? THEY WERE GOING TO HURT PEOPLE.
I WAS REALLY LUCKY THAT MS. MAR AND WONDER MAN W THERE, BECAUSE I DI KNOW HOW I WAS G TO HANDLE ALL OF T BAD GUYS AND NOT ANYONE IN THE STO GET HURT.
I CAN SAY I'M NOT GOING TO USE MY POWERS. I CAN PROMISE NEVER TO DO SUPER-HEROEY THINGS. BUT, PAPA, SOMETIMES STUPID STUFF HAPPENS. IDIOTS PULL OUT GUNS AND...
I CAN'T JUS STAND THERE A WATCH BAD THI GO DOWN JUS BECAUSE I PROM NOT TO DO T THINGS I KN HOW TO DO.
MAYBE...
MAYBE YOU ARE OLD ENOUGH.
BUT I AM STILL HER PAPA.
I AM STIL THE ONE Y WILL HAVE DEAL WITH SHE GETS HURT.

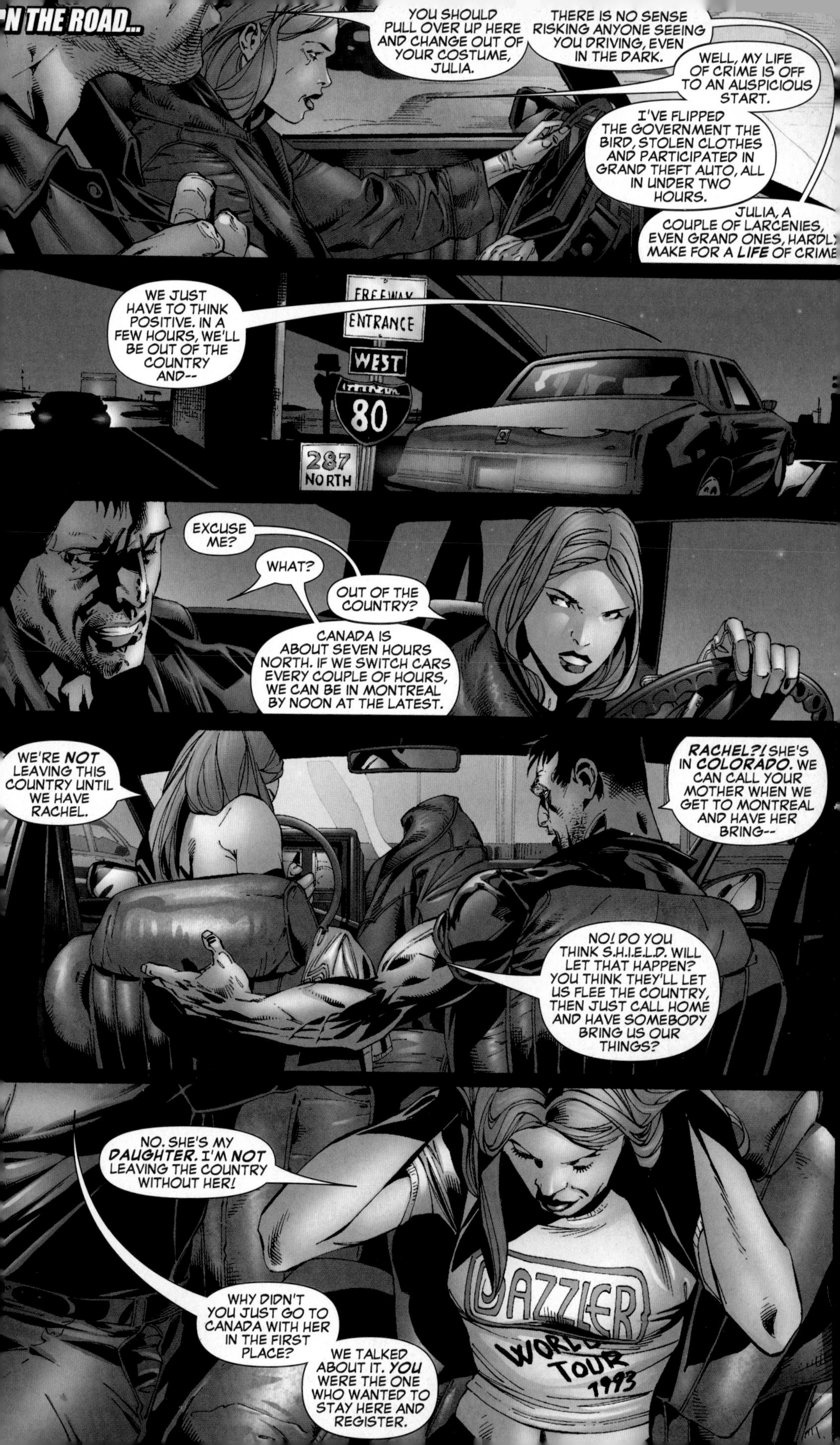
N THE ROAD...
YOU SHOULD PULL OVER UP HERE AND CHANGE OUT OF YOUR COSTUME, JULIA.
THERE IS NO SENSE RISKING ANYONE SEEING YOU DRIVING, EVEN IN THE DARK.
WELL, MY LIFE OF CRIME IS OFF TO AN AUSPICIOUS START.
I'VE FLIPPED THE GOVERNMENT THE BIRD, STOLEN CLOTHES AND PARTICIPATED IN GRAND THEFT AUTO, ALL IN UNDER TWO HOURS.
JULIA, A COUPLE OF LARCENIES, EVEN GRAND ONES, HARDLY MAKE FOR A *LIFE* OF CRIME
WE JUST HAVE TO THINK POSITIVE. IN A FEW HOURS, WE'LL BE OUT OF THE COUNTRY AND--
FREEWAY
ENTRANCE
WEST
80
287 NORTH
EXCUSE ME?
WHAT?
OUT OF THE COUNTRY?
CANADA IS ABOUT SEVEN HOURS NORTH. IF WE SWITCH CARS EVERY COUPLE OF HOURS, WE CAN BE IN MONTREAL BY NOON AT THE LATEST.
WE'RE **NOT** LEAVING THIS COUNTRY UNTIL WE HAVE RACHEL.
RACHEL?! SHE'S IN ***COLORADO.*** WE CAN CALL YOUR MOTHER WHEN WE GET TO MONTREAL AND HAVE HER BRING--
NO! DO YOU THINK S.H.I.E.L.D. WILL LET THAT HAPPEN? YOU THINK THEY'LL LET US FLEE THE COUNTRY, THEN JUST CALL HOME AND HAVE SOMEBODY BRING US OUR THINGS?
NO. SHE'S MY ***DAUGHTER.*** I'M **NOT** LEAVING THE COUNTRY WITHOUT HER!
WHY DIDN'T YOU JUST GO TO CANADA WITH HER IN THE FIRST PLACE?
WE TALKED ABOUT IT. ***YOU*** WERE THE ONE WHO WANTED TO STAY HERE AND REGISTER.
DAZZLER
TOUR
1993

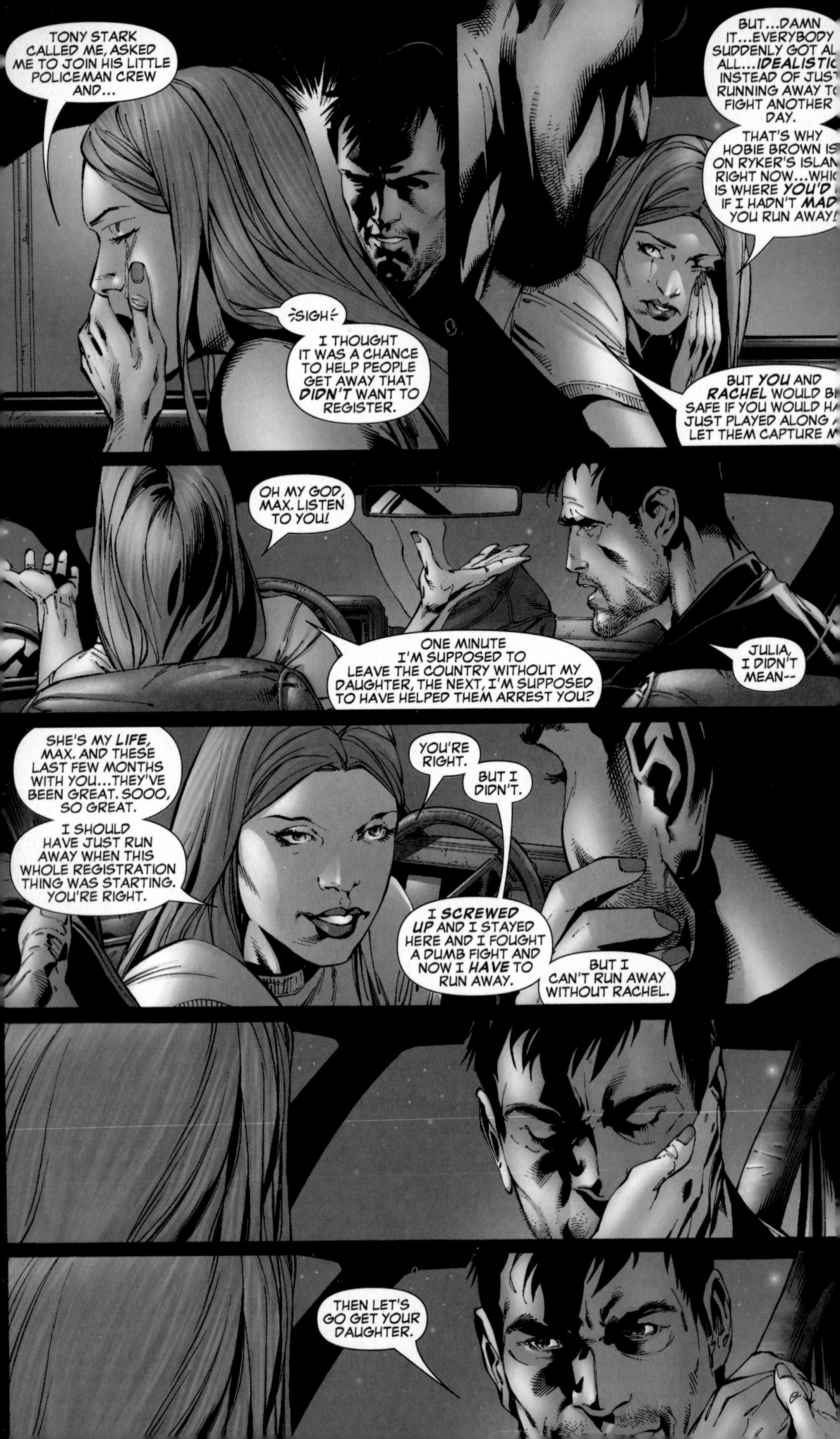
TONY STARK CALLED ME, ASKED ME TO JOIN HIS LITTLE POLICEMAN CREW AND...
-SIGH-
I THOUGHT IT WAS A CHANCE TO HELP PEOPLE GET AWAY THAT DIDN'T WANT TO REGISTER.
BUT...DAMN IT...EVERYBODY SUDDENLY GOT AL ALL...IDEALISTIC INSTEAD OF JUST RUNNING AWAY TO FIGHT ANOTHER DAY.
THAT'S WHY HOBIE BROWN IS ON RYKER'S ISLAN RIGHT NOW...WHIC IS WHERE YOU'D IF I HADN'T MAD YOU RUN AWAY!
BUT YOU AND RACHEL WOULD BE SAFE IF YOU WOULD HA JUST PLAYED ALONG A LET THEM CAPTURE M
OH MY GOD, MAX. LISTEN TO YOU!
ONE MINUTE I'M SUPPOSED TO LEAVE THE COUNTRY WITHOUT MY DAUGHTER, THE NEXT, I'M SUPPOSED TO HAVE HELPED THEM ARREST YOU?
JULIA, I DIDN'T MEAN--
SHE'S MY LIFE, MAX. AND THESE LAST FEW MONTHS WITH YOU...THEY'VE BEEN GREAT. SOOO, SO GREAT.
I SHOULD HAVE JUST RUN AWAY WHEN THIS WHOLE REGISTRATION THING WAS STARTING. YOU'RE RIGHT.
YOU'RE RIGHT.
BUT I DIDN'T.
I SCREWED UP AND I STAYED HERE AND I FOUGHT A DUMB FIGHT AND NOW I HAVE TO RUN AWAY.
BUT I CAN'T RUN AWAY WITHOUT RACHEL.
THEN LET'S GO GET YOUR DAUGHTER.

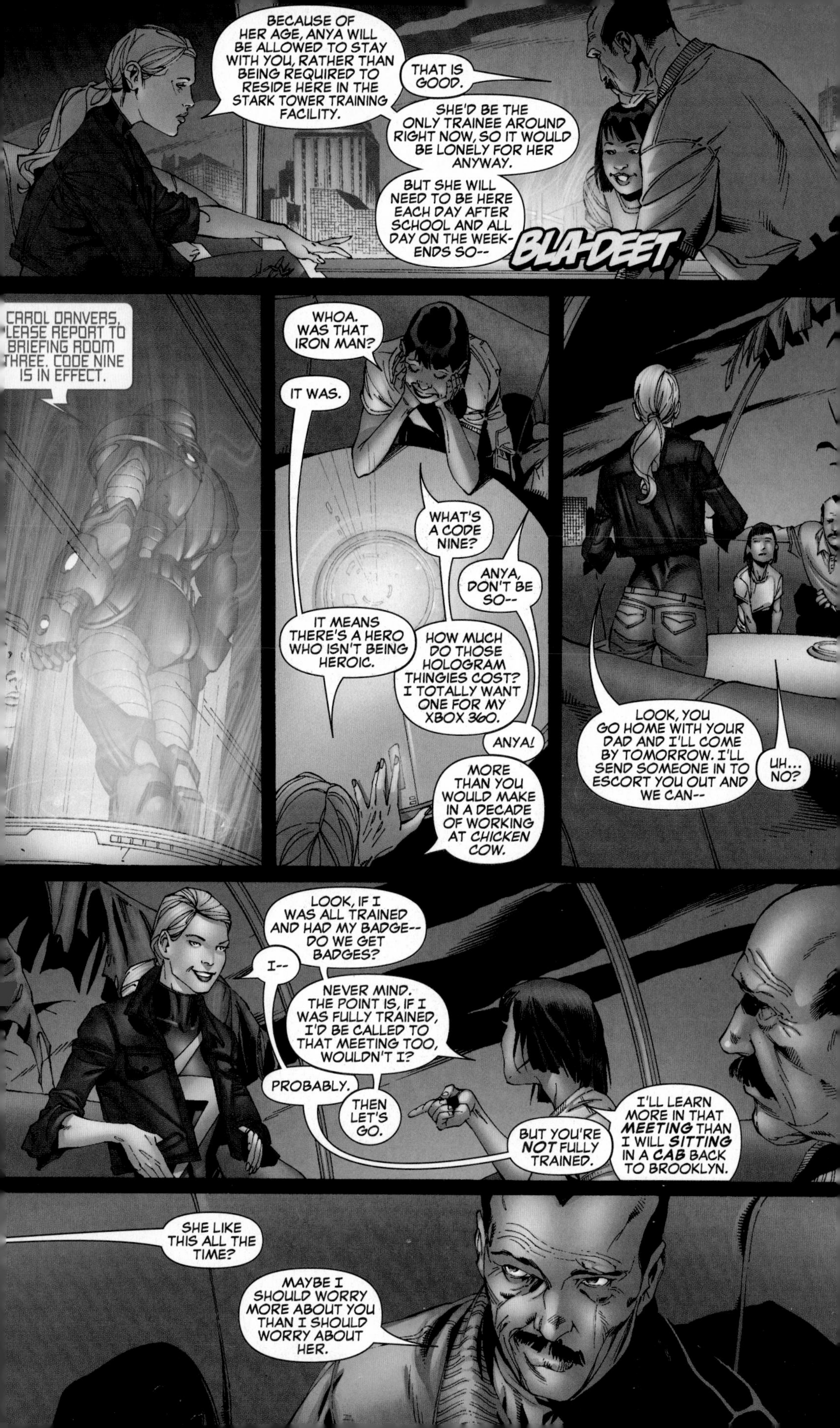
BECAUSE OF HER AGE, ANYA WILL BE ALLOWED TO STAY WITH YOU, RATHER THAN BEING REQUIRED TO RESIDE HERE IN THE STARK TOWER TRAINING FACILITY.
THAT IS GOOD.
SHE'D BE THE ONLY TRAINEE AROUND RIGHT NOW, SO IT WOULD BE LONELY FOR HER ANYWAY.
BUT SHE WILL NEED TO BE HERE EACH DAY AFTER SCHOOL AND ALL DAY ON THE WEEK-ENDS SO--
BLA-DEET
CAROL DANVERS, PLEASE REPORT TO BRIEFING ROOM THREE. CODE NINE IS IN EFFECT.
WHOA. WAS THAT IRON MAN?
IT WAS.
WHAT'S A CODE NINE?
ANYA, DON'T BE SO--
IT MEANS THERE'S A HERO WHO ISN'T BEING HEROIC.
HOW MUCH DO THOSE HOLOGRAM THINGIES COST? I TOTALLY WANT ONE FOR MY XBOX 360.
ANYA!
MORE THAN YOU WOULD MAKE IN A DECADE OF WORKING AT CHICKEN COW.
LOOK, YOU GO HOME WITH YOUR DAD AND I'LL COME BY TOMORROW. I'LL SEND SOMEONE IN TO ESCORT YOU OUT AND WE CAN--
UH... NO?
LOOK, IF I WAS ALL TRAINED AND HAD MY BADGE-- DO WE GET BADGES?
I--
NEVER MIND. THE POINT IS, IF I WAS FULLY TRAINED, I'D BE CALLED TO THAT MEETING TOO, WOULDN'T I?
PROBABLY.
THEN LET'S GO.
BUT YOU'RE NOT FULLY TRAINED.
I'LL LEARN MORE IN THAT MEETING THAN I WILL SITTING IN A CAB BACK TO BROOKLYN.
SHE LIKE THIS ALL THE TIME?
MAYBE I SHOULD WORRY MORE ABOUT YOU THAN I SHOULD WORRY ABOUT HER.

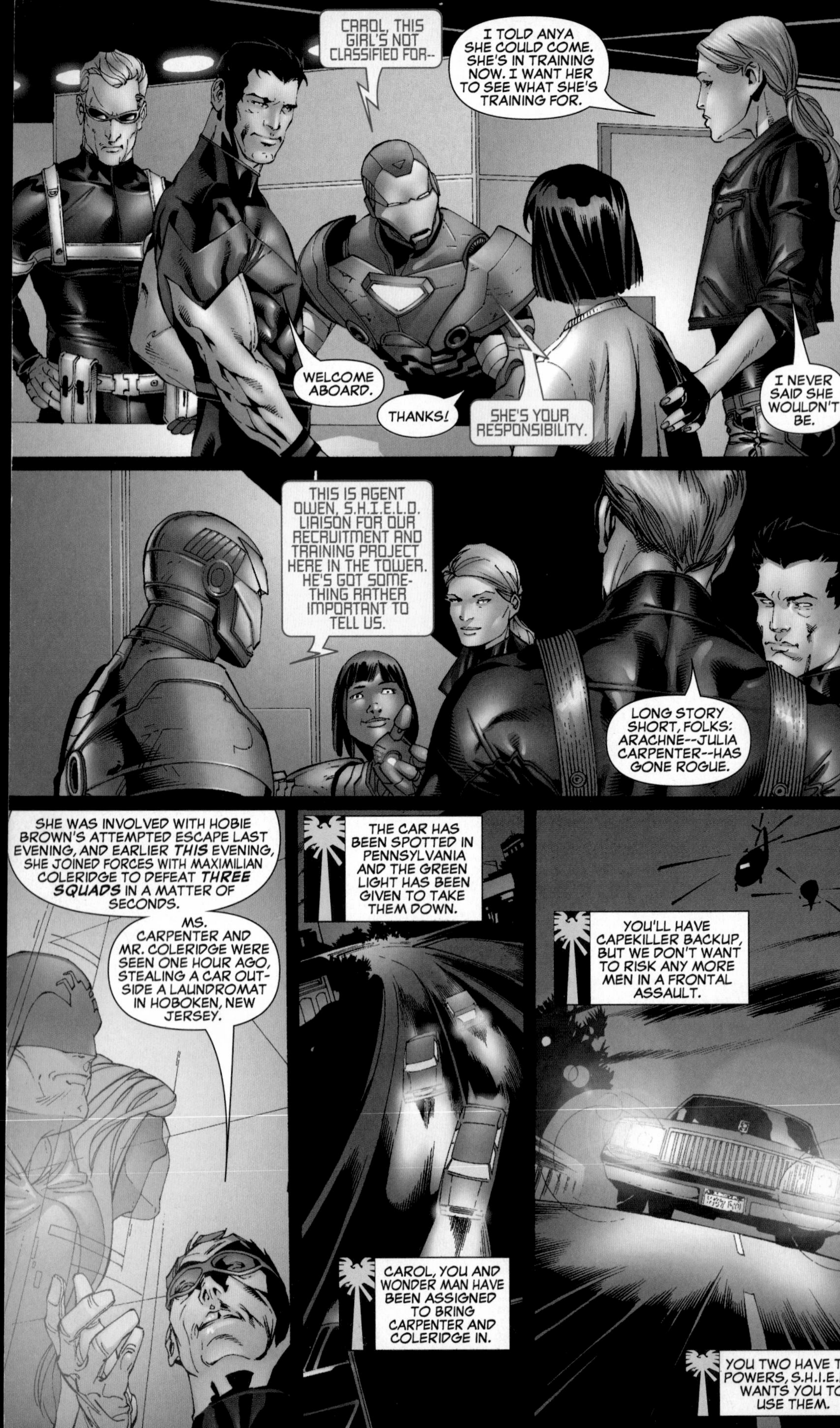
CAROL, THIS GIRL'S NOT CLASSIFIED FOR--
I TOLD ANYA SHE COULD COME. SHE'S IN TRAINING NOW. I WANT HER TO SEE WHAT SHE'S TRAINING FOR.
WELCOME ABOARD.
THANKS!
SHE'S YOUR RESPONSIBILITY.
I NEVER SAID SHE WOULDN'T BE.
THIS IS AGENT OWEN, S.H.I.E.L.D. LIAISON FOR OUR RECRUITMENT AND TRAINING PROJECT HERE IN THE TOWER. HE'S GOT SOMETHING RATHER IMPORTANT TO TELL US.
LONG STORY SHORT, FOLKS: ARACHNE--JULIA CARPENTER--HAS GONE ROGUE.
SHE WAS INVOLVED WITH HOBIE BROWN'S ATTEMPTED ESCAPE LAST EVENING, AND EARLIER *THIS* EVENING, SHE JOINED FORCES WITH MAXIMILIAN COLERIDGE TO DEFEAT ***THREE SQUADS*** IN A MATTER OF SECONDS.
MS. CARPENTER AND MR. COLERIDGE WERE SEEN ONE HOUR AGO, STEALING A CAR OUTSIDE A LAUNDROMAT IN HOBOKEN, NEW JERSEY.
THE CAR HAS BEEN SPOTTED IN PENNSYLVANIA AND THE GREEN LIGHT HAS BEEN GIVEN TO TAKE THEM DOWN.
CAROL, YOU AND WONDER MAN HAVE BEEN ASSIGNED TO BRING CARPENTER AND COLERIDGE IN.
YOU'LL HAVE CAPEKILLER BACKUP, BUT WE DON'T WANT TO RISK ANY MORE MEN IN A FRONTAL ASSAULT.
YOU TWO HAVE T POWERS, S.H.I.E. WANTS YOU TO USE THEM.

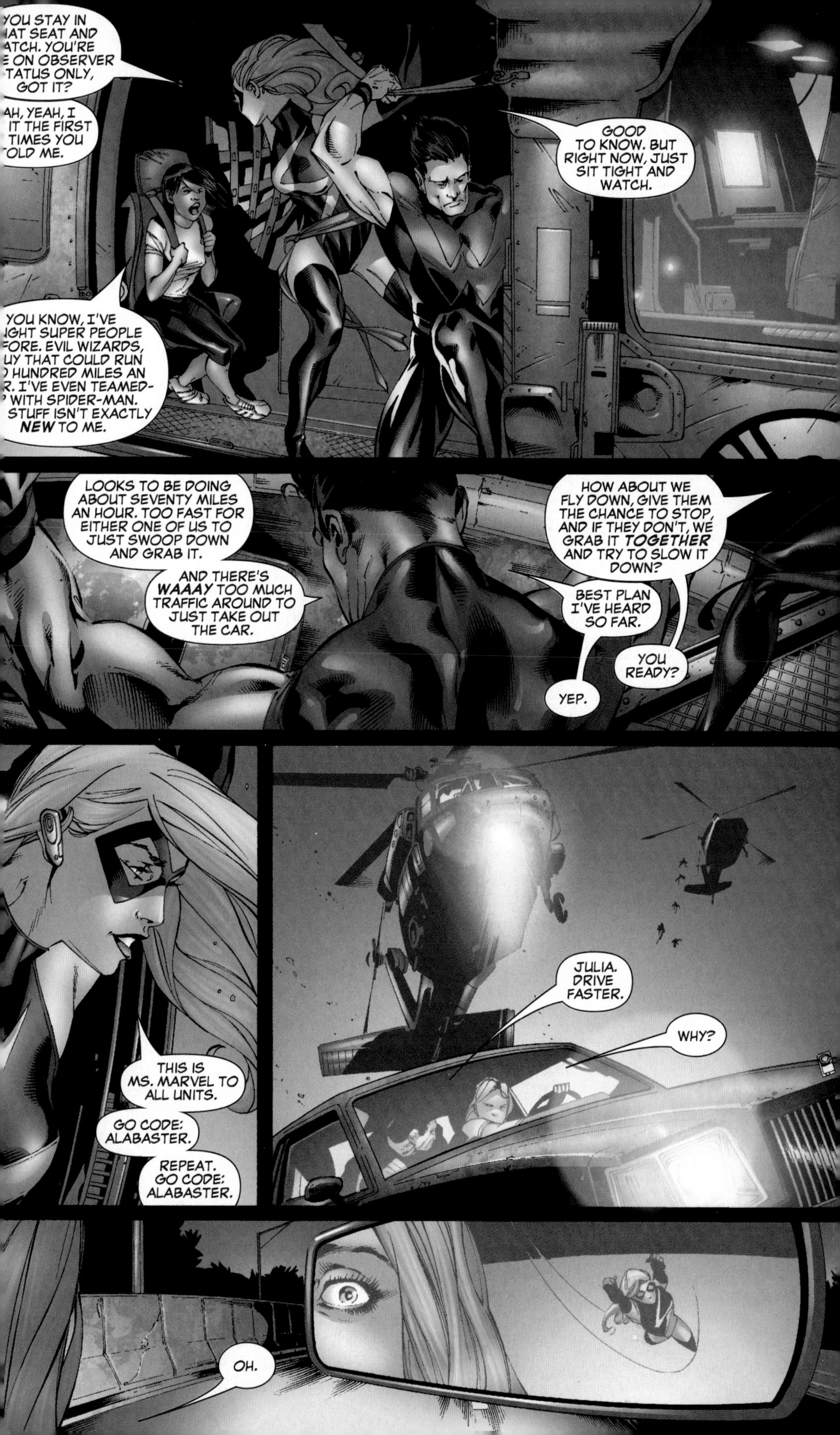

YOU STAY IN
IAT SEAT AND
ATCH. YOU'RE
E ON OBSERVER
TATUS ONLY,
GOT IT?
AH, YEAH, I
IT THE FIRST
TIMES YOU
TOLD ME.
GOOD TO KNOW. BUT RIGHT NOW, JUST SIT TIGHT AND WATCH.
YOU KNOW, I'VE
IGHT SUPER PEOPLE
FORE. EVIL WIZARDS,
UY THAT COULD RUN
HUNDRED MILES AN
R. I'VE EVEN TEAMED-
WITH SPIDER-MAN.
STUFF ISN'T EXACTLY
NEW TO ME.
LOOKS TO BE DOING ABOUT SEVENTY MILES AN HOUR. TOO FAST FOR EITHER ONE OF US TO JUST SWOOP DOWN AND GRAB IT.
AND THERE'S **WAAAY** TOO MUCH TRAFFIC AROUND TO JUST TAKE OUT THE CAR.
HOW ABOUT WE FLY DOWN, GIVE THEM THE CHANCE TO STOP, AND IF THEY DON'T, WE GRAB IT ***TOGETHER*** AND TRY TO SLOW IT DOWN?
BEST PLAN I'VE HEARD SO FAR.
YOU READY?
YEP.
THIS IS MS. MARVEL TO ALL UNITS.
GO CODE: ALABASTER.
REPEAT. GO CODE: ALABASTER.
JULIA. DRIVE FASTER.
WHY?
OH.

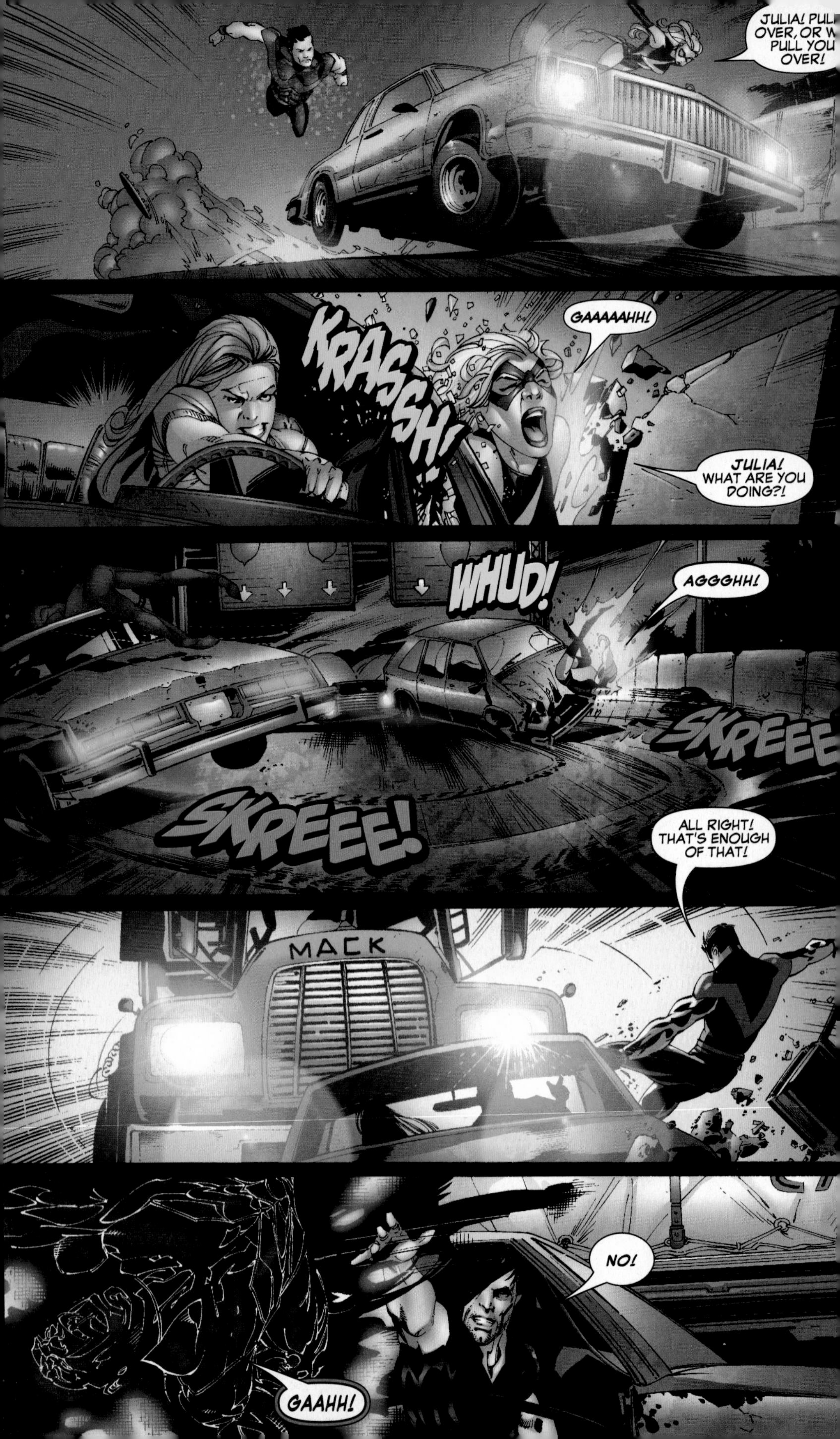

JULIA! PULL OVER, OR W PULL YOU OVER!
KRASSH!
GAAAAAHH!
JULIA! WHAT ARE YOU DOING?!
WHUD!
AGGGHH!
SKREEE
SKREEE!
ALL RIGHT! THAT'S ENOUGH OF THAT!
MACK
NO!
GAAHH!

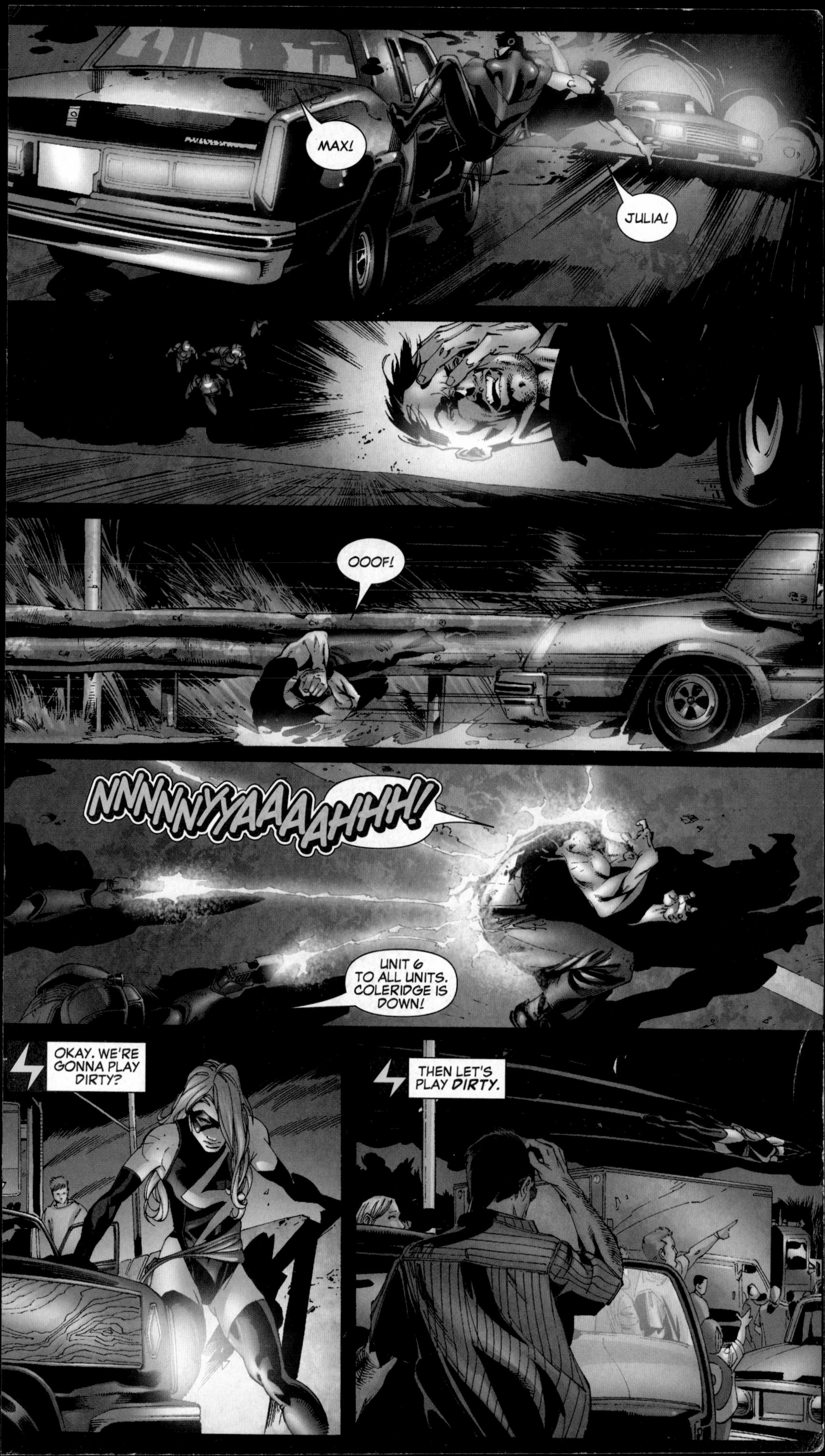
MAX!
JULIA!
OOOF!
NNNNNYYAAAAAHHH!
UNIT 6 TO ALL UNITS. COLERIDGE IS DOWN!
OKAY. WE'RE GONNA PLAY DIRTY?
THEN LET'S PLAY DIRTY.

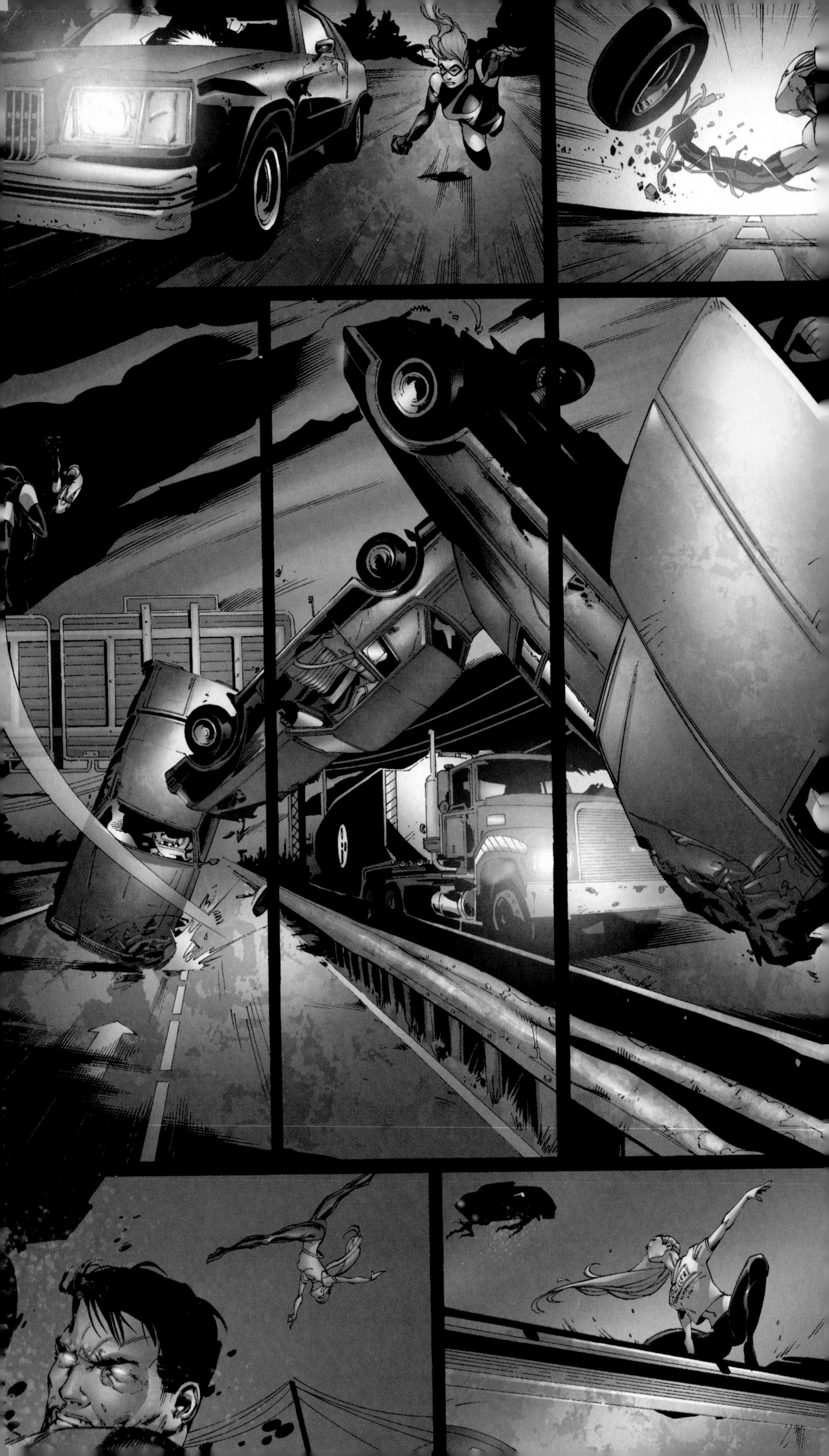

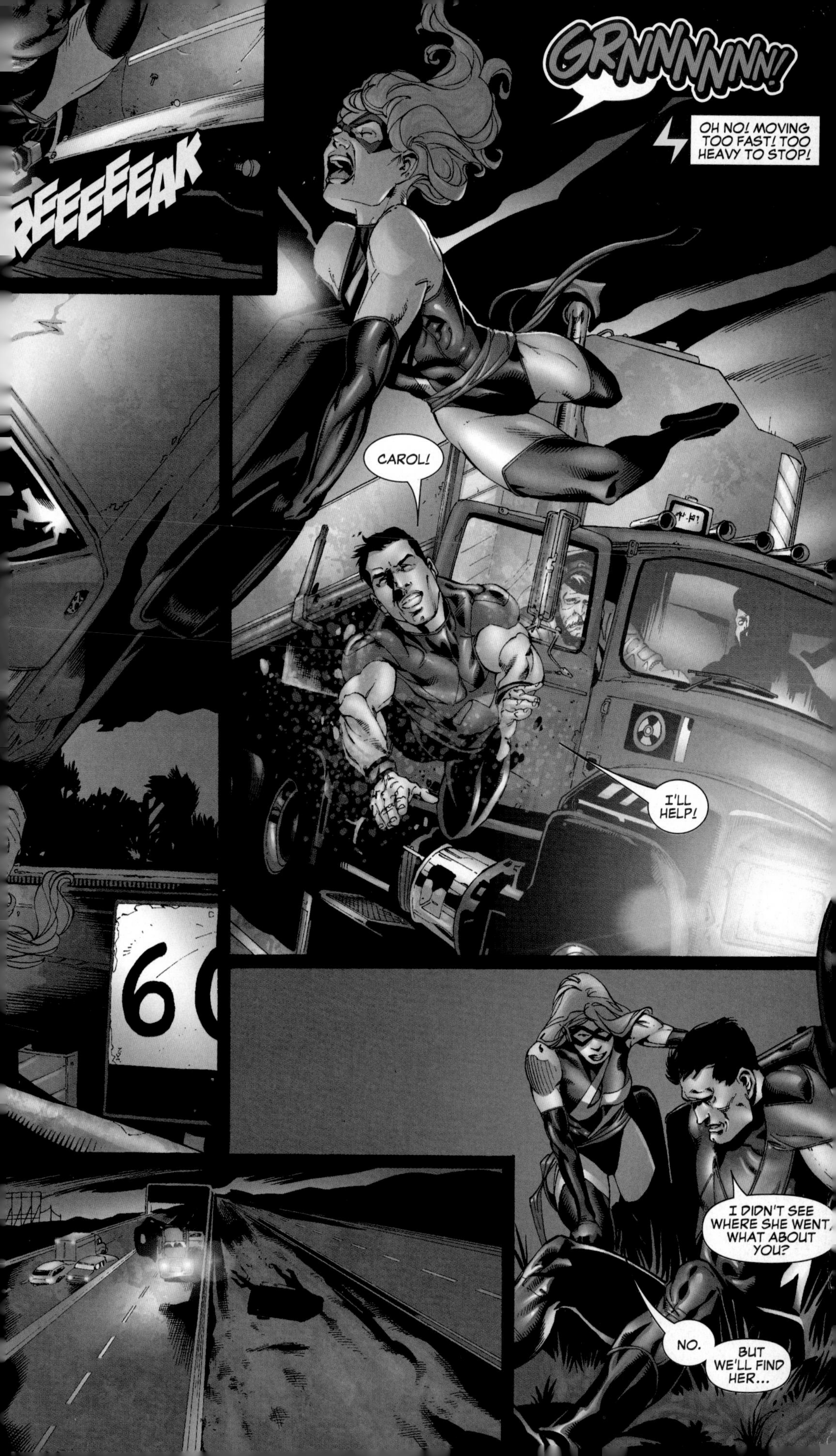
REEEEEAK
GRNNNNNN!
OH NO! MOVING TOO FAST! TOO HEAVY TO STOP!
CAROL!
I'LL HELP!
60
I DIDN'T SEE WHERE SHE WENT. WHAT ABOUT YOU?
NO.
BUT WE'LL FIND HER...

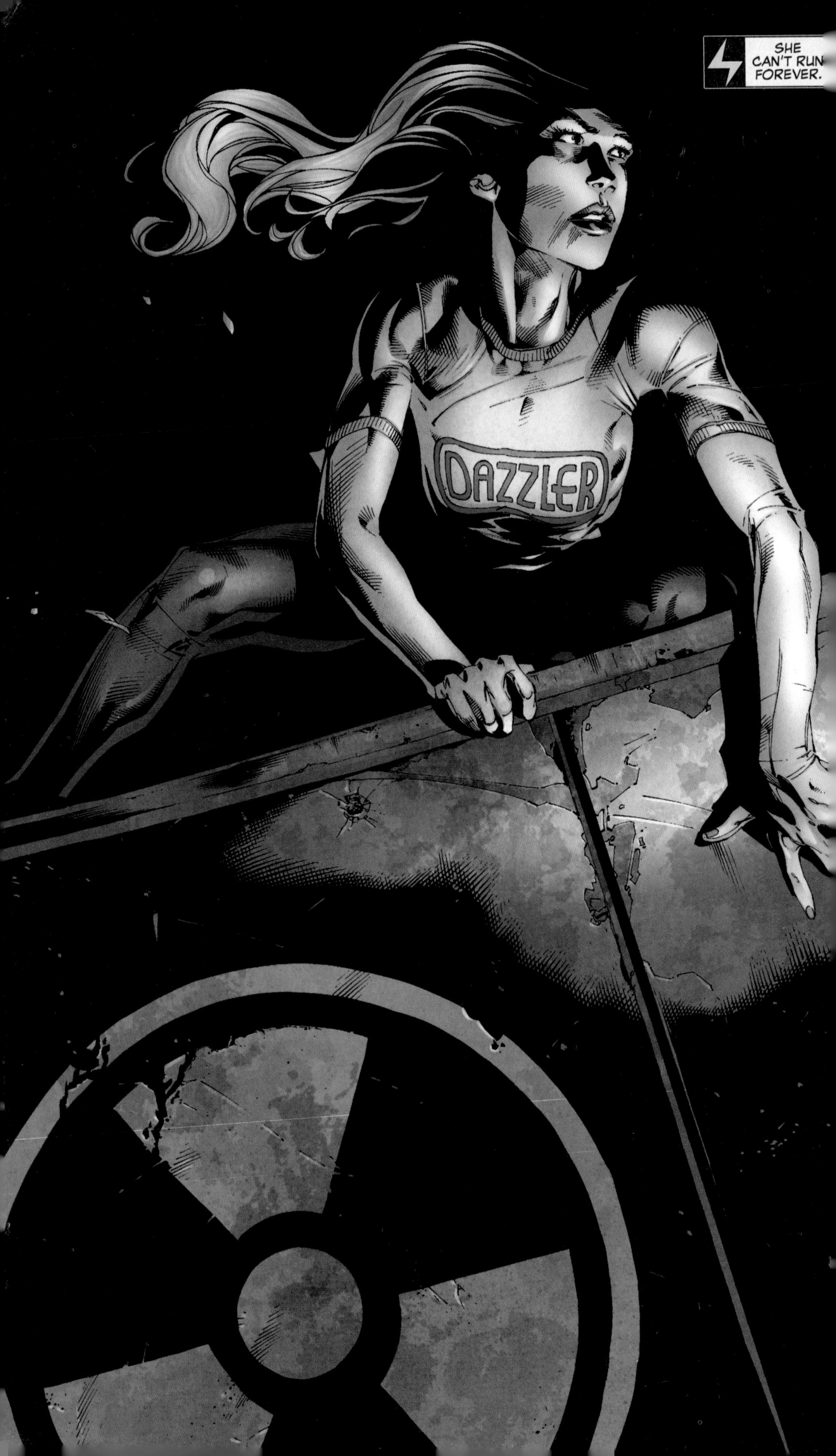

SHE CAN'T RUN FOREVER.
DAZZLER

MS. MARVEL
A MARVEL COMICS EVENT

CIVIL WAR

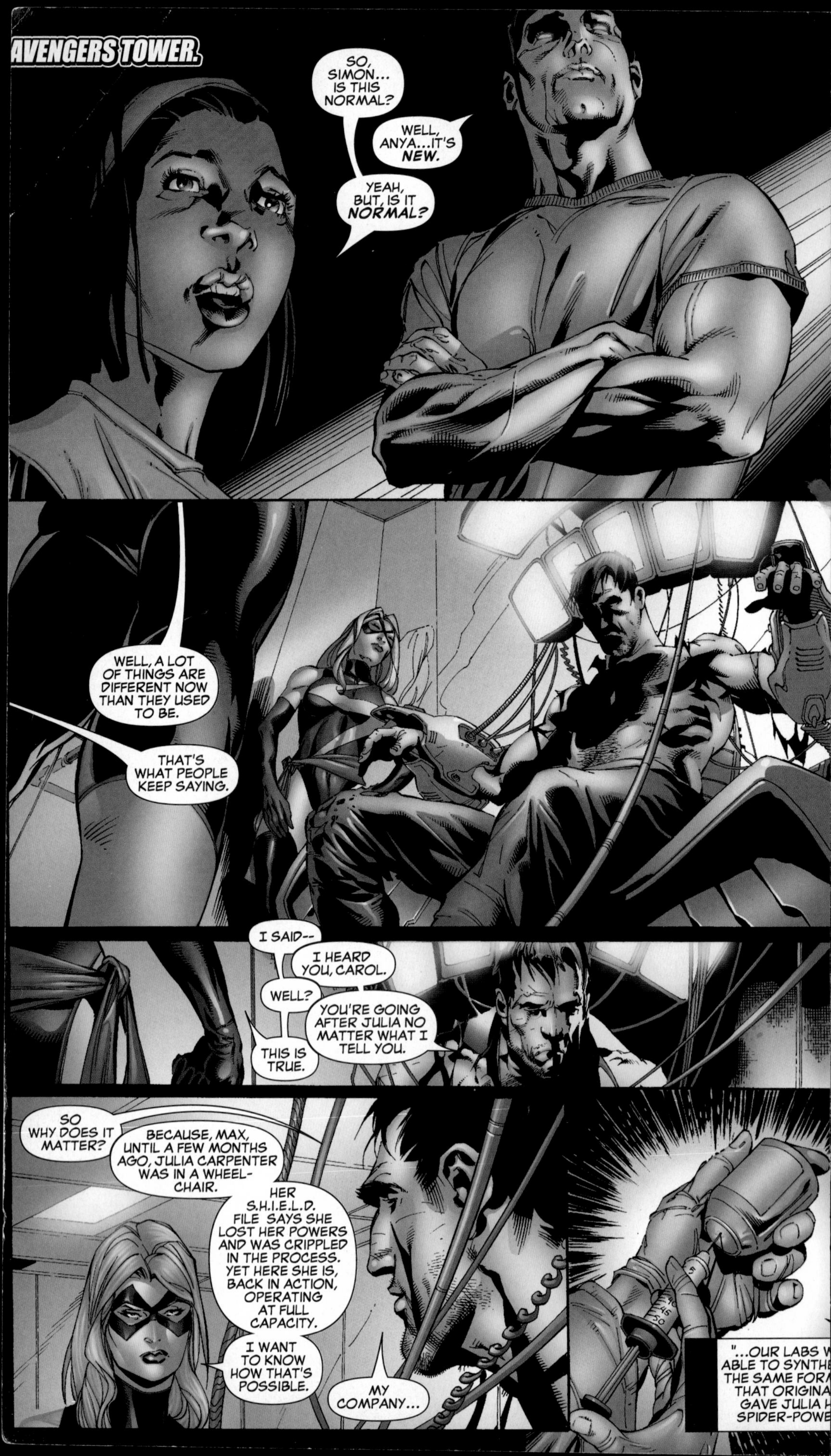
AVENGERS TOWER.
SO, SIMON... IS THIS NORMAL?
WELL, ANYA...IT'S NEW.
YEAH, BUT, IS IT NORMAL?
WELL, A LOT OF THINGS ARE DIFFERENT NOW THAN THEY USED TO BE.
THAT'S WHAT PEOPLE KEEP SAYING.
I SAID--
I HEARD YOU, CAROL.
WELL?
YOU'RE GOING AFTER JULIA NO MATTER WHAT I TELL YOU.
THIS IS TRUE.
SO WHY DOES IT MATTER?
BECAUSE, MAX, UNTIL A FEW MONTHS AGO, JULIA CARPENTER WAS IN A WHEEL-CHAIR.
HER S.H.I.E.L.D. FILE SAYS SHE LOST HER POWERS AND WAS CRIPPLED IN THE PROCESS. YET HERE SHE IS, BACK IN ACTION, OPERATING AT FULL CAPACITY.
I WANT TO KNOW HOW THAT'S POSSIBLE.
MY COMPANY...

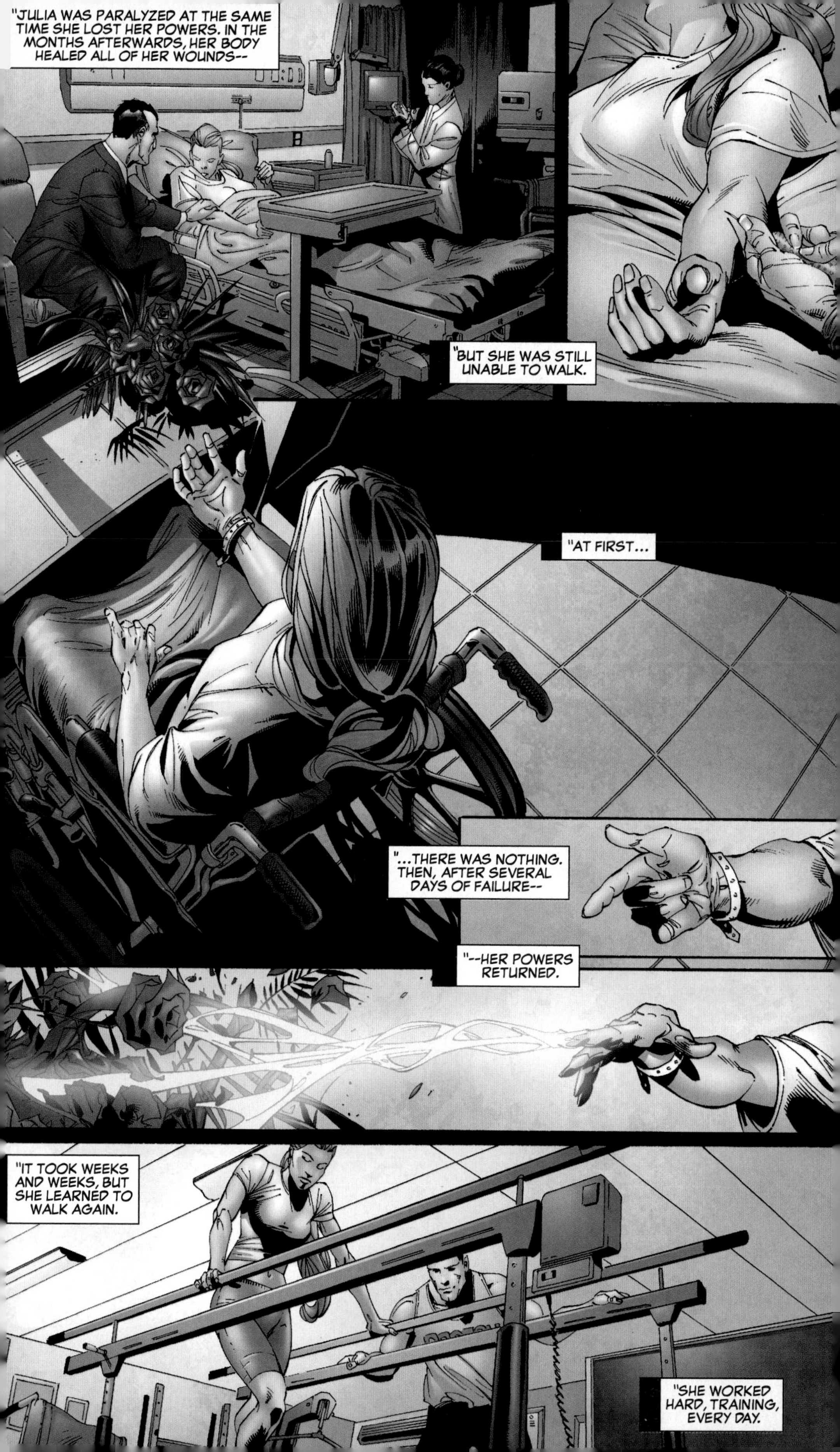
"JULIA WAS PARALYZED AT THE SAME TIME SHE LOST HER POWERS. IN THE MONTHS AFTERWARDS, HER BODY HEALED ALL OF HER WOUNDS--
"BUT SHE WAS STILL UNABLE TO WALK.
"AT FIRST...
"...THERE WAS NOTHING. THEN, AFTER SEVERAL DAYS OF FAILURE--
"--HER POWERS RETURNED.
"IT TOOK WEEKS AND WEEKS, BUT SHE LEARNED TO WALK AGAIN.
"SHE WORKED HARD, TRAINING, EVERY DAY.

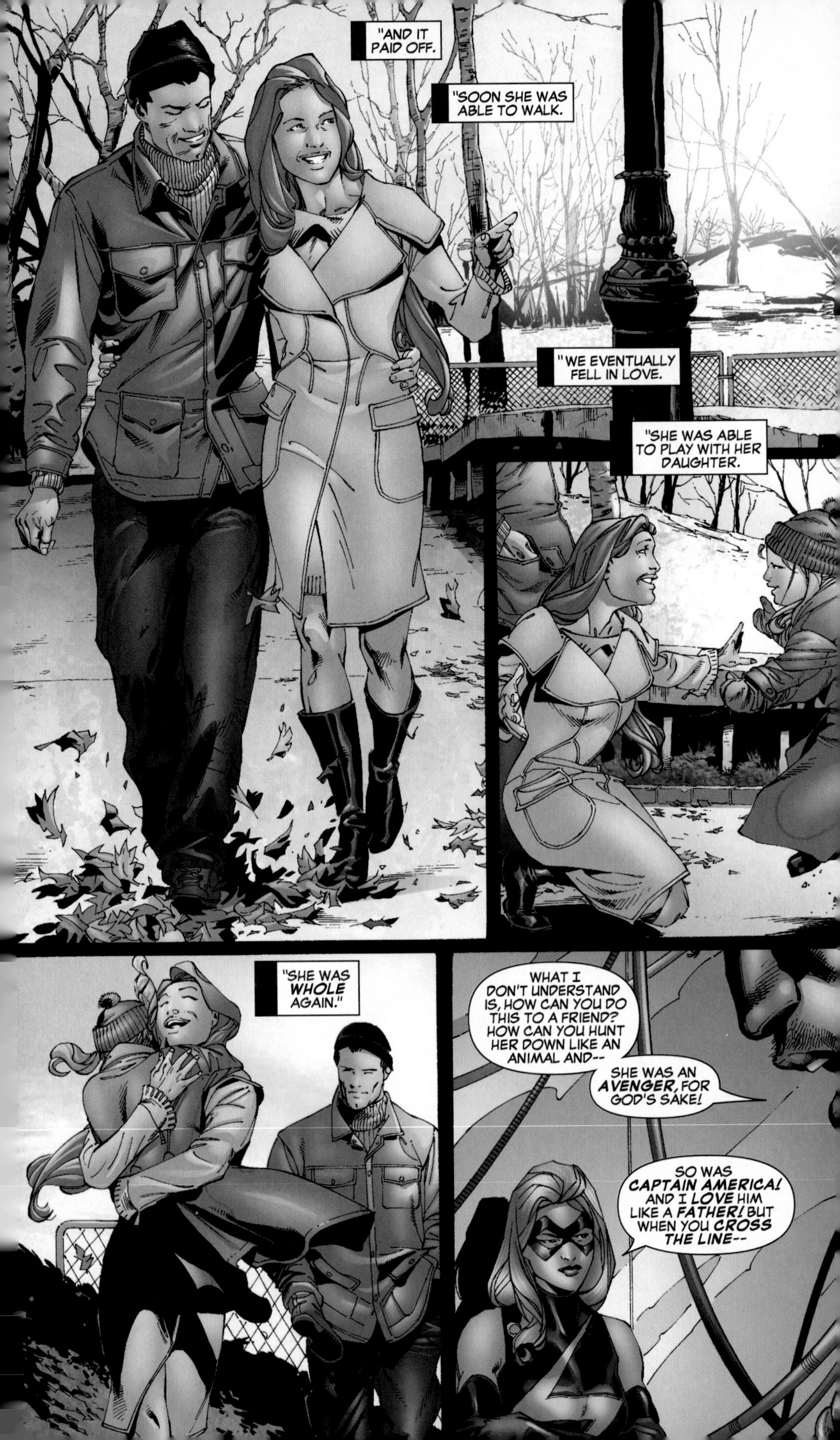
"AND IT PAID OFF.
"SOON SHE WAS ABLE TO WALK.
"WE EVENTUALLY FELL IN LOVE.
"SHE WAS ABLE TO PLAY WITH HER DAUGHTER.
"SHE WAS **WHOLE** AGAIN."
WHAT I DON'T UNDERSTAND IS, HOW CAN YOU DO THIS TO A FRIEND? HOW CAN YOU HUNT HER DOWN LIKE AN ANIMAL AND--
SHE WAS AN **AVENGER**, FOR GOD'S SAKE!
SO WAS **CAPTAIN AMERICA!** AND I **LOVE** HIM LIKE A **FATHER!** BUT WHEN YOU **CROSS THE LINE**--

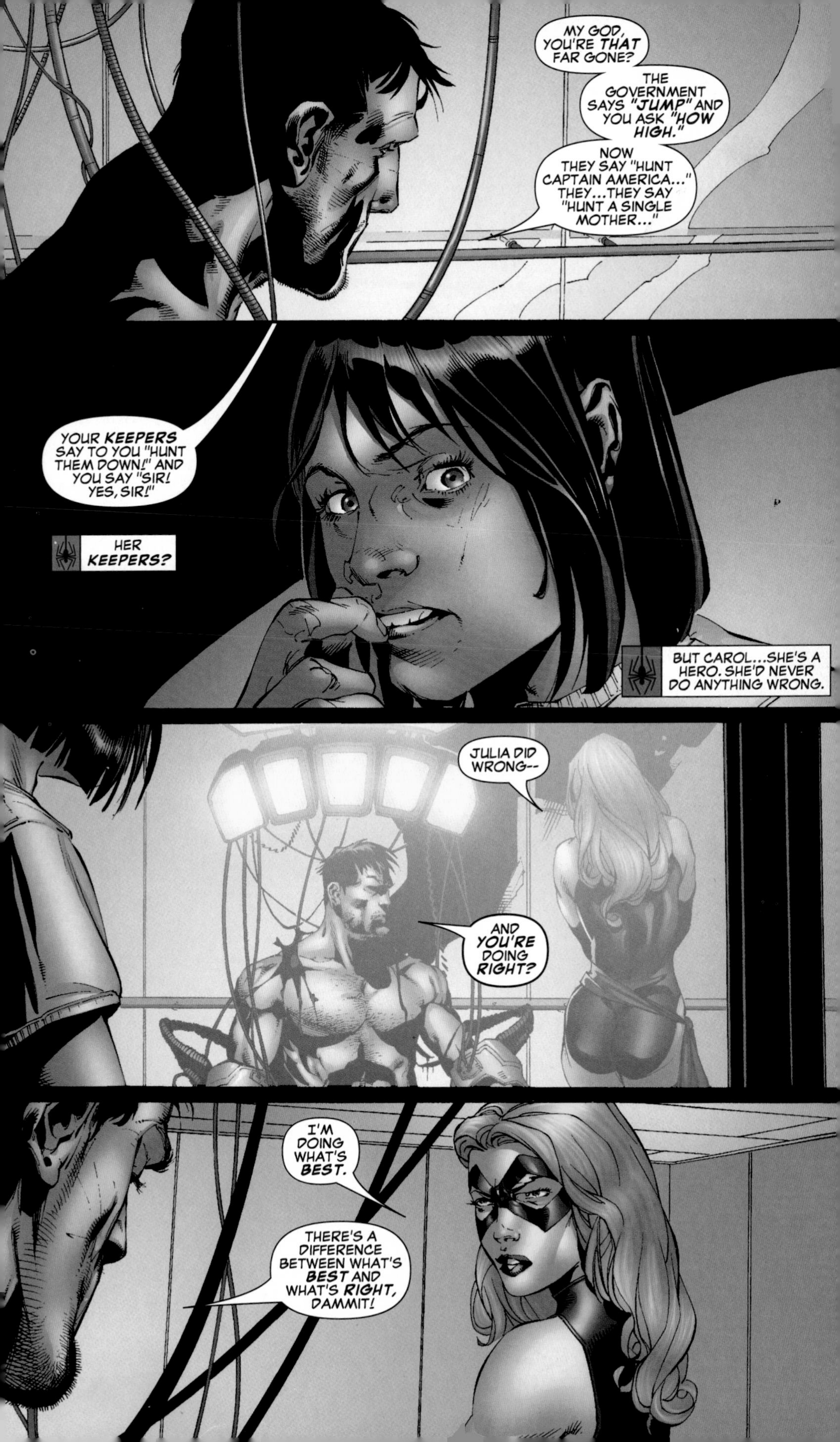
MY GOD, YOU'RE *THAT* FAR GONE?
THE GOVERNMENT SAYS *"JUMP"* AND YOU ASK *"HOW HIGH."*
NOW THEY SAY "HUNT CAPTAIN AMERICA..." THEY...THEY SAY "HUNT A SINGLE MOTHER..."
YOUR **KEEPERS** SAY TO YOU "HUNT THEM DOWN!" AND YOU SAY "SIR! YES, SIR!"
HER ***KEEPERS?***
BUT CAROL...SHE'S A HERO. SHE'D NEVER DO ANYTHING WRONG.
JULIA DID WRONG--
AND ***YOU'RE*** DOING ***RIGHT?***
I'M DOING WHAT'S ***BEST.***
THERE'S A DIFFERENCE BETWEEN WHAT'S ***BEST*** AND WHAT'S ***RIGHT,*** DAMMIT!

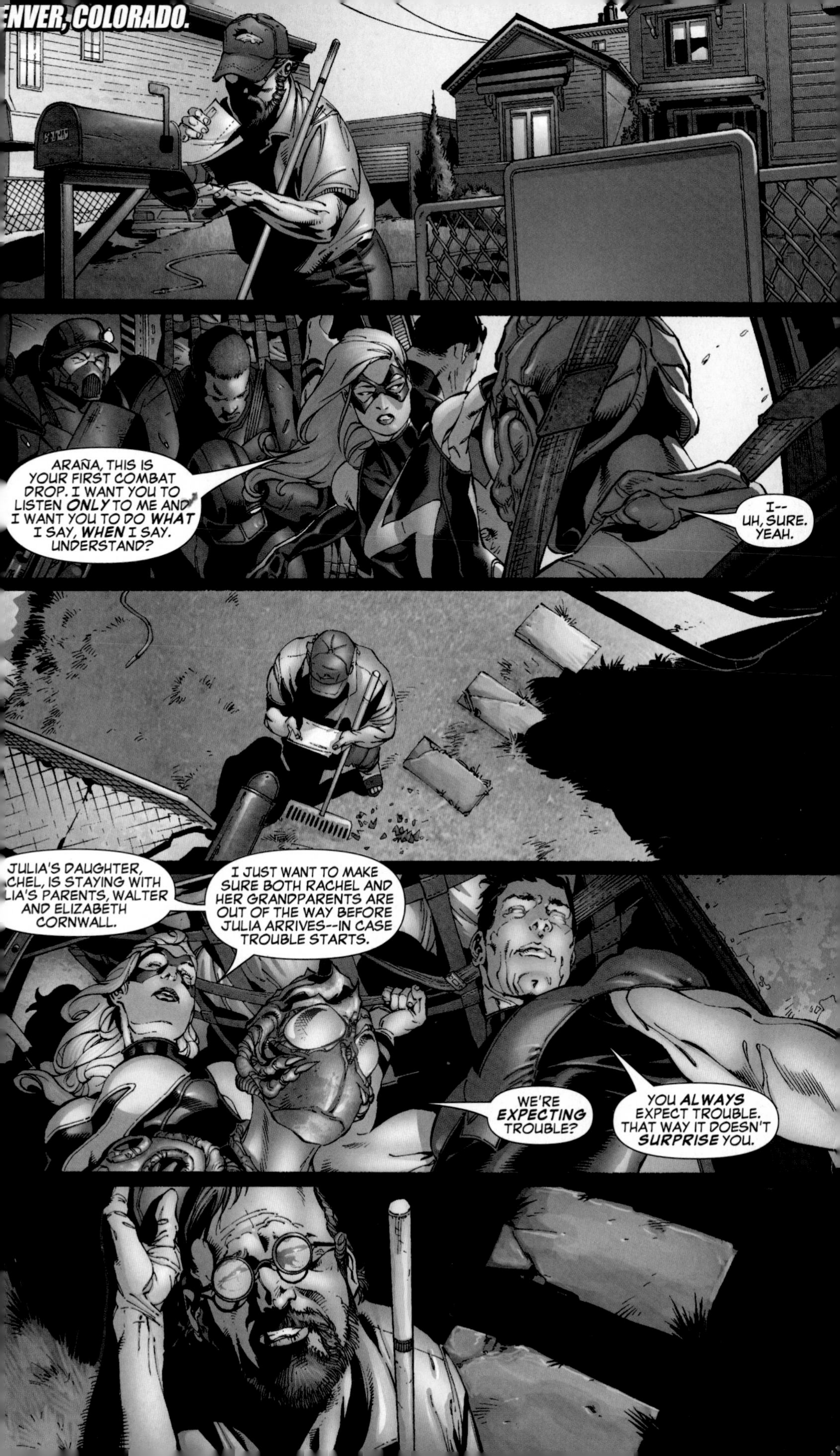
ENVER, COLORADO.
ARAÑA, THIS IS YOUR FIRST COMBAT DROP. I WANT YOU TO LISTEN ONLY TO ME AND I WANT YOU TO DO WHAT I SAY, WHEN I SAY. UNDERSTAND?
I-- UH, SURE. YEAH.
JULIA'S DAUGHTER, CHEL, IS STAYING WITH LIA'S PARENTS, WALTER AND ELIZABETH CORNWALL.
I JUST WANT TO MAKE SURE BOTH RACHEL AND HER GRANDPARENTS ARE OUT OF THE WAY BEFORE JULIA ARRIVES--IN CASE TROUBLE STARTS.
WE'RE EXPECTING TROUBLE?
YOU ALWAYS EXPECT TROUBLE. THAT WAY IT DOESN'T SURPRISE YOU.

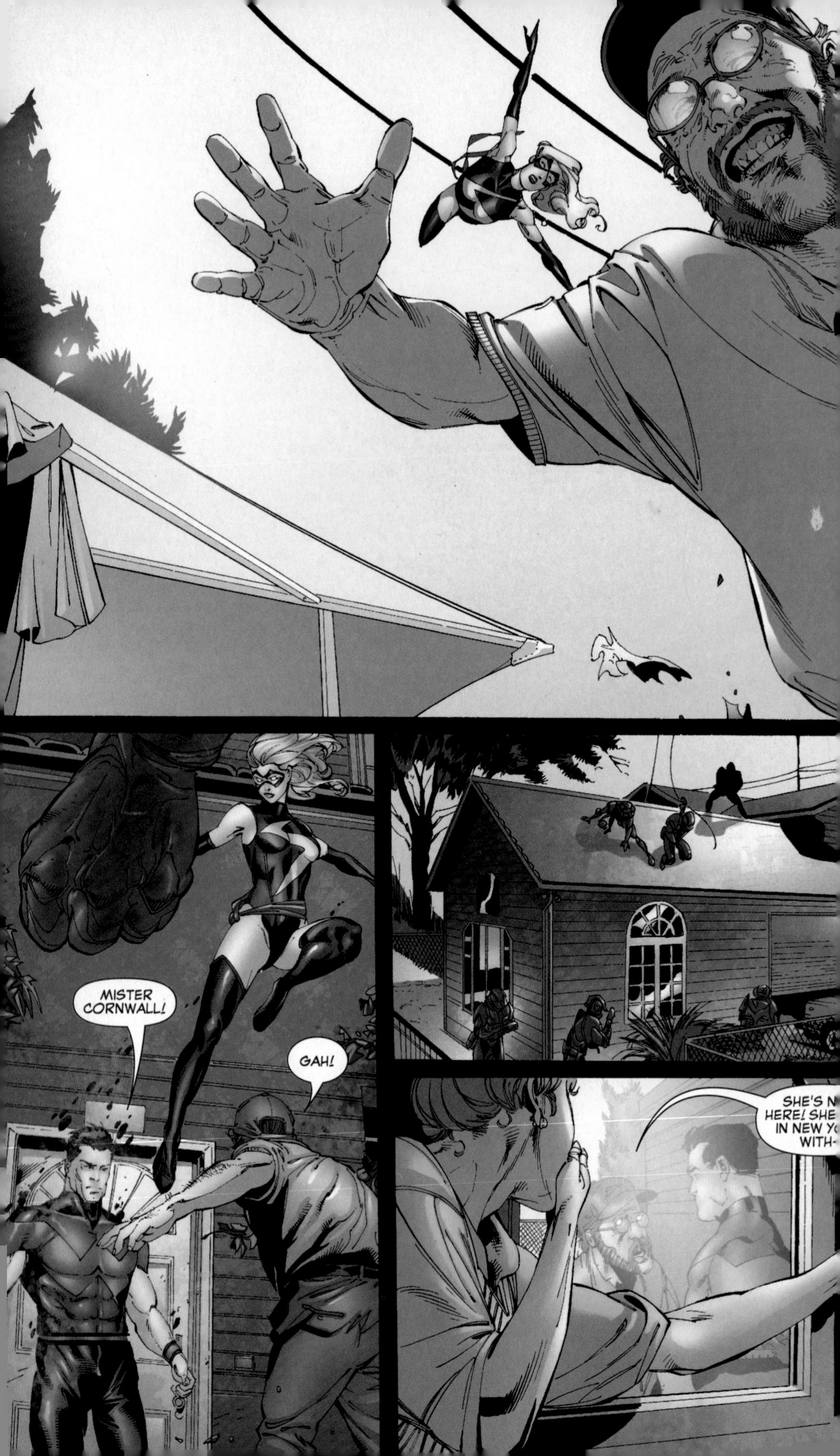
MISTER CORNWALL!
GAH!
SHE'S N
HERE! SHE
IN NEW Y
WITH-

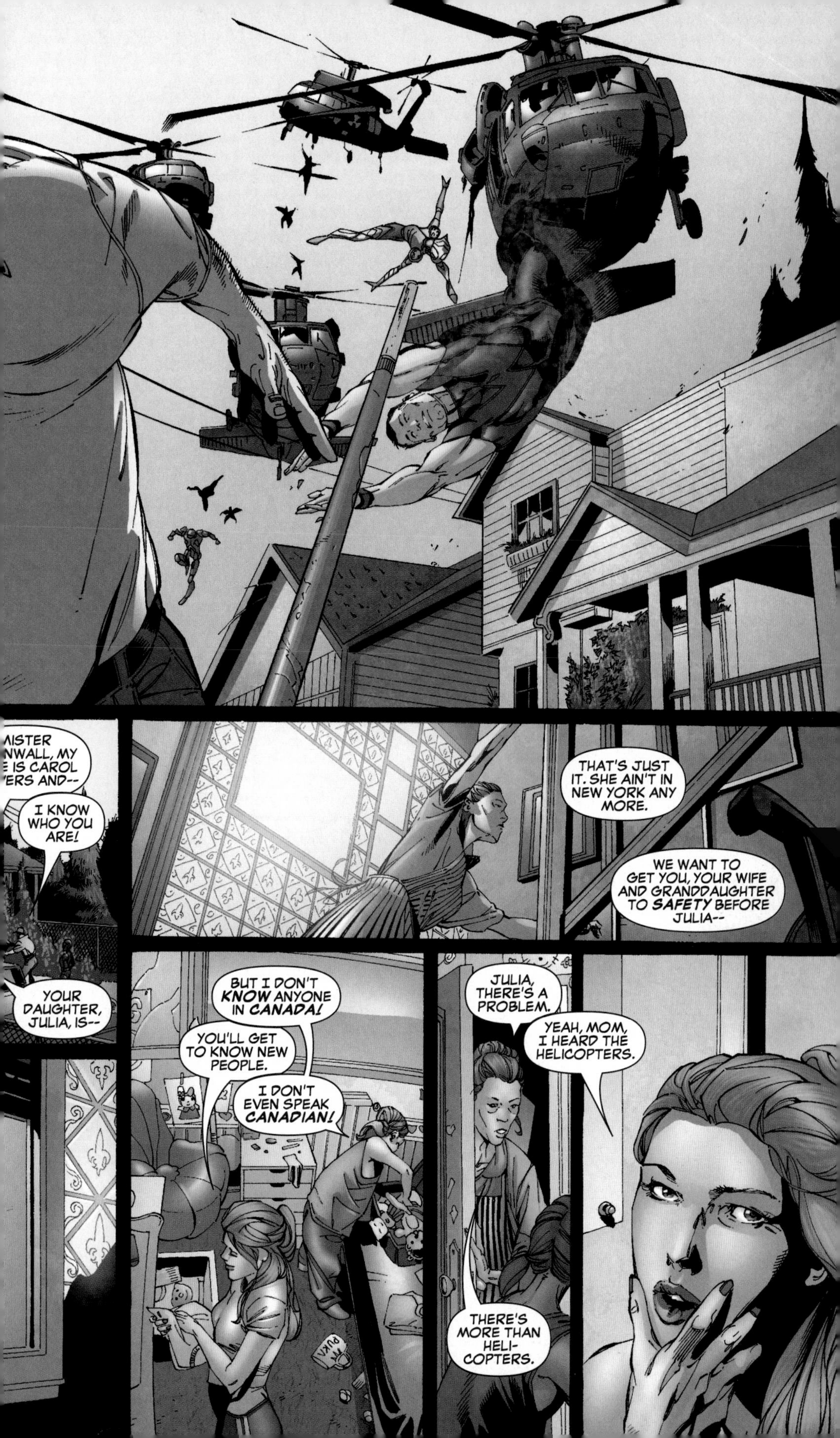
MISTER
NWALL, MY
E IS CAROL
ERS AND--
I KNOW WHO YOU ARE!
THAT'S JUST IT. SHE AIN'T IN NEW YORK ANY MORE.
WE WANT TO GET YOU, YOUR WIFE AND GRANDDAUGHTER TO SAFETY BEFORE JULIA--
YOUR DAUGHTER, JULIA, IS--
BUT I DON'T KNOW ANYONE IN CANADA!
YOU'LL GET TO KNOW NEW PEOPLE.
I DON'T EVEN SPEAK CANADIAN!
JULIA, THERE'S A PROBLEM.
YEAH, MOM, I HEARD THE HELICOPTERS.
THERE'S MORE THAN HELI-COPTERS.

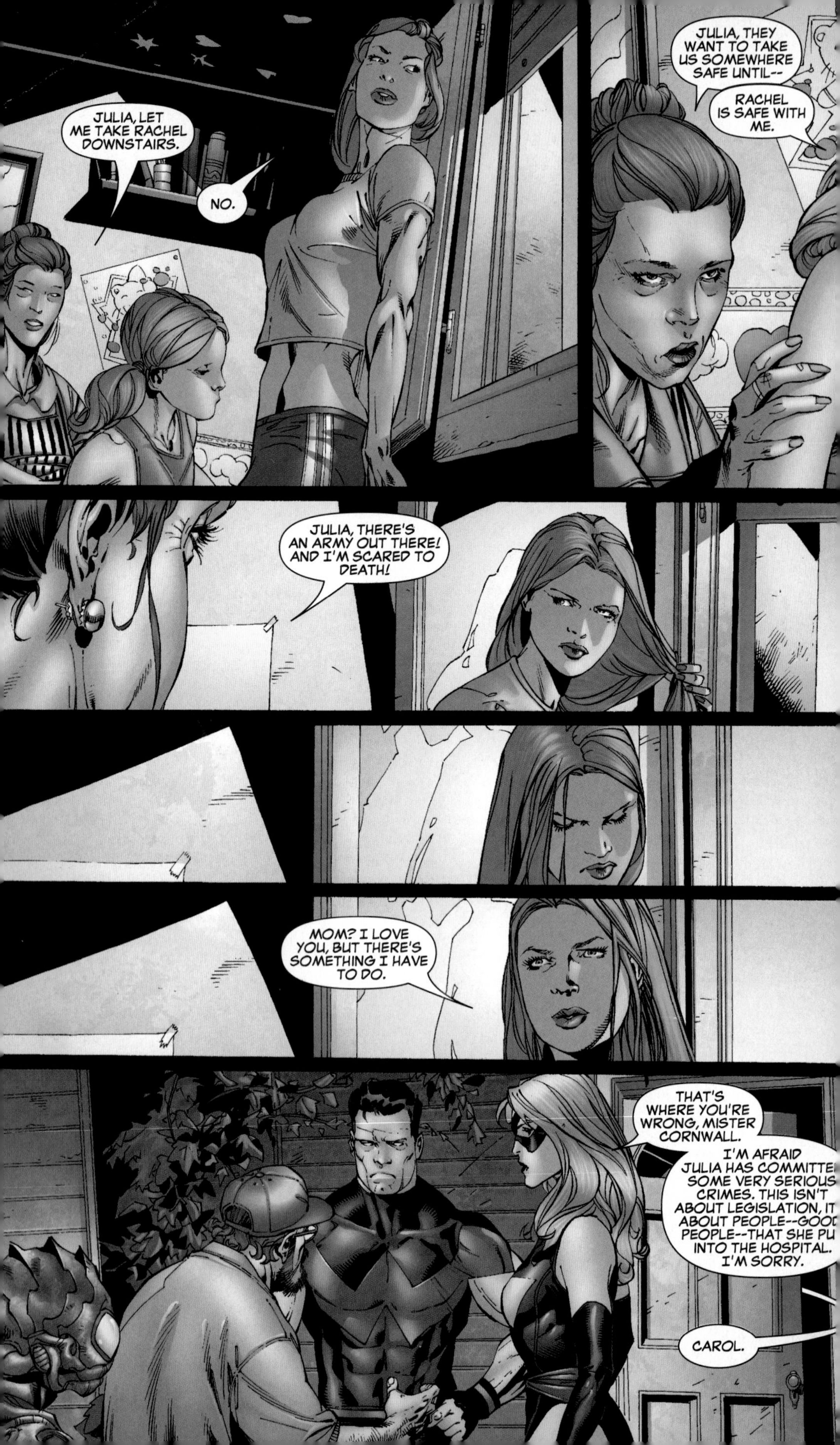
JULIA, LET ME TAKE RACHEL DOWNSTAIRS.
NO.
JULIA, THEY WANT TO TAKE US SOMEWHERE SAFE UNTIL--
RACHEL IS SAFE WITH ME.
JULIA, THERE'S AN ARMY OUT THERE! AND I'M SCARED TO DEATH!
MOM? I LOVE YOU, BUT THERE'S SOMETHING I HAVE TO DO.
THAT'S WHERE YOU'RE WRONG, MISTER CORNWALL.
I'M AFRAID JULIA HAS COMMITTE SOME VERY SERIOUS CRIMES. THIS ISN'T ABOUT LEGISLATION, IT ABOUT PEOPLE--GOOD PEOPLE--THAT SHE PU INTO THE HOSPITAL. I'M SORRY.
CAROL.

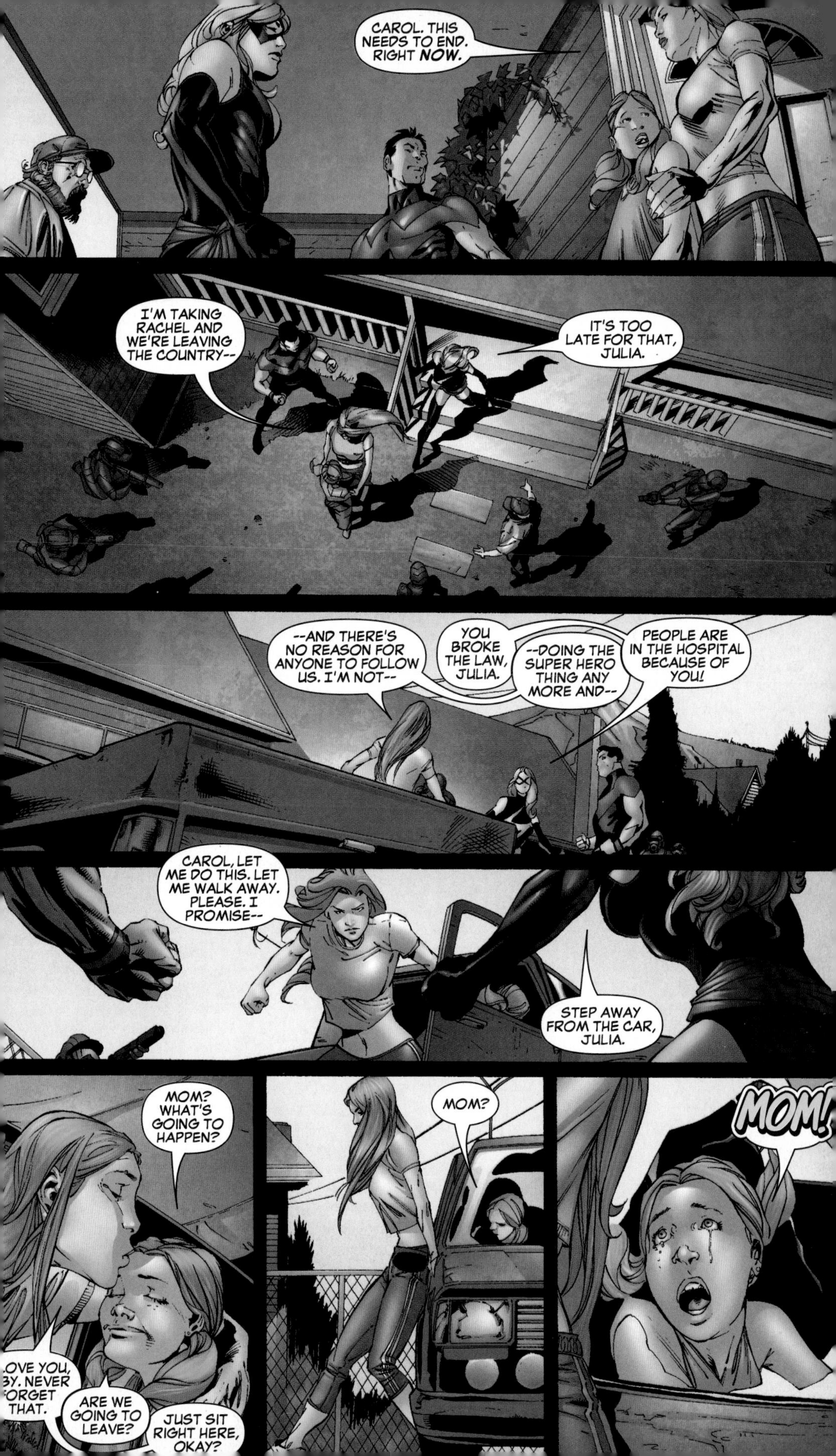

CAROL. THIS NEEDS TO END. RIGHT **NOW.**
I'M TAKING RACHEL AND WE'RE LEAVING THE COUNTRY--
IT'S TOO LATE FOR THAT, JULIA.
--AND THERE'S NO REASON FOR ANYONE TO FOLLOW US. I'M NOT--
YOU BROKE THE LAW, JULIA.
--DOING THE SUPER HERO THING ANY MORE AND--
PEOPLE ARE IN THE HOSPITAL BECAUSE OF YOU!
CAROL, LET ME DO THIS. LET ME WALK AWAY. PLEASE. I PROMISE--
STEP AWAY FROM THE CAR, JULIA.
MOM? WHAT'S GOING TO HAPPEN?
OVE YOU, BY. NEVER ORGET THAT.
ARE WE GOING TO LEAVE?
JUST SIT RIGHT HERE, OKAY?
MOM?
MOM!

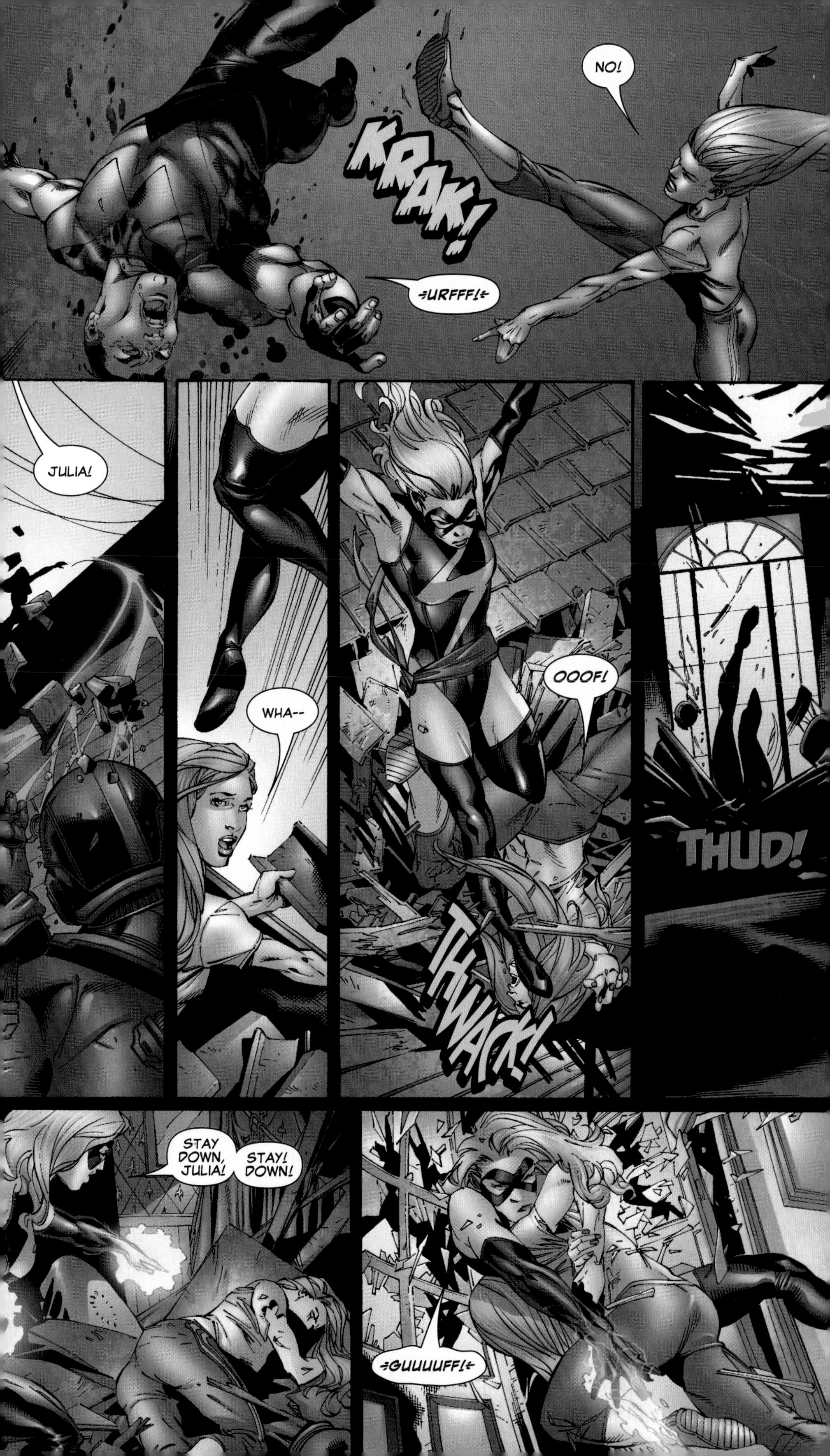
NO!
KRAK!
URFFF!
JULIA!
WHA--
OOOF!
THWACK!
THUD!
STAY DOWN, JULIA!
STAY! DOWN!
GUUUUFF!

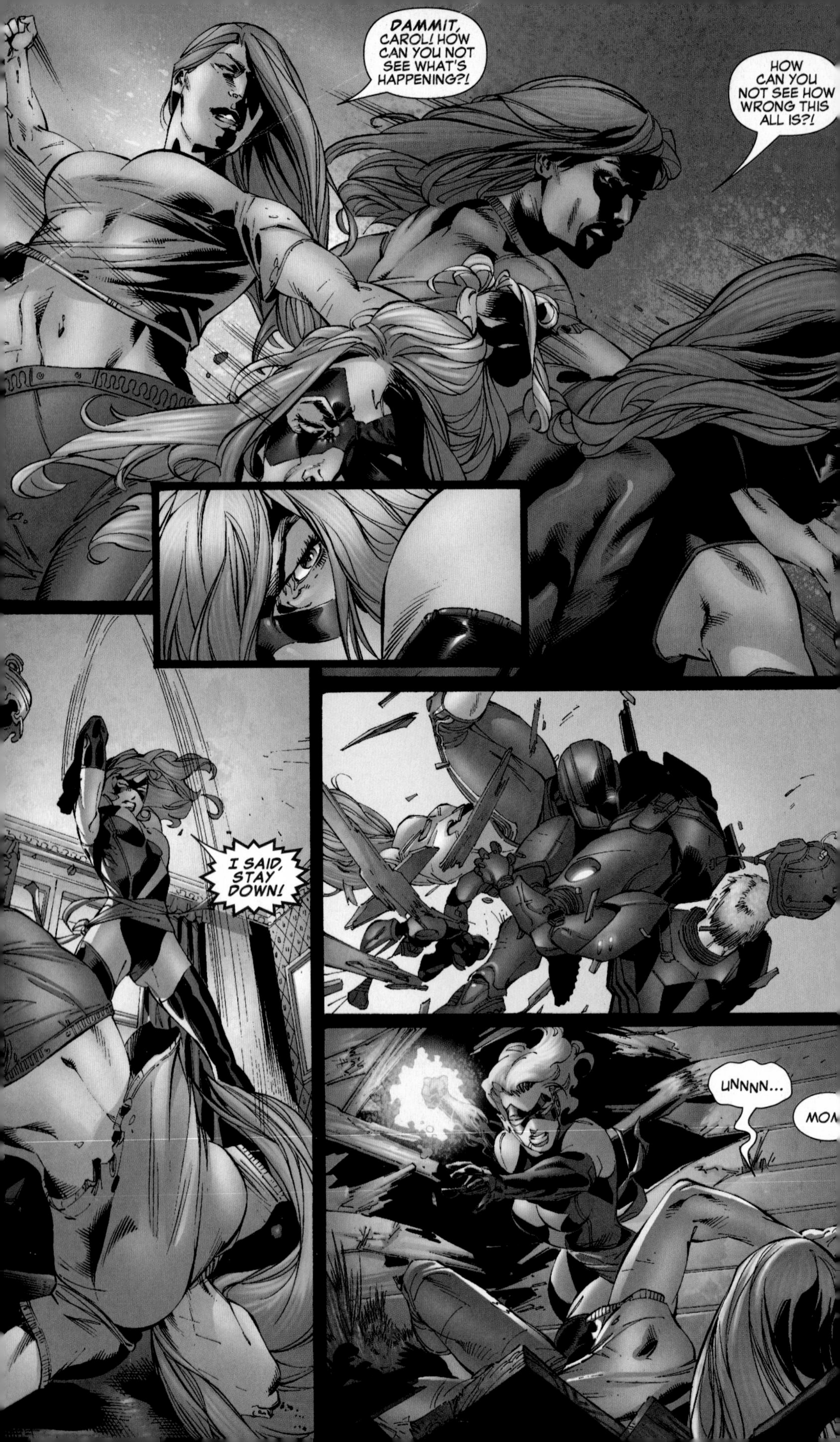

DAMMIT, CAROL! HOW CAN YOU NOT SEE WHAT'S HAPPENING?!
HOW CAN YOU NOT SEE HOW WRONG THIS ALL IS?!
I SAID, STAY DOWN!
UNNNN...
MOM

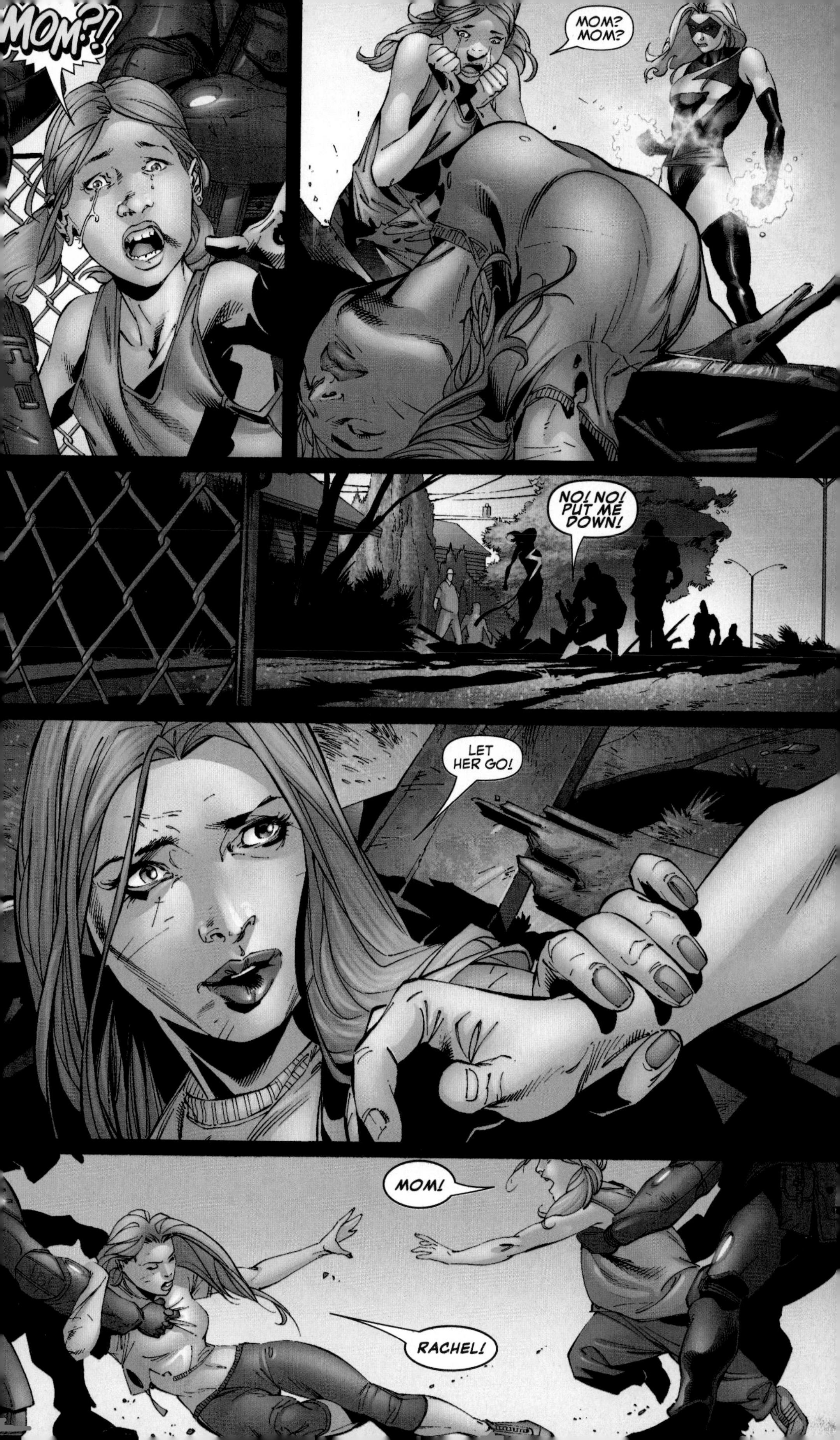
MOM?!
MOM? MOM?
NO! NO! PUT ME DOWN!
LET HER GO!
MOM!
RACHEL!

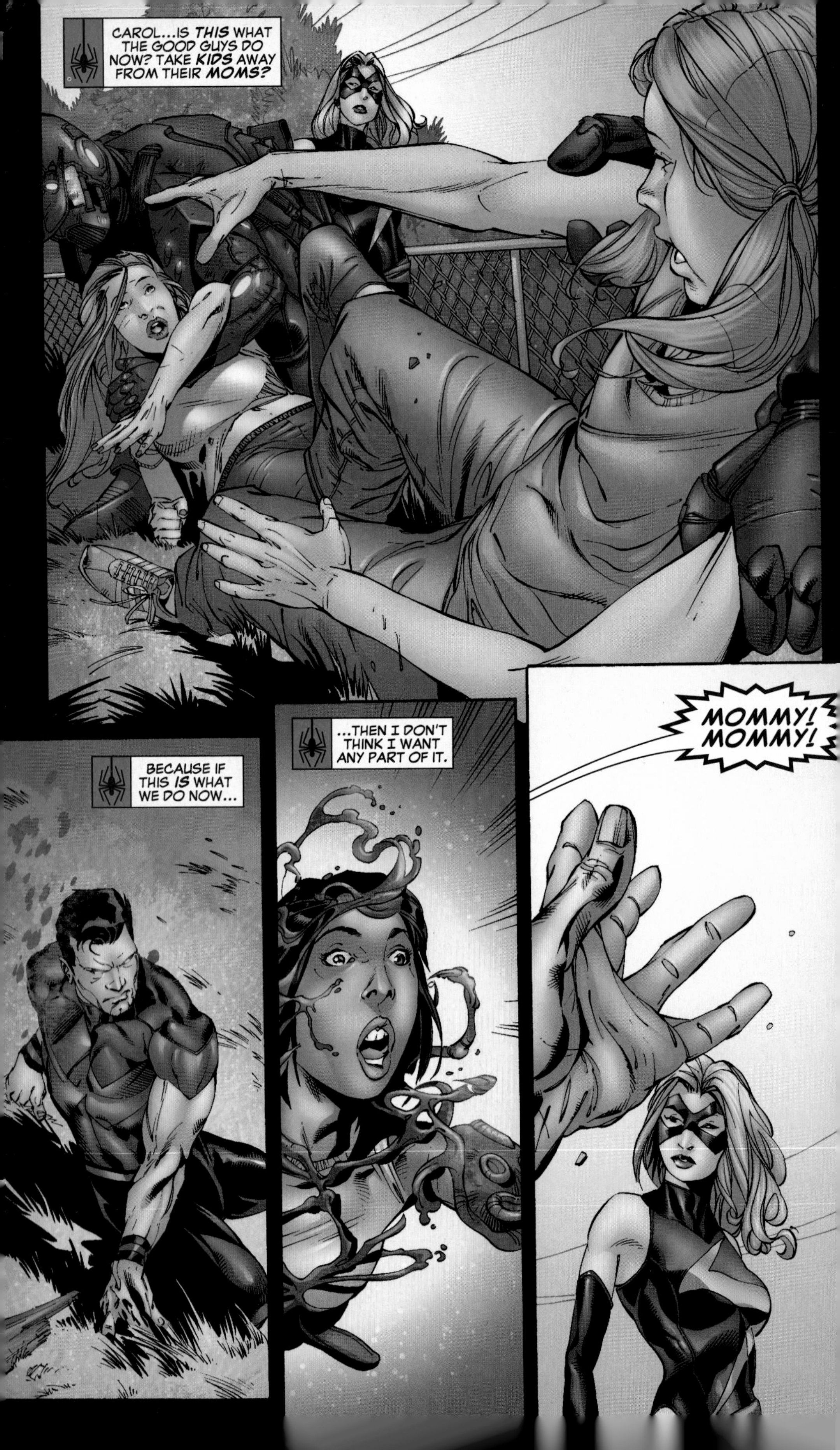
CAROL...IS THIS WHAT THE GOOD GUYS DO NOW? TAKE KIDS AWAY FROM THEIR MOMS?
BECAUSE IF THIS IS WHAT WE DO NOW...
...THEN I DON'T THINK I WANT ANY PART OF IT.
MOMMY! MOMMY!

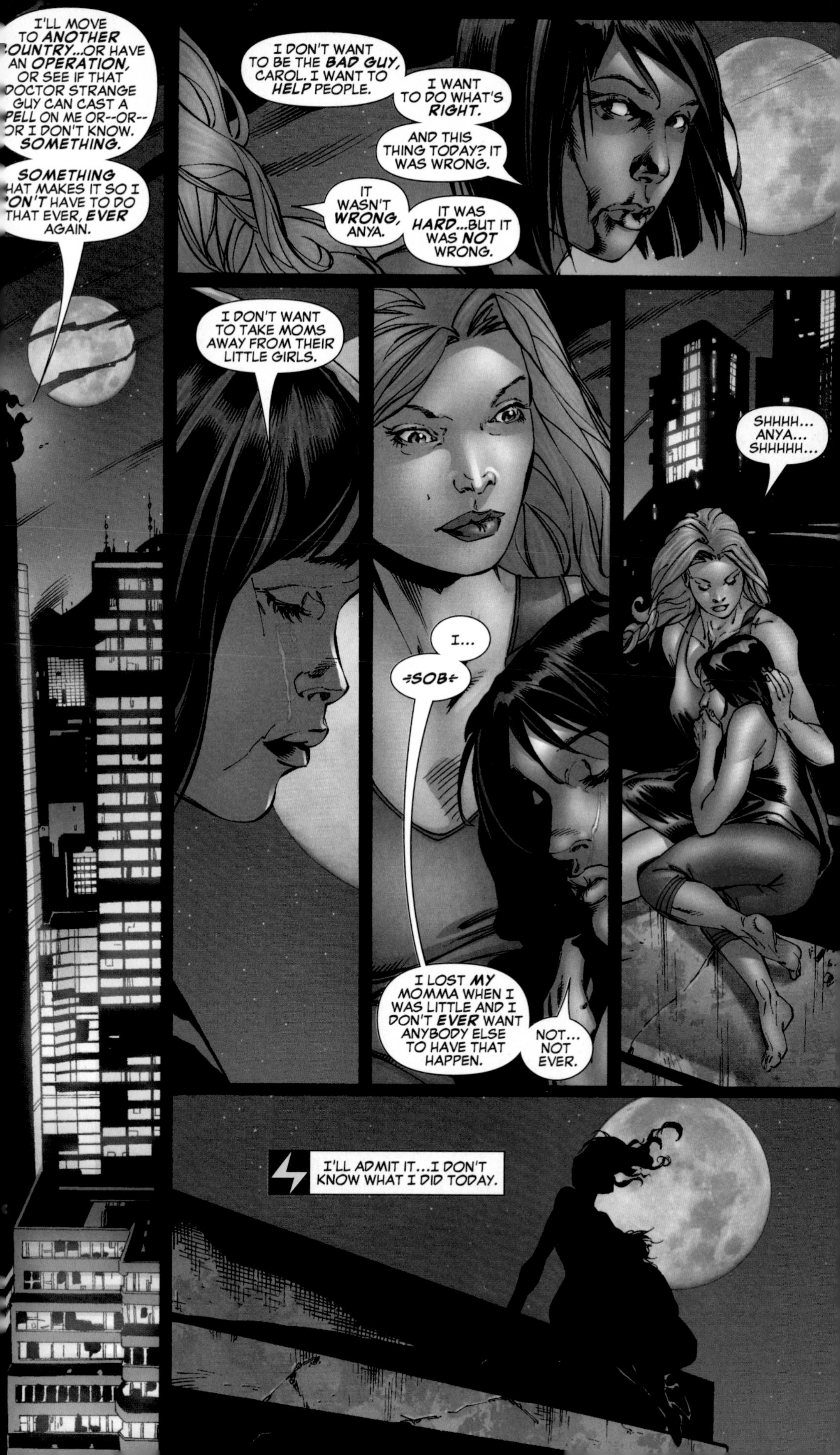
I'LL MOVE TO ANOTHER OUNTRY...OR HAVE AN OPERATION, OR SEE IF THAT DOCTOR STRANGE GUY CAN CAST A PELL ON ME OR--OR-- OR I DON'T KNOW. SOMETHING.
SOMETHING HAT MAKES IT SO I ON'T HAVE TO DO THAT EVER, EVER AGAIN.
I DON'T WANT TO BE THE BAD GUY, CAROL. I WANT TO HELP PEOPLE.
I WANT TO DO WHAT'S RIGHT.
AND THIS THING TODAY? IT WAS WRONG.
IT WASN'T WRONG, ANYA.
IT WAS HARD...BUT IT WAS NOT WRONG.
I DON'T WANT TO TAKE MOMS AWAY FROM THEIR LITTLE GIRLS.
I...
SOB
I LOST MY MOMMA WHEN I WAS LITTLE AND I DON'T EVER WANT ANYBODY ELSE TO HAVE THAT HAPPEN.
NOT... NOT EVER.
SHHHH... ANYA... SHHHHH...
I'LL ADMIT IT...I DON'T KNOW WHAT I DID TODAY.

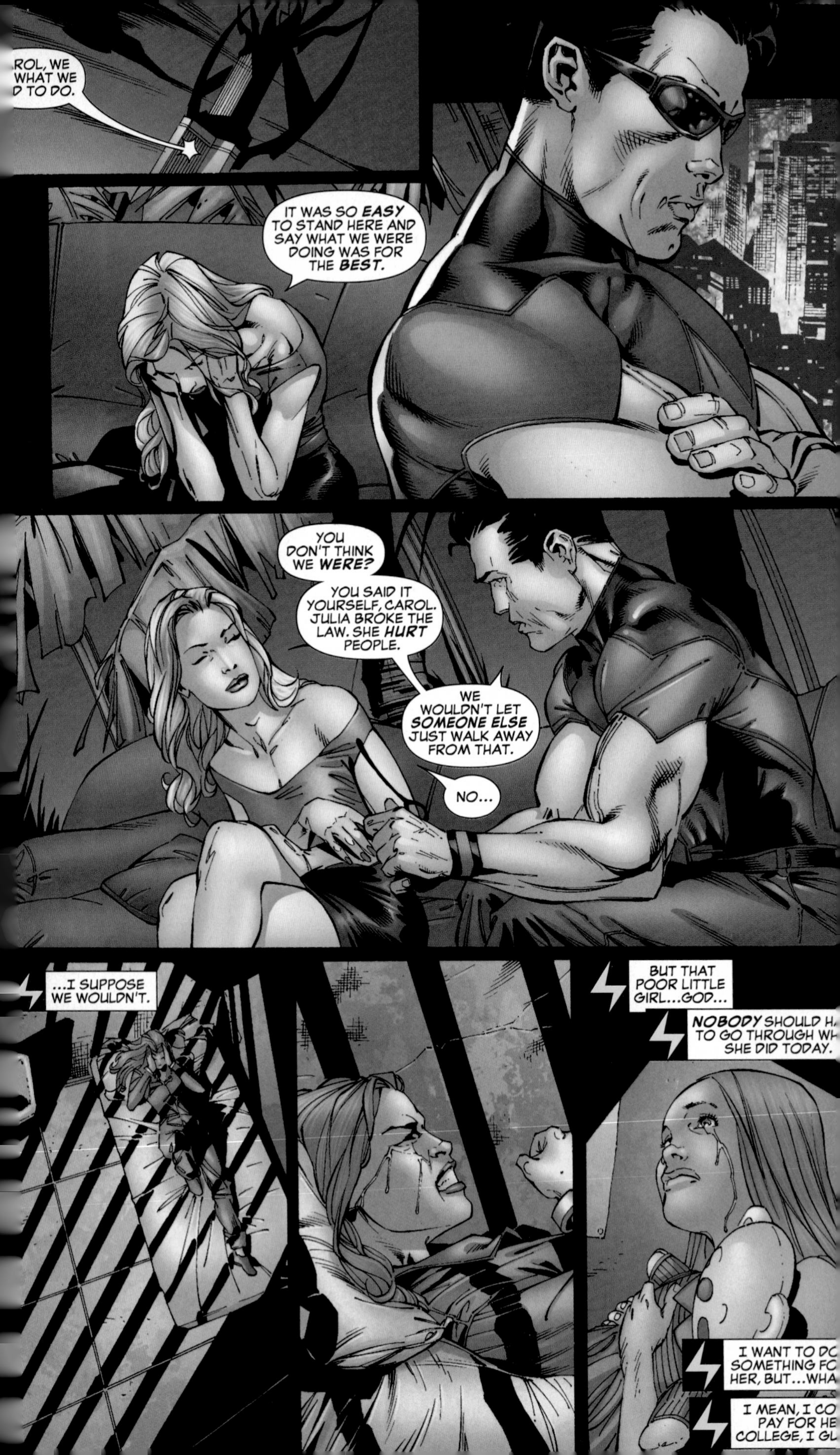

AROL, WE
WHAT WE
D TO DO.
IT WAS SO EASY TO STAND HERE AND SAY WHAT WE WERE DOING WAS FOR THE BEST.
YOU DON'T THINK WE WERE?
YOU SAID IT YOURSELF, CAROL. JULIA BROKE THE LAW. SHE HURT PEOPLE.
WE WOULDN'T LET SOMEONE ELSE JUST WALK AWAY FROM THAT.
NO...
...I SUPPOSE WE WOULDN'T.
BUT THAT POOR LITTLE GIRL...GOD...
NOBODY SHOULD H
TO GO THROUGH WH
SHE DID TODAY.
I WANT TO DO
SOMETHING FO
HER, BUT...WHA
I MEAN, I CO
PAY FOR HE
COLLEGE, I GU

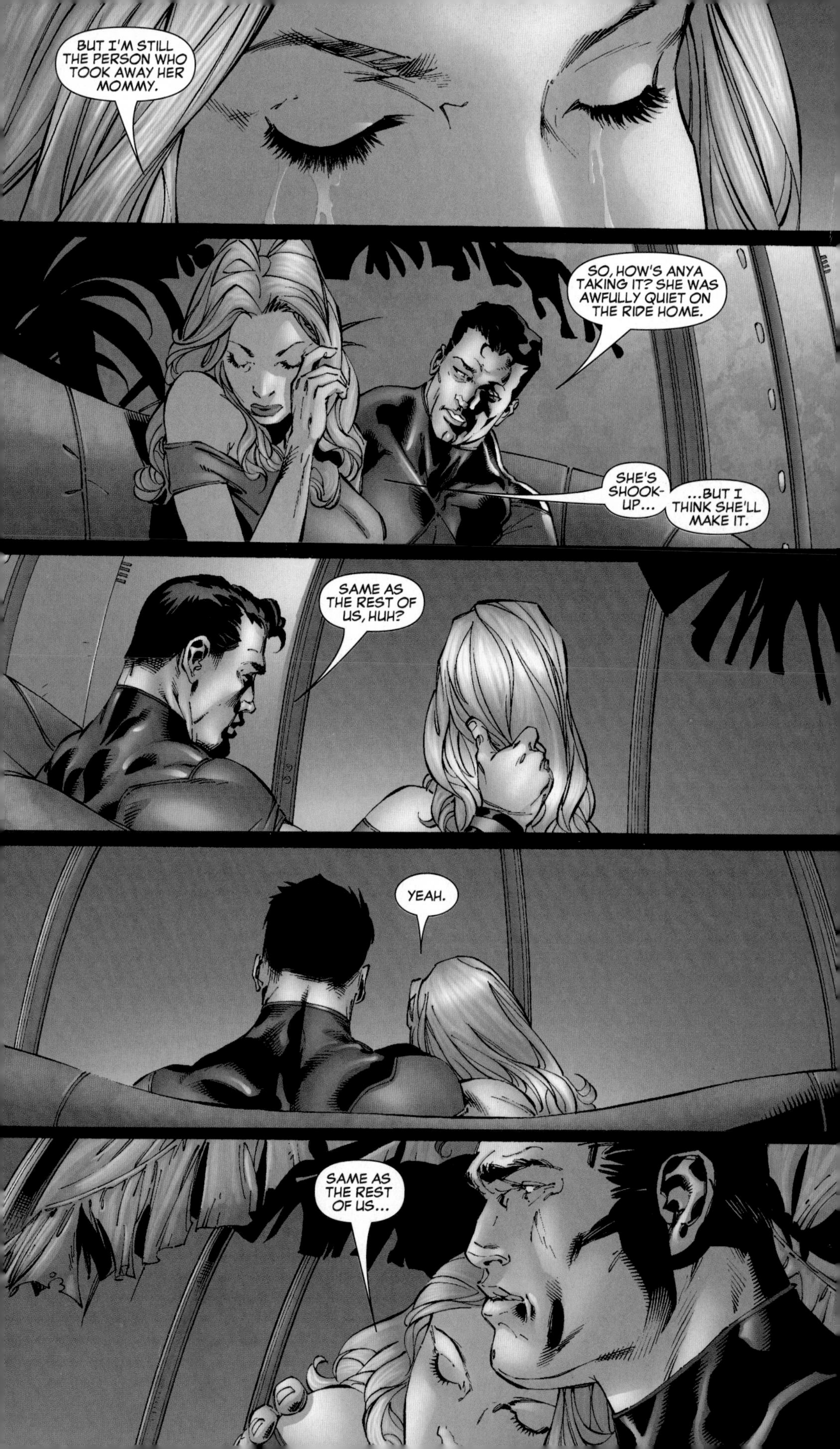

BUT I'M STILL THE PERSON WHO TOOK AWAY HER MOMMY.
SO, HOW'S ANYA TAKING IT? SHE WAS AWFULLY QUIET ON THE RIDE HOME.
SHE'S SHOOK-UP...
...BUT I THINK SHE'LL MAKE IT.
SAME AS THE REST OF US, HUH?
YEAH.
SAME AS THE REST OF US...

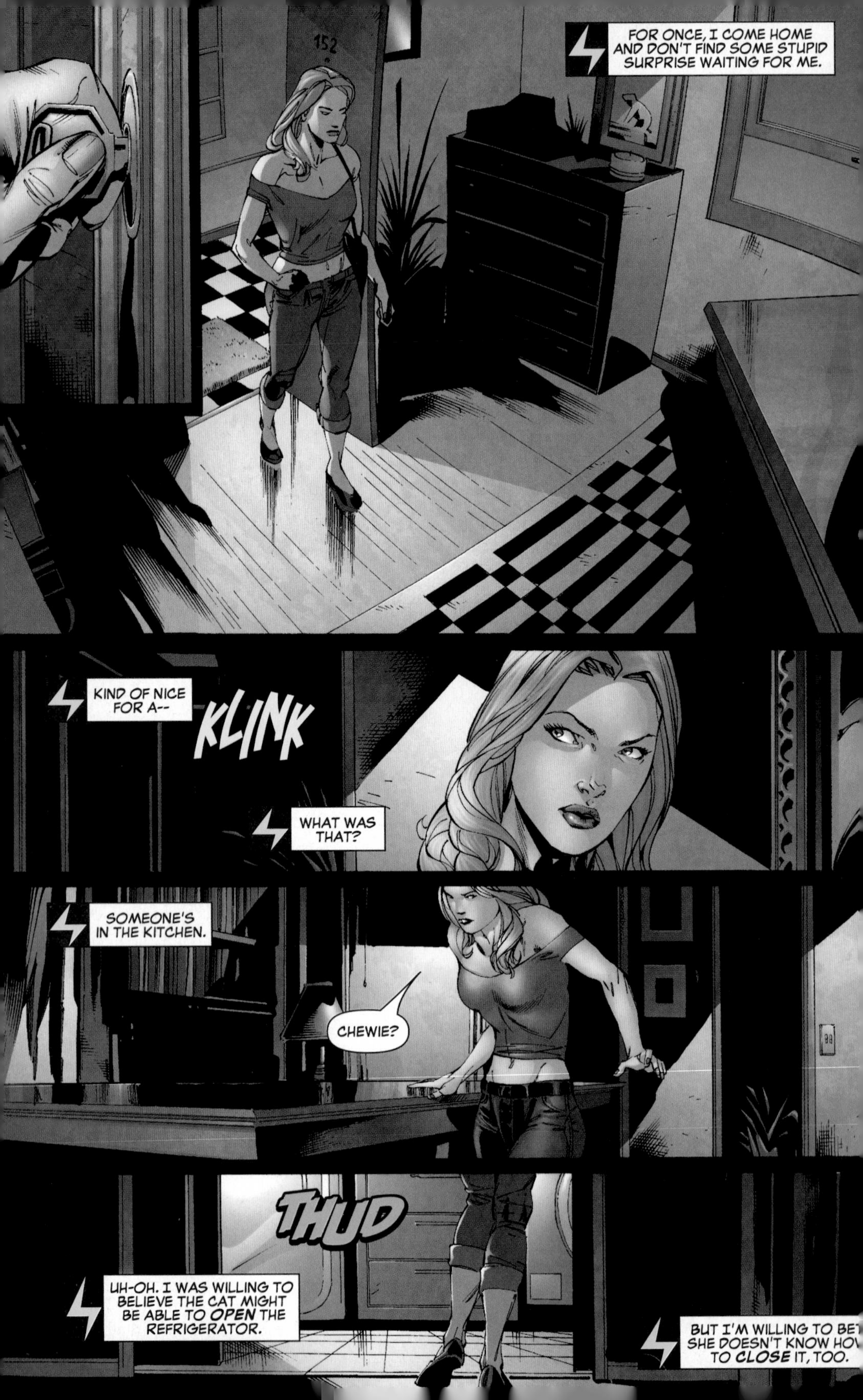
FOR ONCE, I COME HOME AND DON'T FIND SOME STUPID SURPRISE WAITING FOR ME.
152
KIND OF NICE FOR A--
KLINK
WHAT WAS THAT?
SOMEONE'S IN THE KITCHEN.
CHEWIE?
THUD
UH-OH. I WAS WILLING TO BELIEVE THE CAT MIGHT BE ABLE TO *OPEN* THE REFRIGERATOR.
BUT I'M WILLING TO BET SHE DOESN'T KNOW HOW TO *CLOSE* IT, TOO.

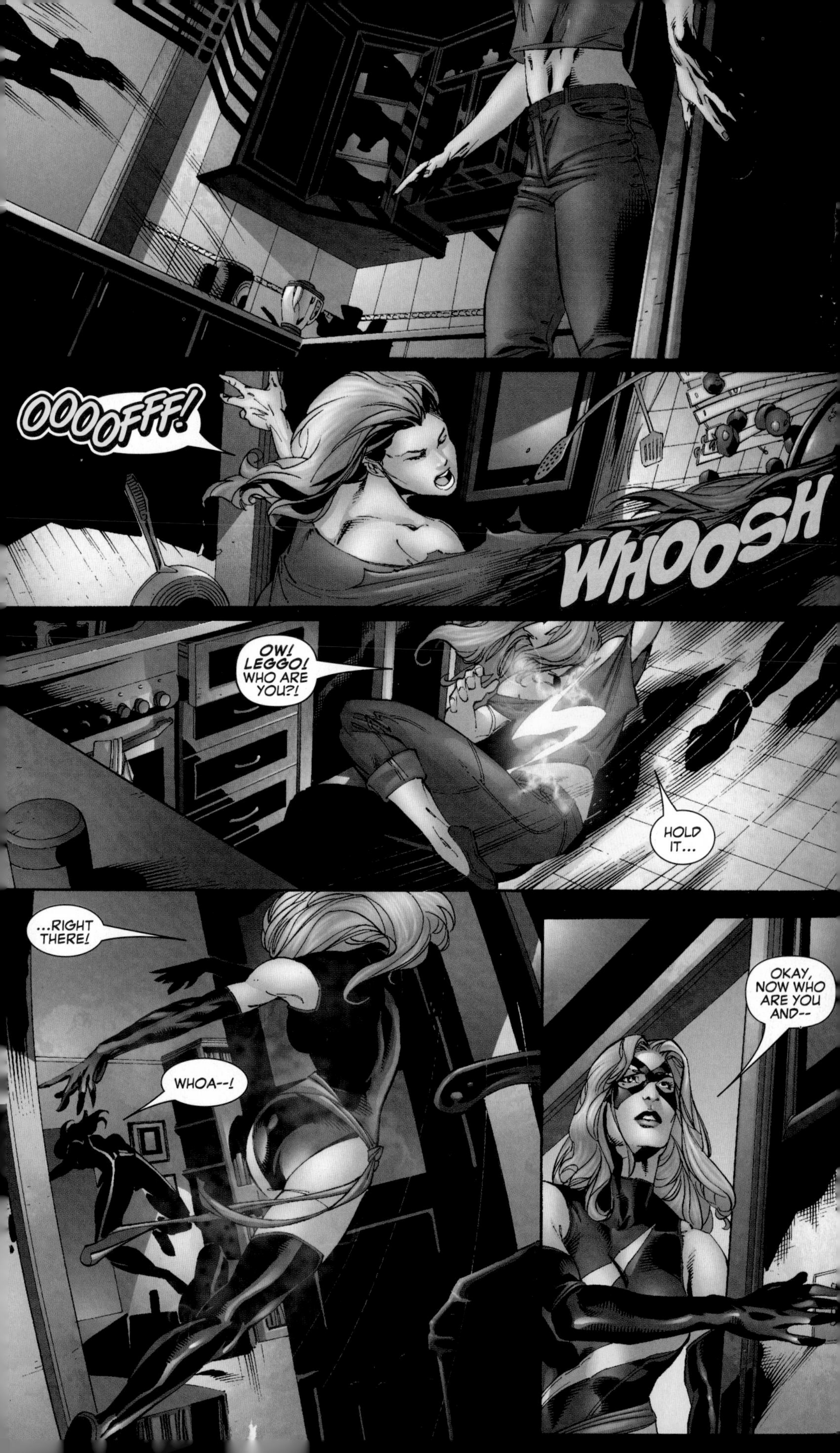

OOOOFFF!
WHOOSH
OW! LEGGO! WHO ARE YOU?!
HOLD IT...
...RIGHT THERE!
WHOA--!
OKAY, NOW WHO ARE YOU AND--

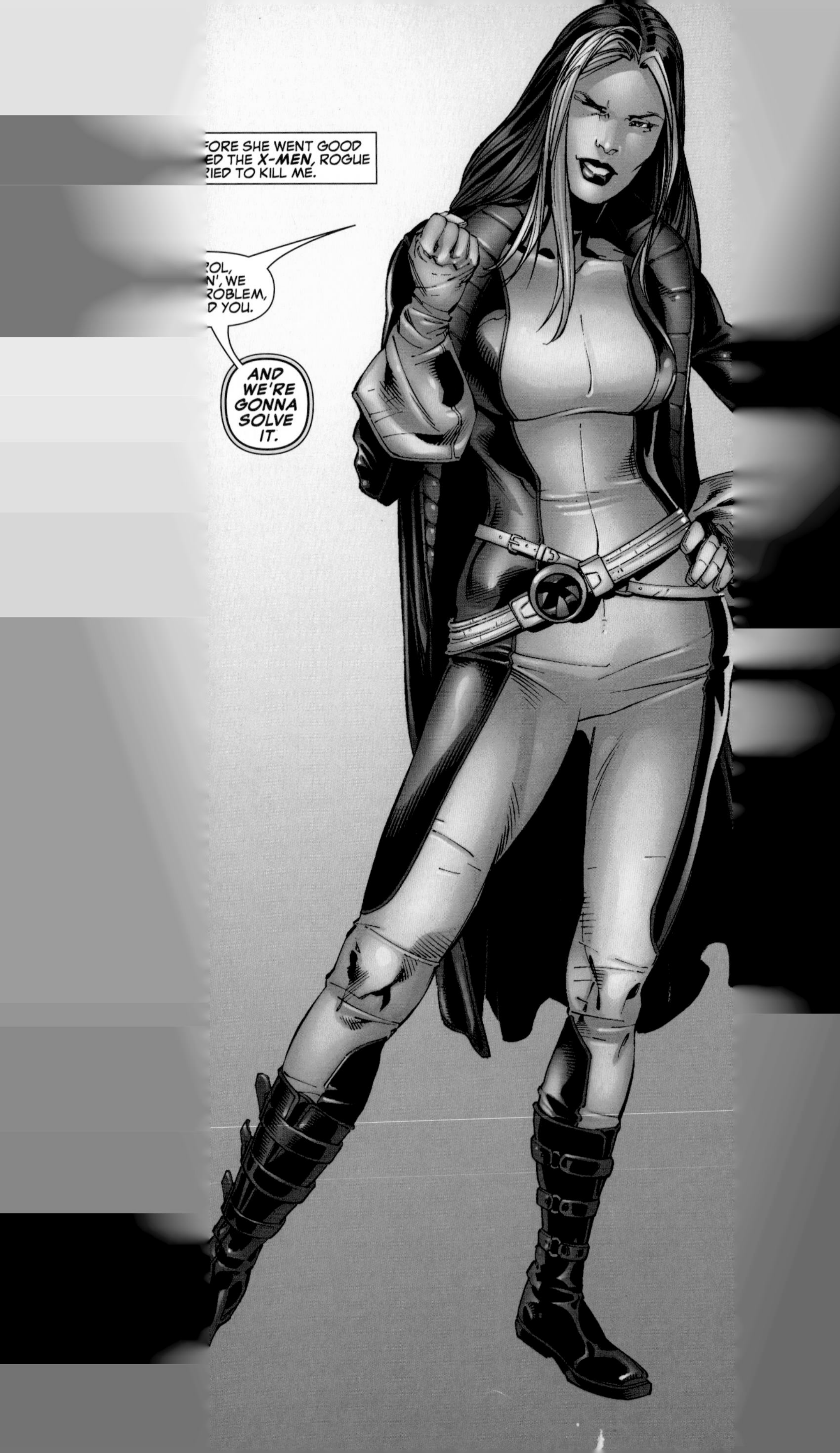

FORE SHE WENT GOOD
ED THE **X-MEN,** ROGUE
RIED TO KILL ME.
ROL,
N', WE
ROBLEM,
D YOU.
AND WE'RE GONNA SOLVE IT.

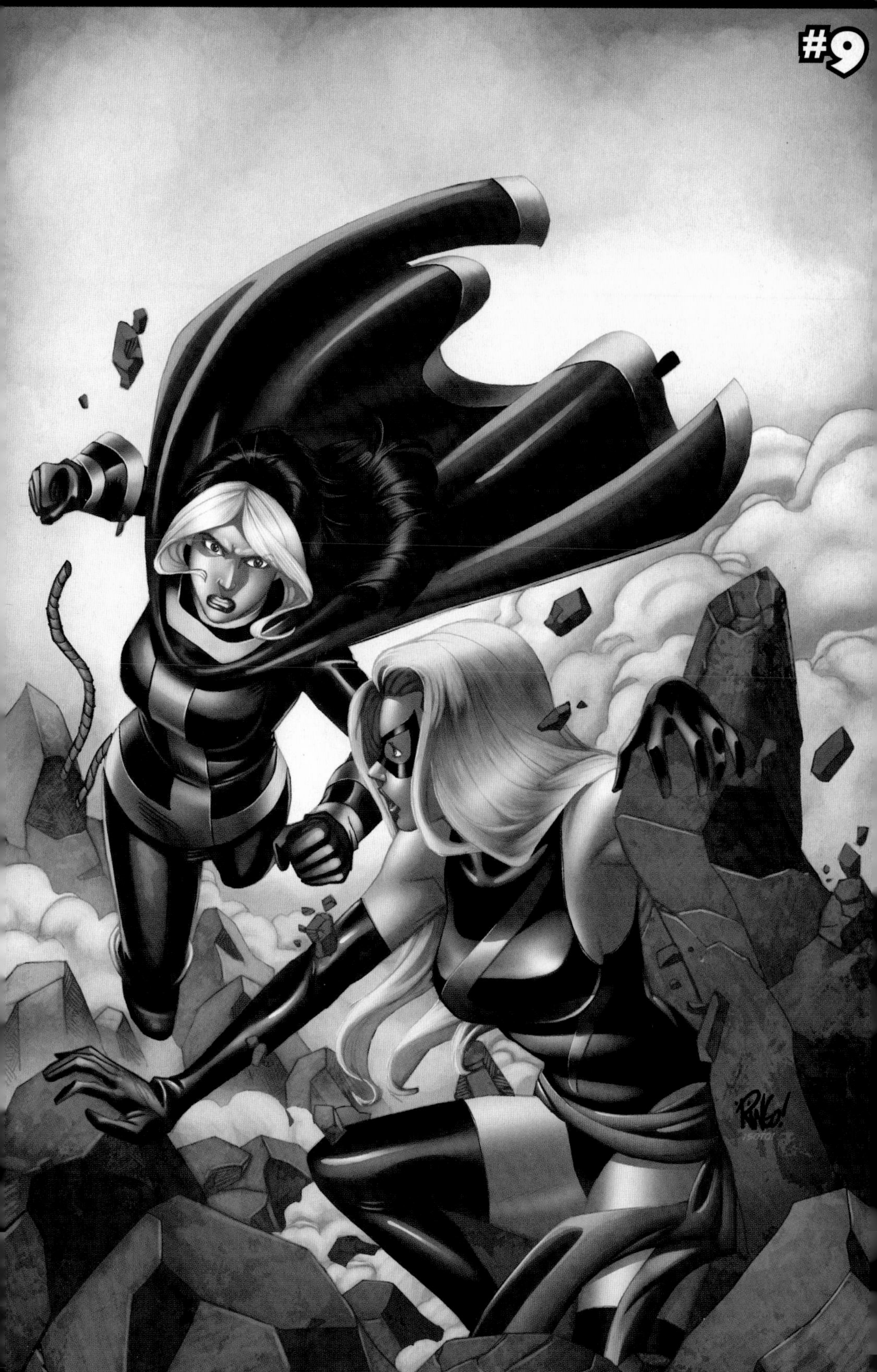
#9

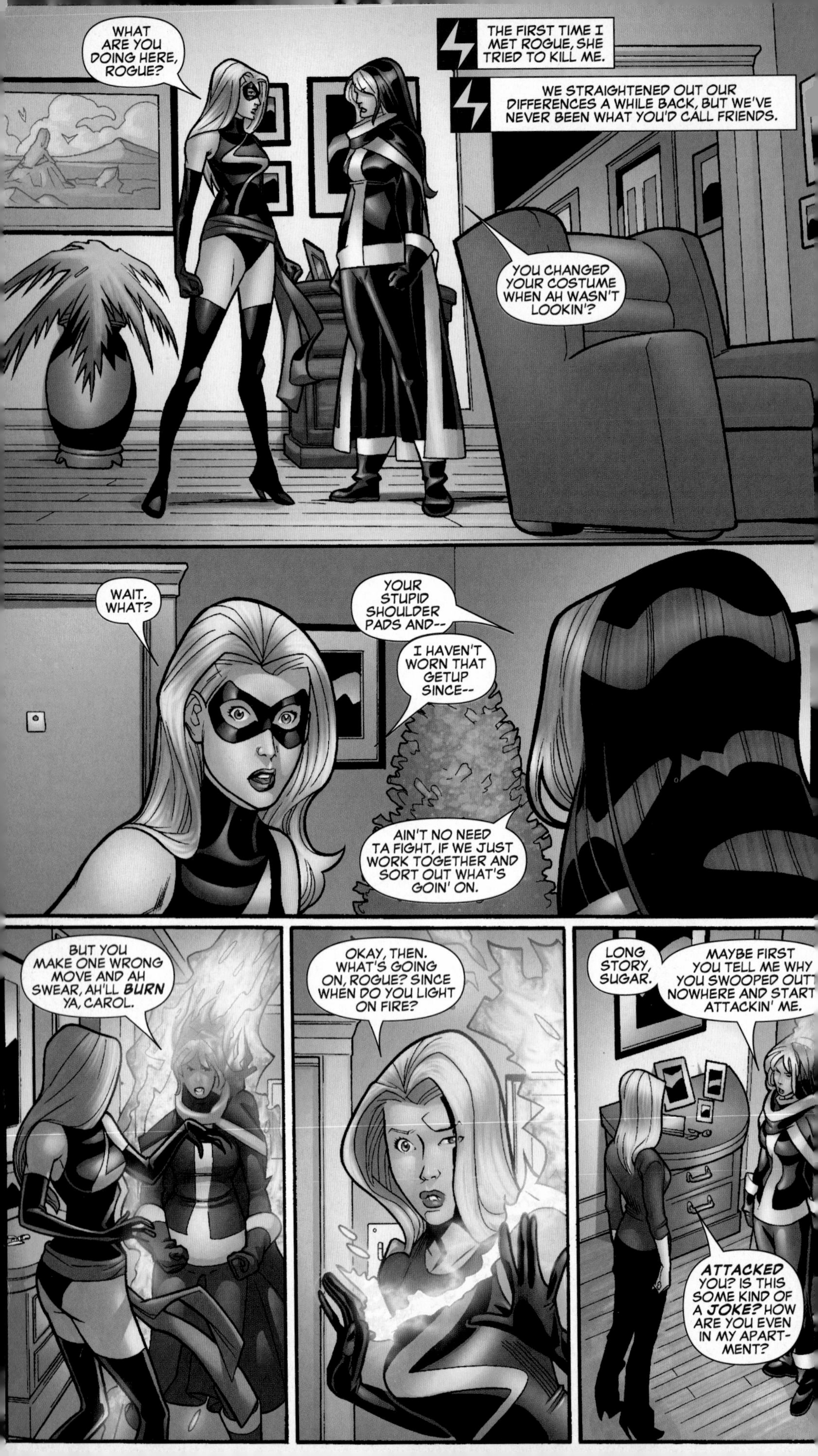
WHAT ARE YOU DOING HERE, ROGUE?
THE FIRST TIME I MET ROGUE, SHE TRIED TO KILL ME.
WE STRAIGHTENED OUT OUR DIFFERENCES A WHILE BACK, BUT WE'VE NEVER BEEN WHAT YOU'D CALL FRIENDS.
YOU CHANGED YOUR COSTUME WHEN AH WASN'T LOOKIN'?
WAIT. WHAT?
YOUR STUPID SHOULDER PADS AND--
I HAVEN'T WORN THAT GETUP SINCE--
AIN'T NO NEED TA FIGHT, IF WE JUST WORK TOGETHER AND SORT OUT WHAT'S GOIN' ON.
BUT YOU MAKE ONE WRONG MOVE AND AH SWEAR, AH'LL **BURN** YA, CAROL.
OKAY, THEN. WHAT'S GOING ON, ROGUE? SINCE WHEN DO YOU LIGHT ON FIRE?
LONG STORY, SUGAR.
MAYBE FIRST YOU TELL ME WHY YOU SWOOPED OUT NOWHERE AND START ATTACKIN' ME.
ATTACKED YOU? IS THIS SOME KIND OF A ***JOKE?*** HOW ARE YOU EVEN IN MY APARTMENT?

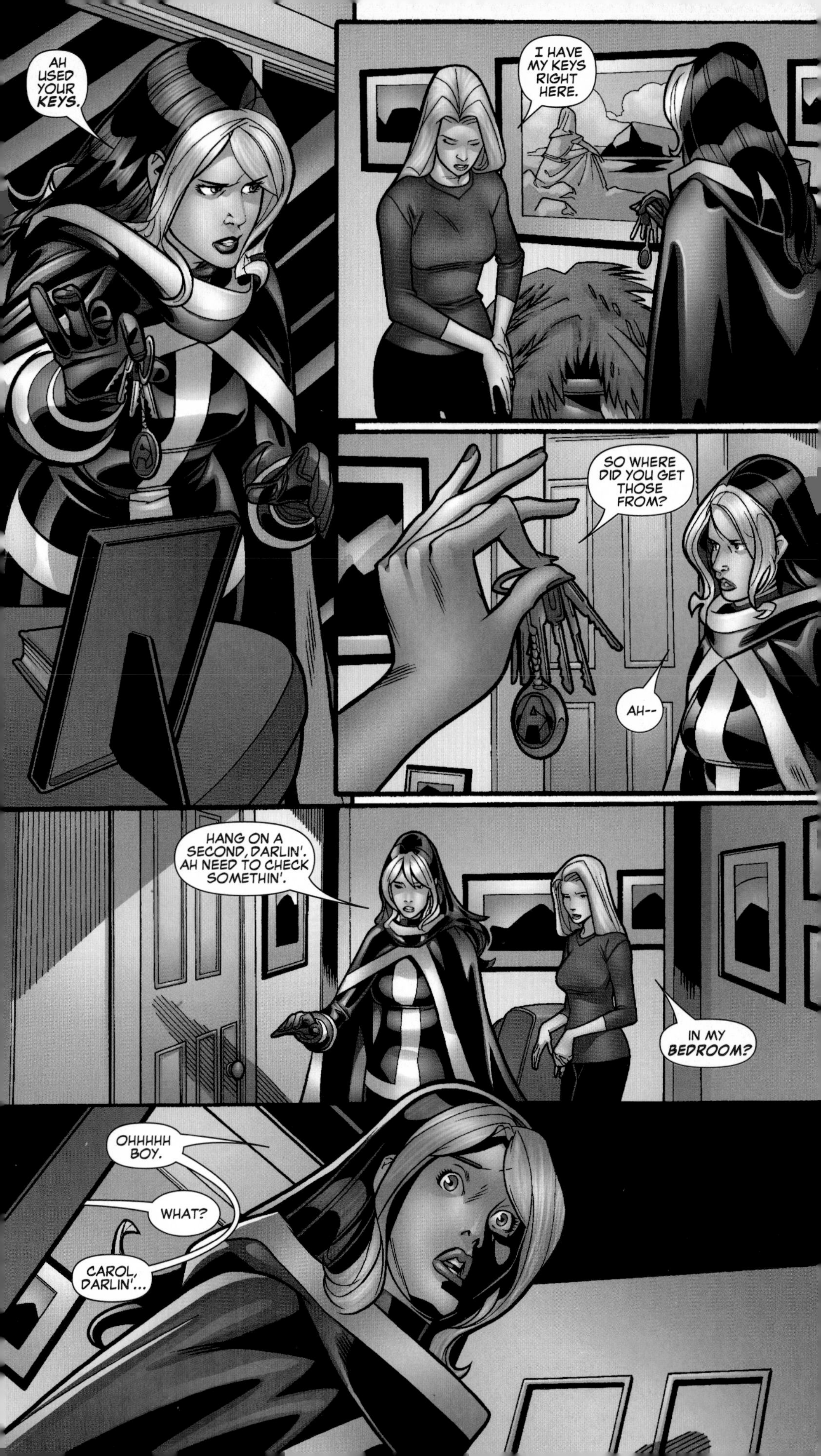
AH USED YOUR KEYS.
I HAVE MY KEYS RIGHT HERE.
SO WHERE DID YOU GET THOSE FROM?
AH--
HANG ON A SECOND, DARLIN'. AH NEED TO CHECK SOMETHIN'.
IN MY BEDROOM?
OHHHHH BOY.
WHAT?
CAROL, DARLIN'...

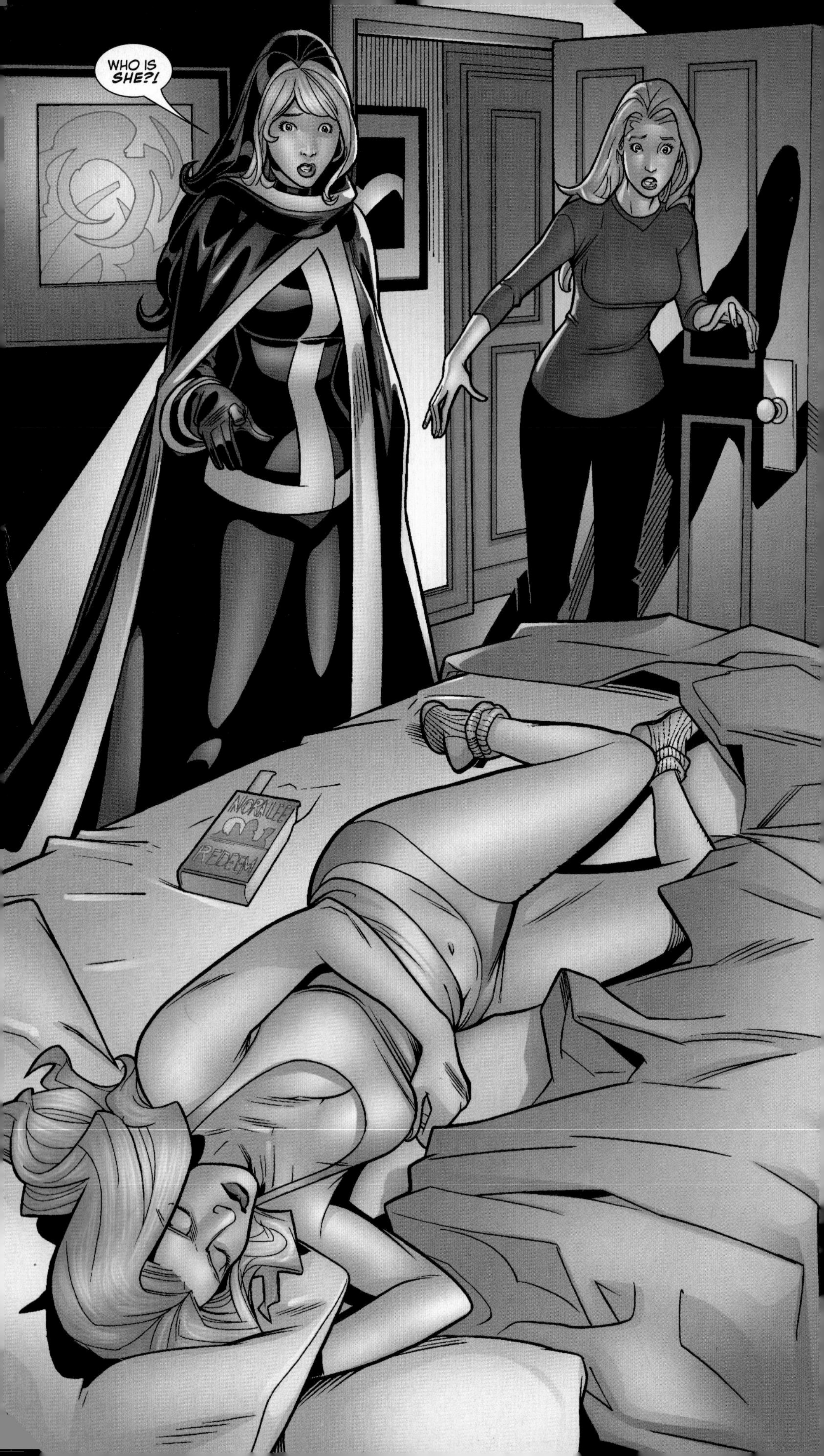
WHO IS SHE?!
NORALEE
REDEEM

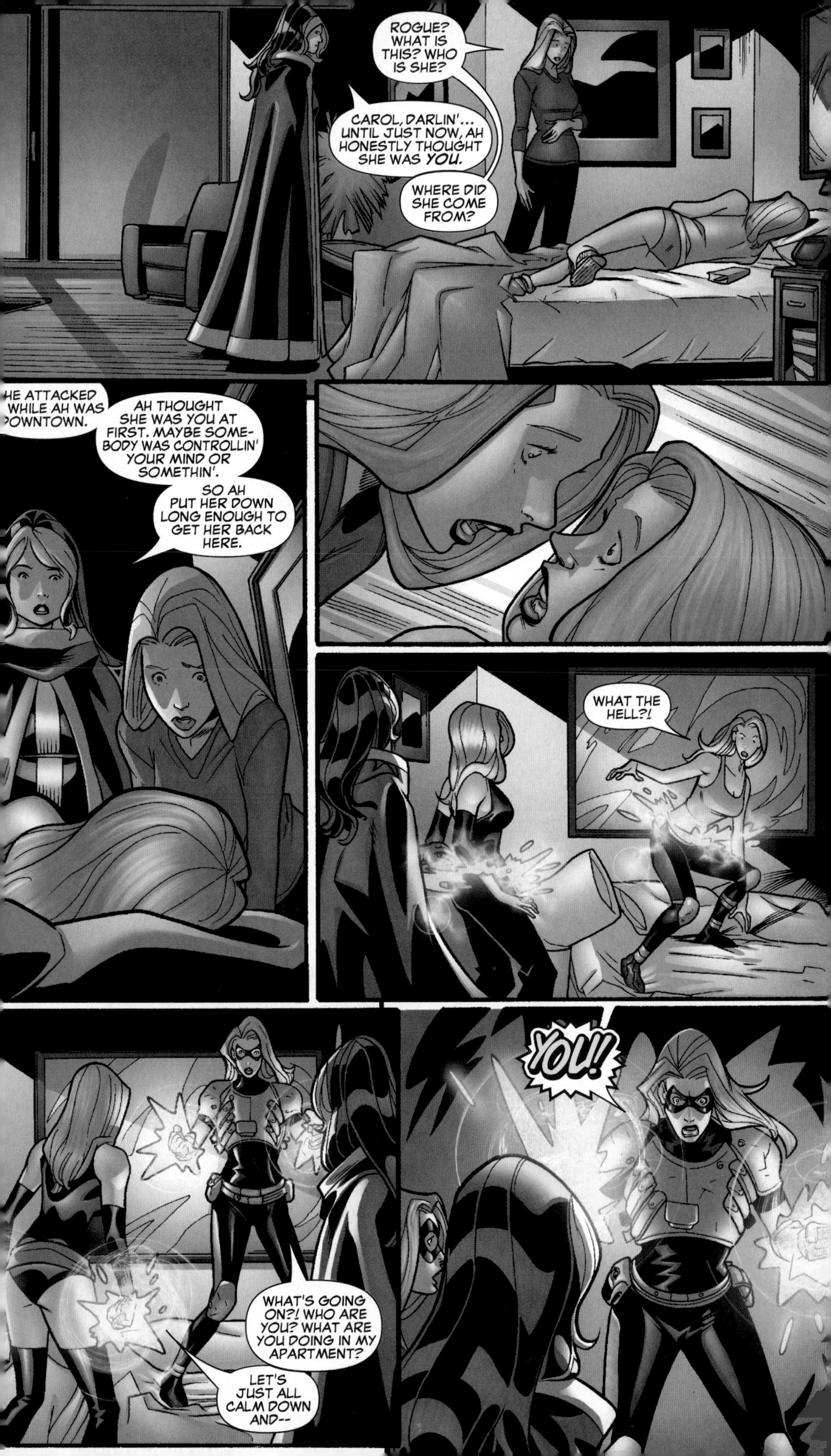
ROGUE? WHAT IS THIS? WHO IS SHE?
CAROL, DARLIN'... UNTIL JUST NOW, AH HONESTLY THOUGHT SHE WAS YOU.
WHERE DID SHE COME FROM?
HE ATTACKED WHILE AH WAS DOWNTOWN.
AH THOUGHT SHE WAS YOU AT FIRST. MAYBE SOMEBODY WAS CONTROLLIN' YOUR MIND OR SOMETHIN'.
SO AH PUT HER DOWN LONG ENOUGH TO GET HER BACK HERE.
WHAT THE HELL?!
WHAT'S GOING ON?! WHO ARE YOU? WHAT ARE YOU DOING IN MY APARTMENT?
LET'S JUST ALL CALM DOWN AND--
YOU!!

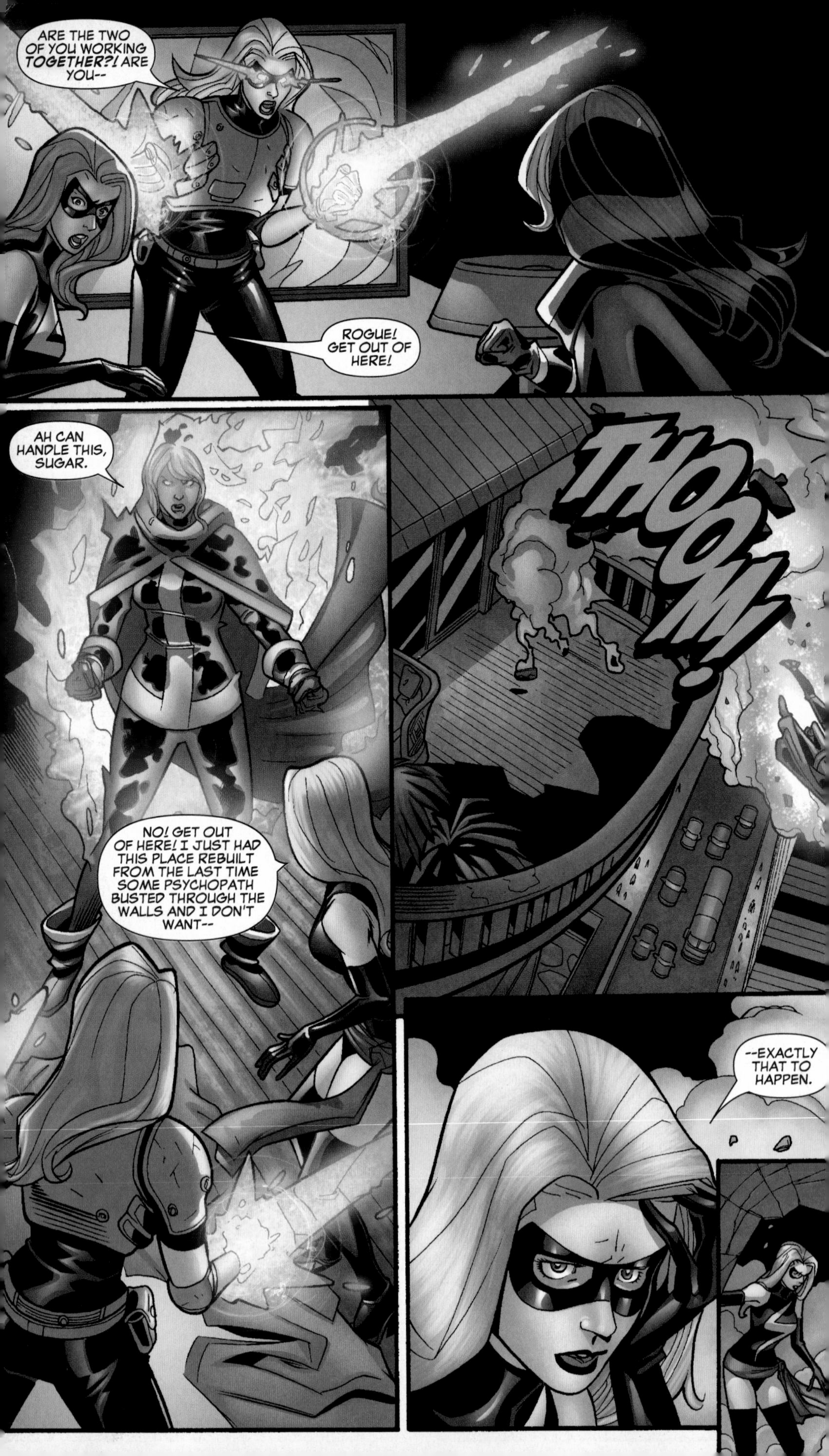

ARE THE TWO OF YOU WORKING *TOGETHER?!* ARE YOU--
ROGUE! GET OUT OF HERE!
AH CAN HANDLE THIS, SUGAR.
NO! GET OUT OF HERE! I JUST HAD THIS PLACE REBUILT FROM THE LAST TIME SOME PSYCHOPATH BUSTED THROUGH THE WALLS AND I DON'T WANT--
THOOM!
--EXACTLY THAT TO HAPPEN.

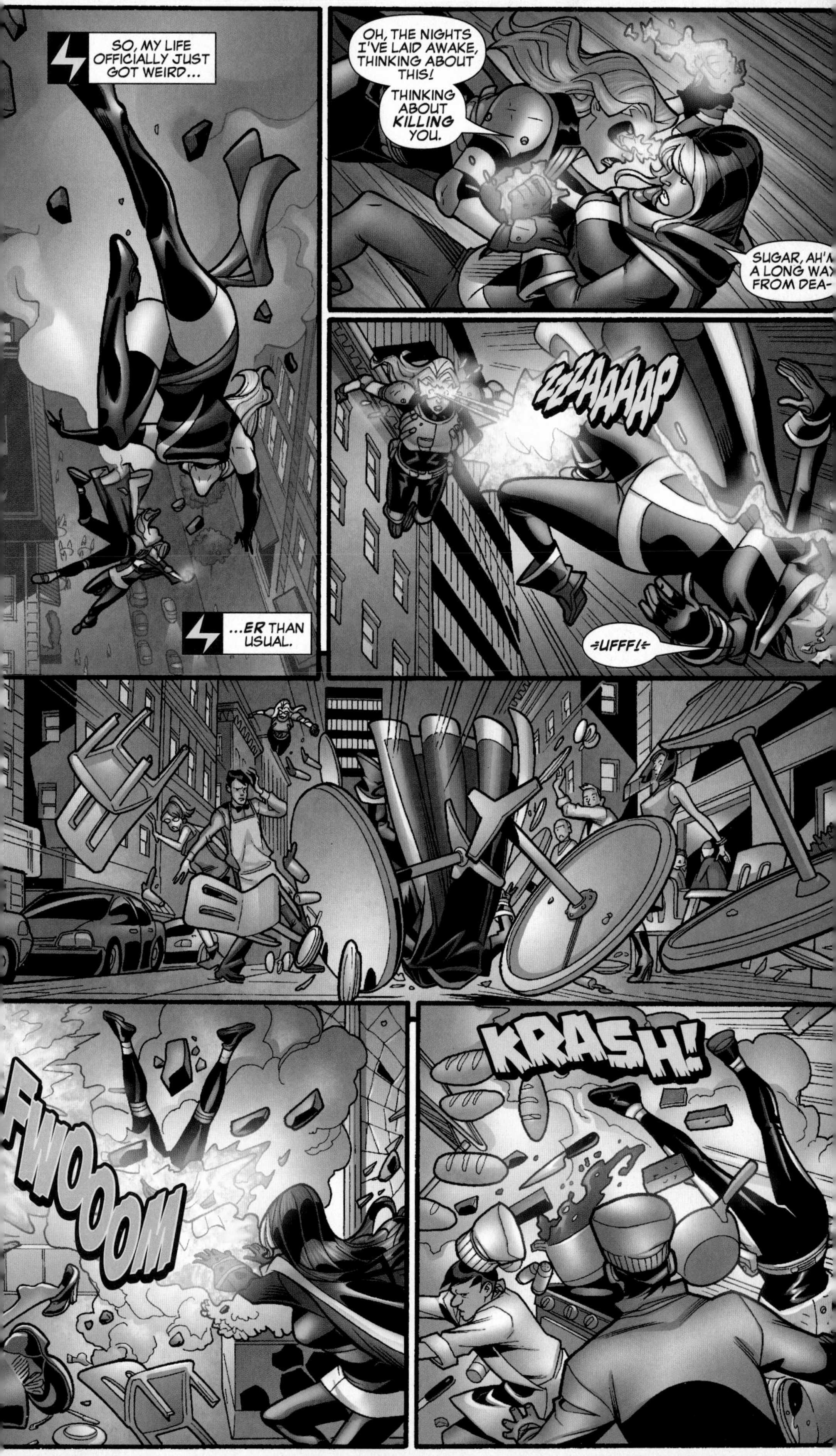
SO, MY LIFE OFFICIALLY JUST GOT WEIRD...
...ER THAN USUAL.
OH, THE NIGHTS I'VE LAID AWAKE, THINKING ABOUT THIS!
THINKING ABOUT KILLING YOU.
SUGAR, AH'M A LONG WAY FROM DEA-
ZZZAAAAP
UFFF!
FWOOOM
KRASH!

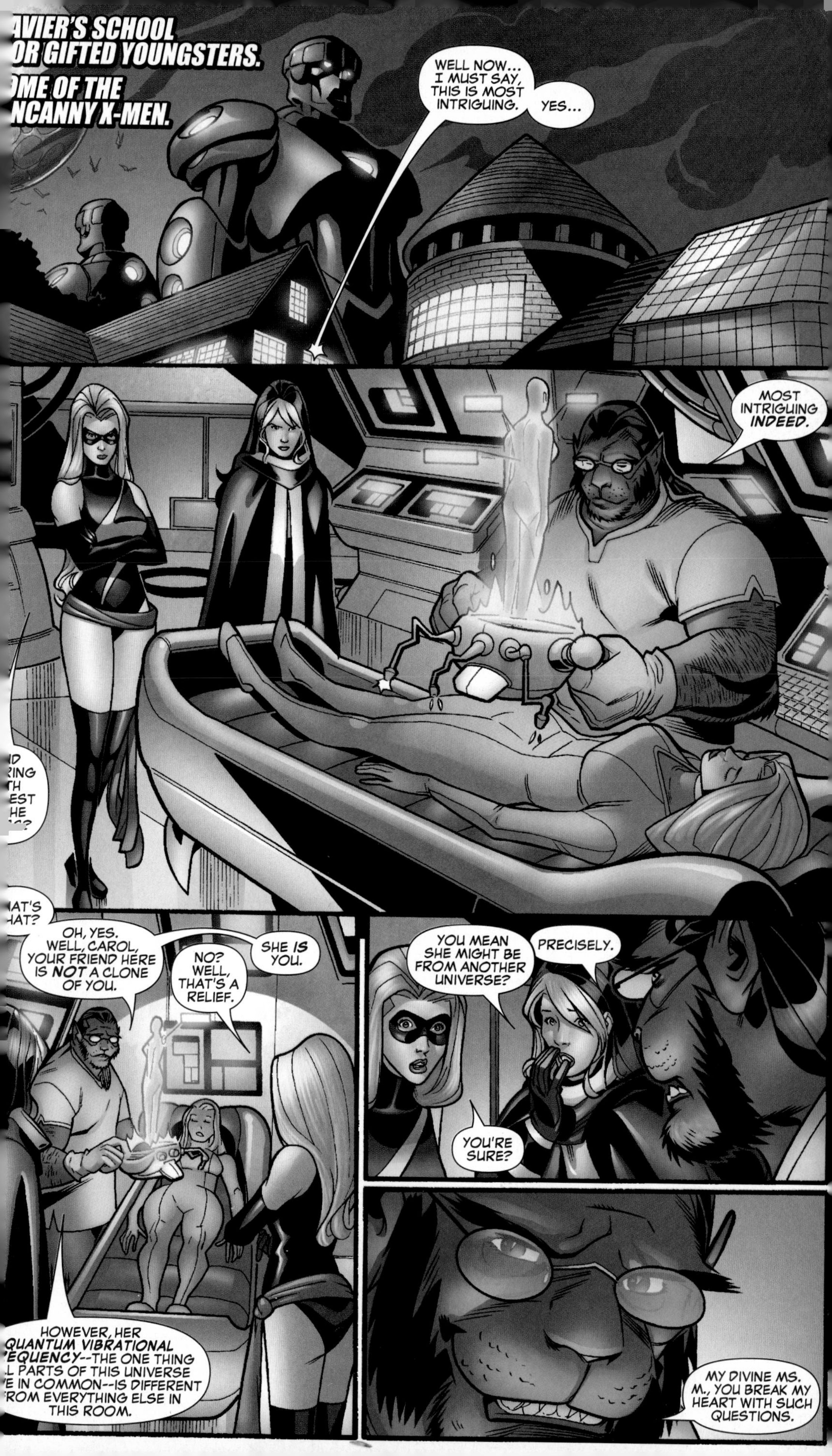

AVIER'S SCHOOL
OR GIFTED YOUNGSTERS.
OME OF THE
NCANNY X-MEN.
WELL NOW... I MUST SAY, THIS IS MOST INTRIGUING.
YES...
MOST INTRIGUING INDEED.
OH, YES. WELL, CAROL, YOUR FRIEND HERE IS NOT A CLONE OF YOU.
NO? WELL, THAT'S A RELIEF.
SHE IS YOU.
HOWEVER, HER QUANTUM VIBRATIONAL EQUENCY--THE ONE THING L PARTS OF THIS UNIVERSE E IN COMMON--IS DIFFERENT FROM EVERYTHING ELSE IN THIS ROOM.
YOU MEAN SHE MIGHT BE FROM ANOTHER UNIVERSE?
PRECISELY.
YOU'RE SURE?
MY DIVINE MS. M., YOU BREAK MY HEART WITH SUCH QUESTIONS.

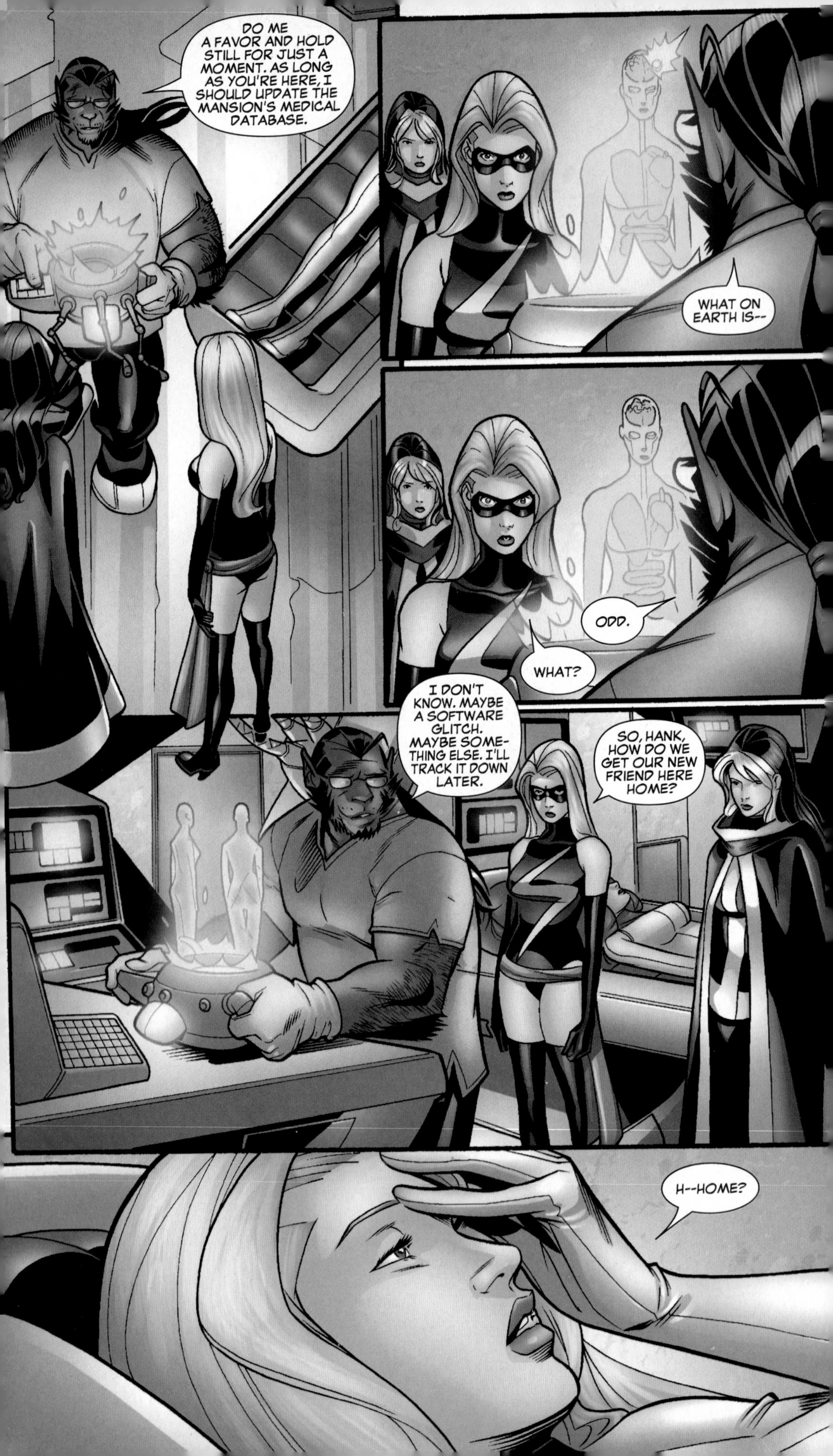
DO ME A FAVOR AND HOLD STILL FOR JUST A MOMENT. AS LONG AS YOU'RE HERE, I SHOULD UPDATE THE MANSION'S MEDICAL DATABASE.
WHAT ON EARTH IS--
ODD.
WHAT?
I DON'T KNOW. MAYBE A SOFTWARE GLITCH. MAYBE SOMETHING ELSE. I'LL TRACK IT DOWN LATER.
SO, HANK, HOW DO WE GET OUR NEW FRIEND HERE HOME?
H--HOME?

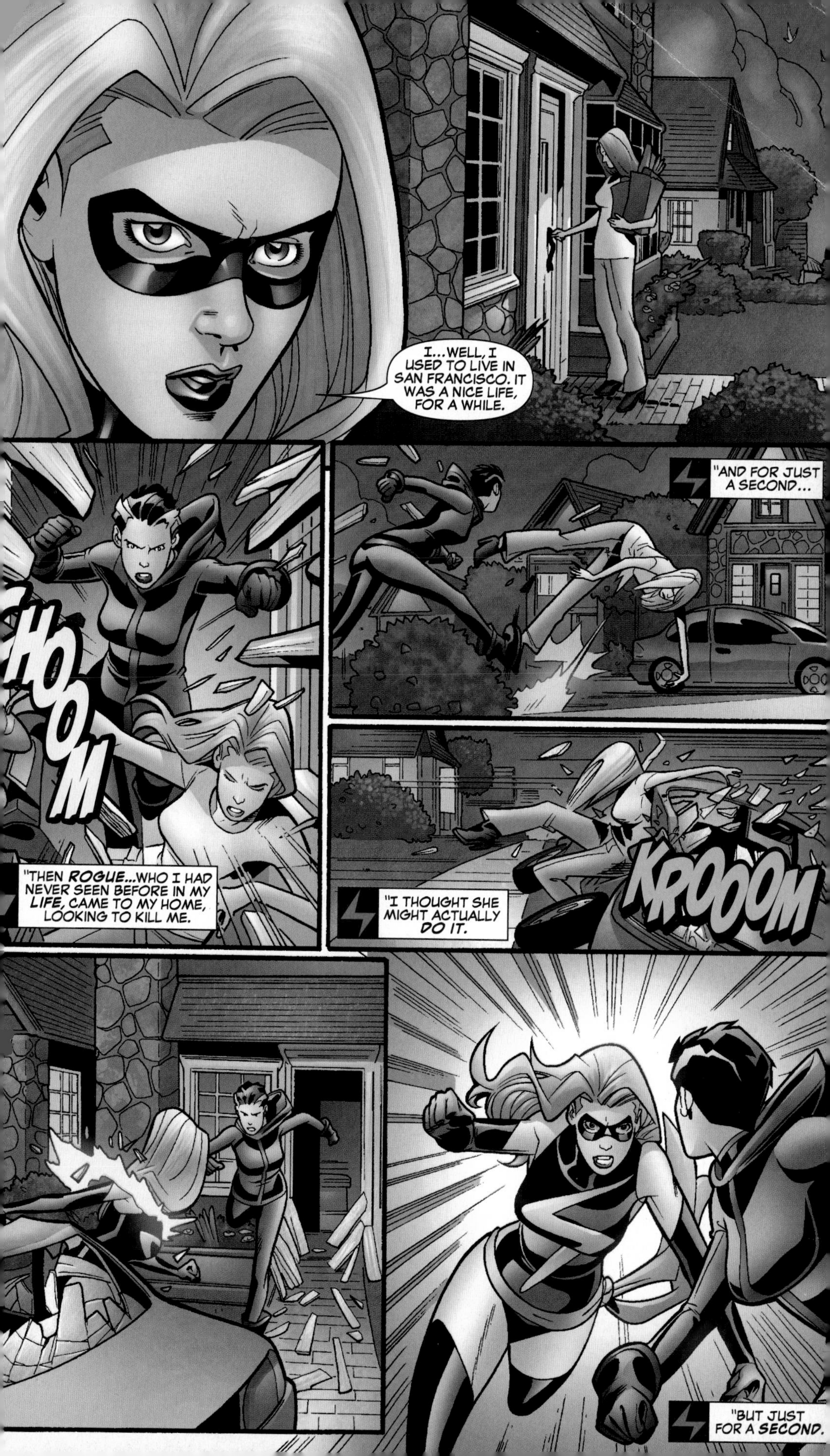
I...WELL, I USED TO LIVE IN SAN FRANCISCO. IT WAS A NICE LIFE, FOR A WHILE.
CHOOM
"THEN ROGUE...WHO I HAD NEVER SEEN BEFORE IN MY LIFE, CAME TO MY HOME, LOOKING TO KILL ME.
"AND FOR JUST A SECOND...
KROOOM
"I THOUGHT SHE MIGHT ACTUALLY DO IT.
"BUT JUST FOR A SECOND.

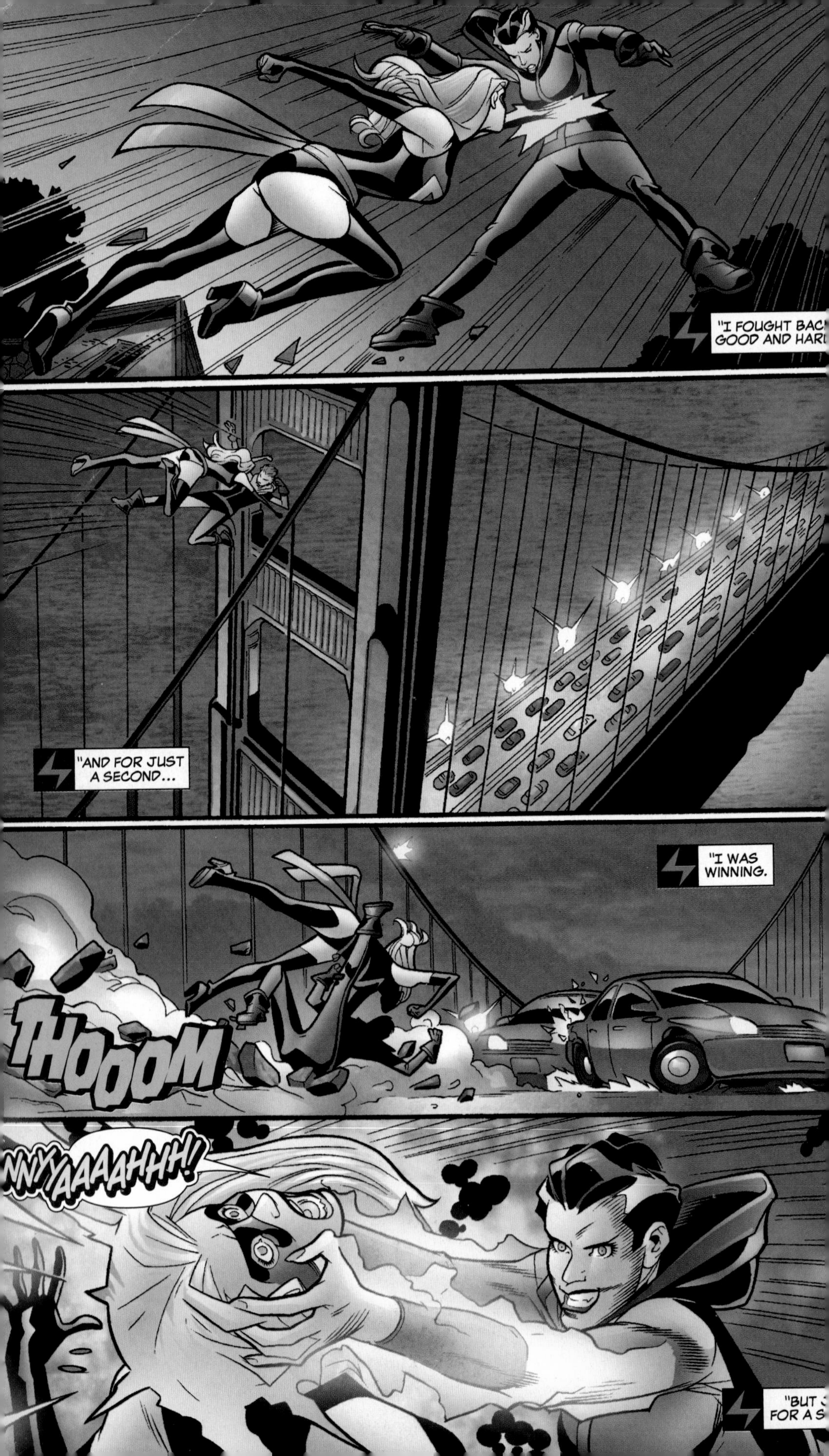
"I FOUGHT BAC
GOOD AND HAR
"AND FOR JUST A SECOND...
"I WAS WINNING.
THOOOM
NNYYAAAAHHH!
"BUT
FOR A S

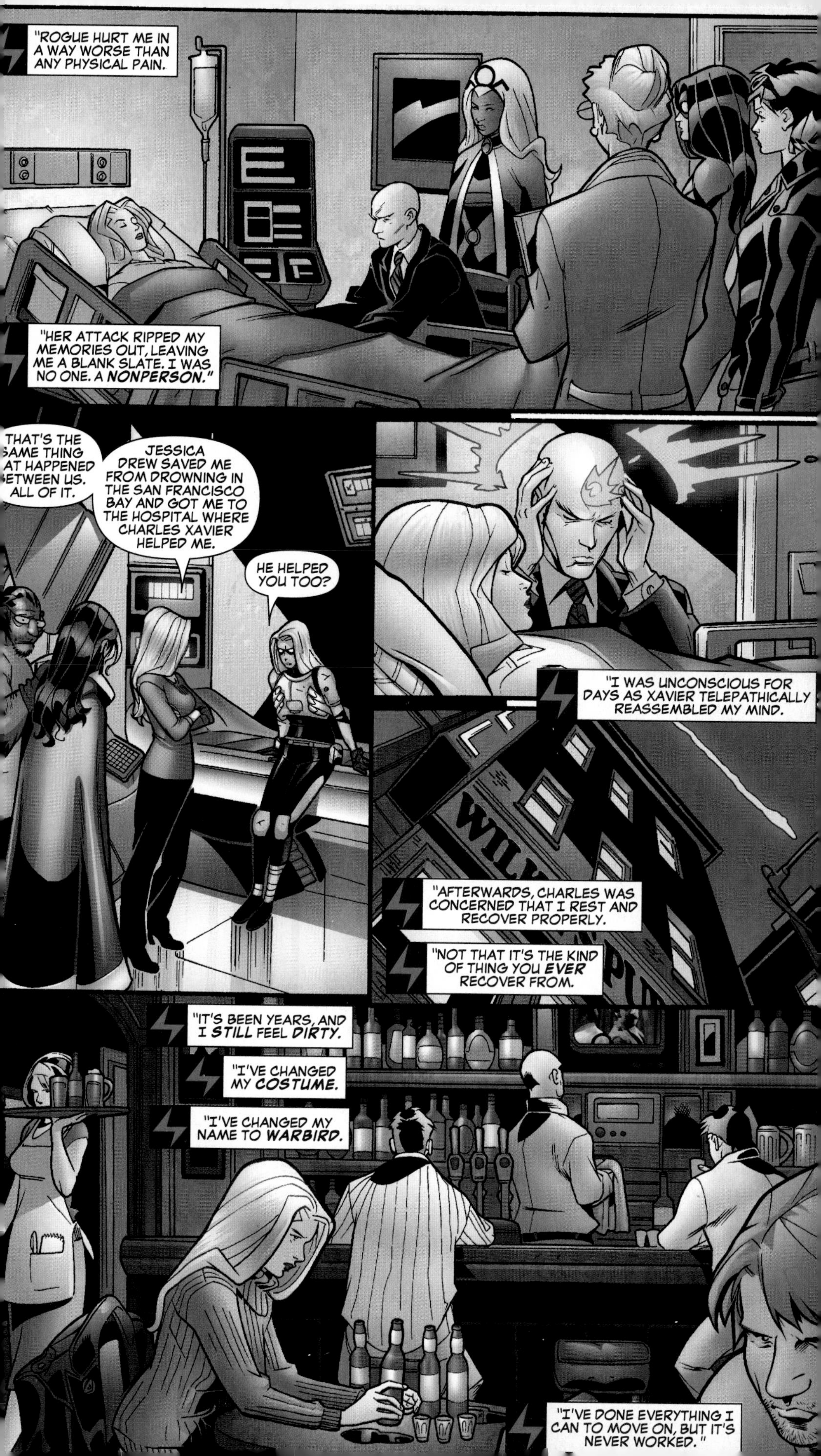

"ROGUE HURT ME IN A WAY WORSE THAN ANY PHYSICAL PAIN.
"HER ATTACK RIPPED MY MEMORIES OUT, LEAVING ME A BLANK SLATE. I WAS NO ONE. A NONPERSON."
THAT'S THE SAME THING AT HAPPENED BETWEEN US. ALL OF IT.
JESSICA DREW SAVED ME FROM DROWNING IN THE SAN FRANCISCO BAY AND GOT ME TO THE HOSPITAL WHERE CHARLES XAVIER HELPED ME.
HE HELPED YOU TOO?
"I WAS UNCONSCIOUS FOR DAYS AS XAVIER TELEPATHICALLY REASSEMBLED MY MIND.
"AFTERWARDS, CHARLES WAS CONCERNED THAT I REST AND RECOVER PROPERLY.
"NOT THAT IT'S THE KIND OF THING YOU EVER RECOVER FROM.
"IT'S BEEN YEARS, AND I STILL FEEL DIRTY.
"I'VE CHANGED MY COSTUME.
"I'VE CHANGED MY NAME TO WARBIRD.
"I'VE DONE EVERYTHING I CAN TO MOVE ON, BUT IT'S NEVER WORKED."

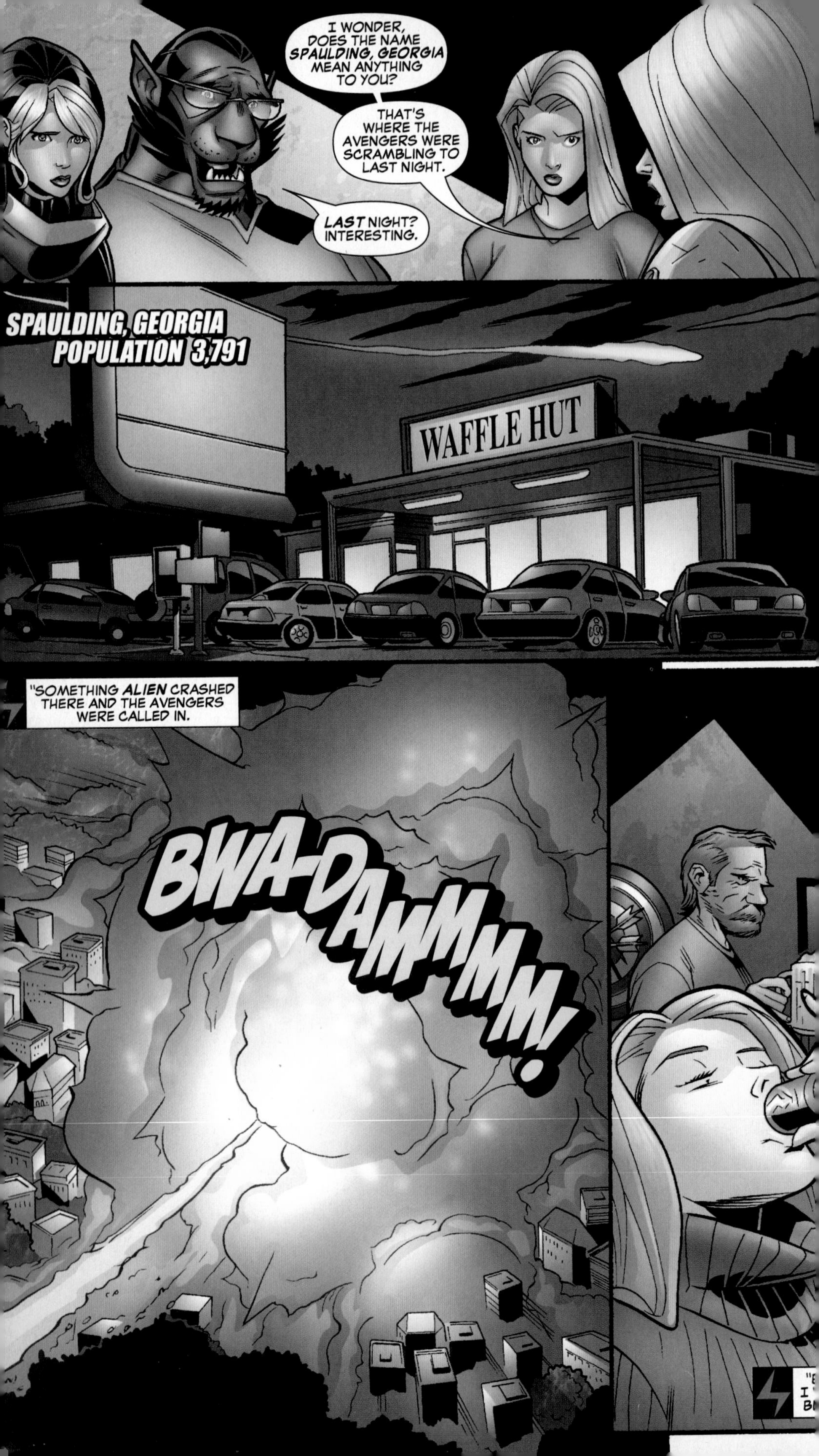

I WONDER, DOES THE NAME SPAULDING, GEORGIA MEAN ANYTHING TO YOU?
THAT'S WHERE THE AVENGERS WERE SCRAMBLING TO LAST NIGHT.
LAST NIGHT? INTERESTING.
SPAULDING, GEORGIA POPULATION 3,791
WAFFLE HUT
"SOMETHING ALIEN CRASHED THERE AND THE AVENGERS WERE CALLED IN.
BWA-DAMMMMM!

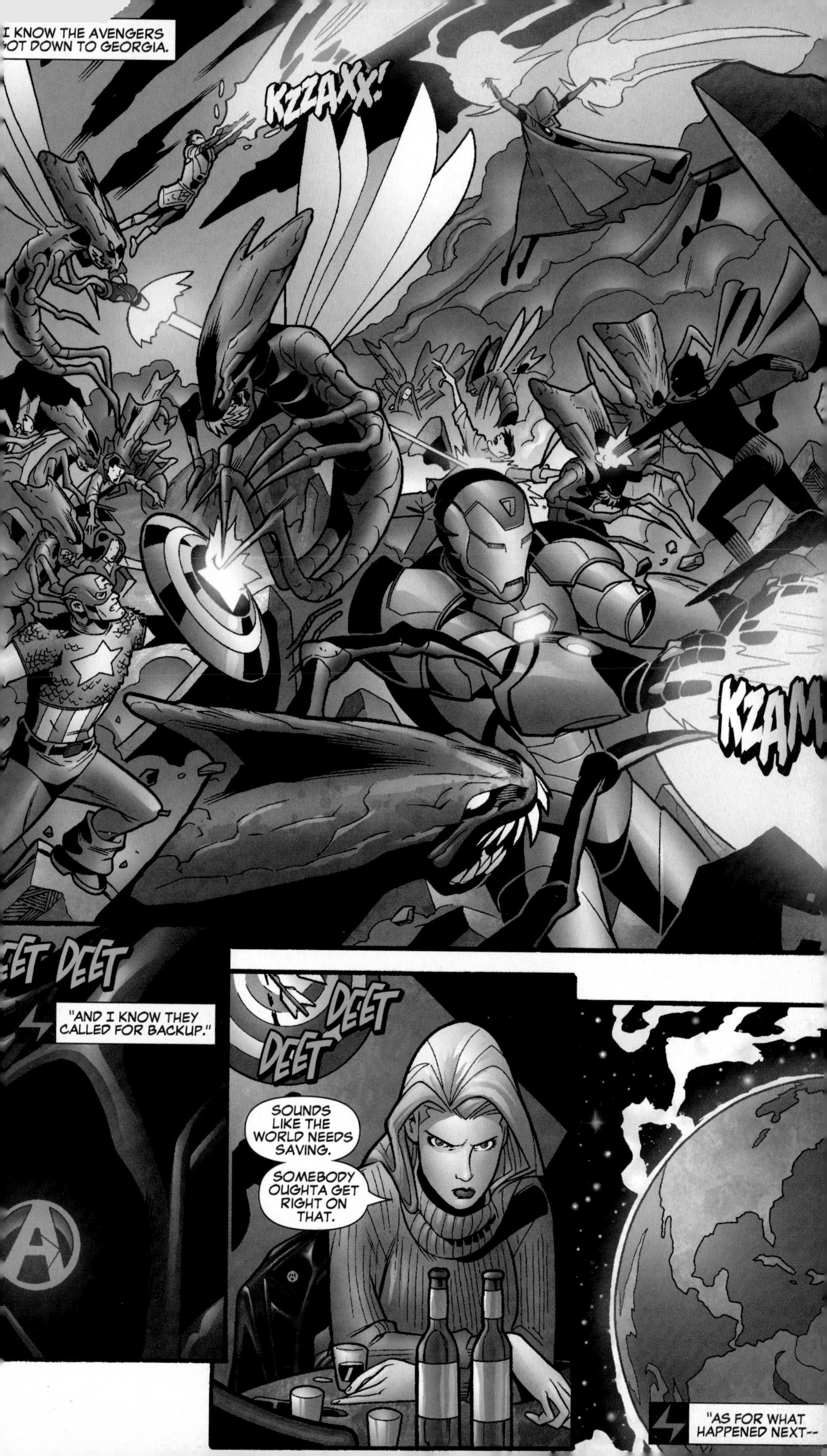
I KNOW THE AVENGERS GOT DOWN TO GEORGIA.
KZZAXX!
KZAM
DEET DEET
"AND I KNOW THEY CALLED FOR BACKUP."
DEET DEET
SOUNDS LIKE THE WORLD NEEDS SAVING.
SOMEBODY OUGHTA GET RIGHT ON THAT.
"AS FOR WHAT HAPPENED NEXT--

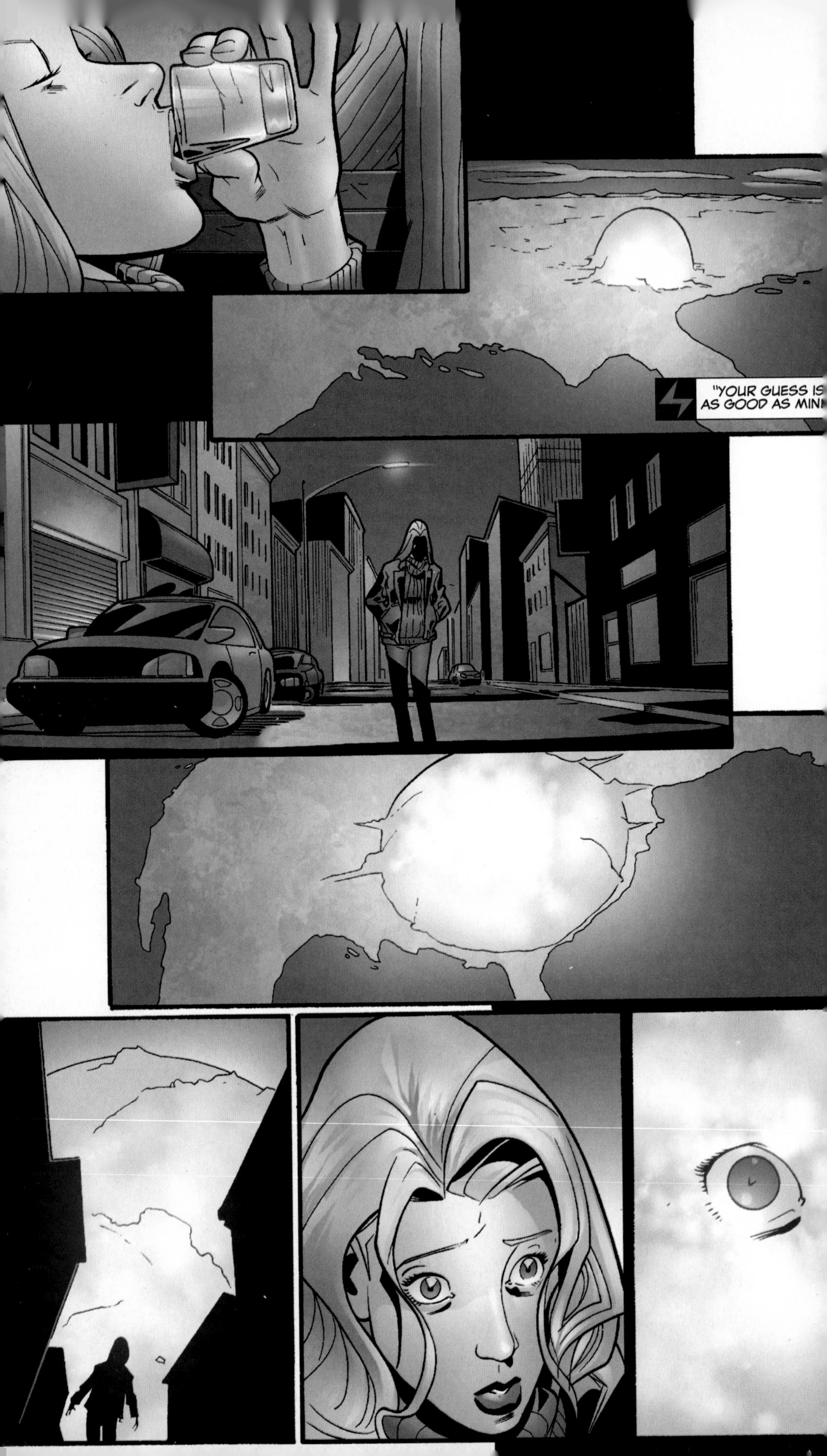
"YOUR GUESS IS
AS GOOD AS MIN

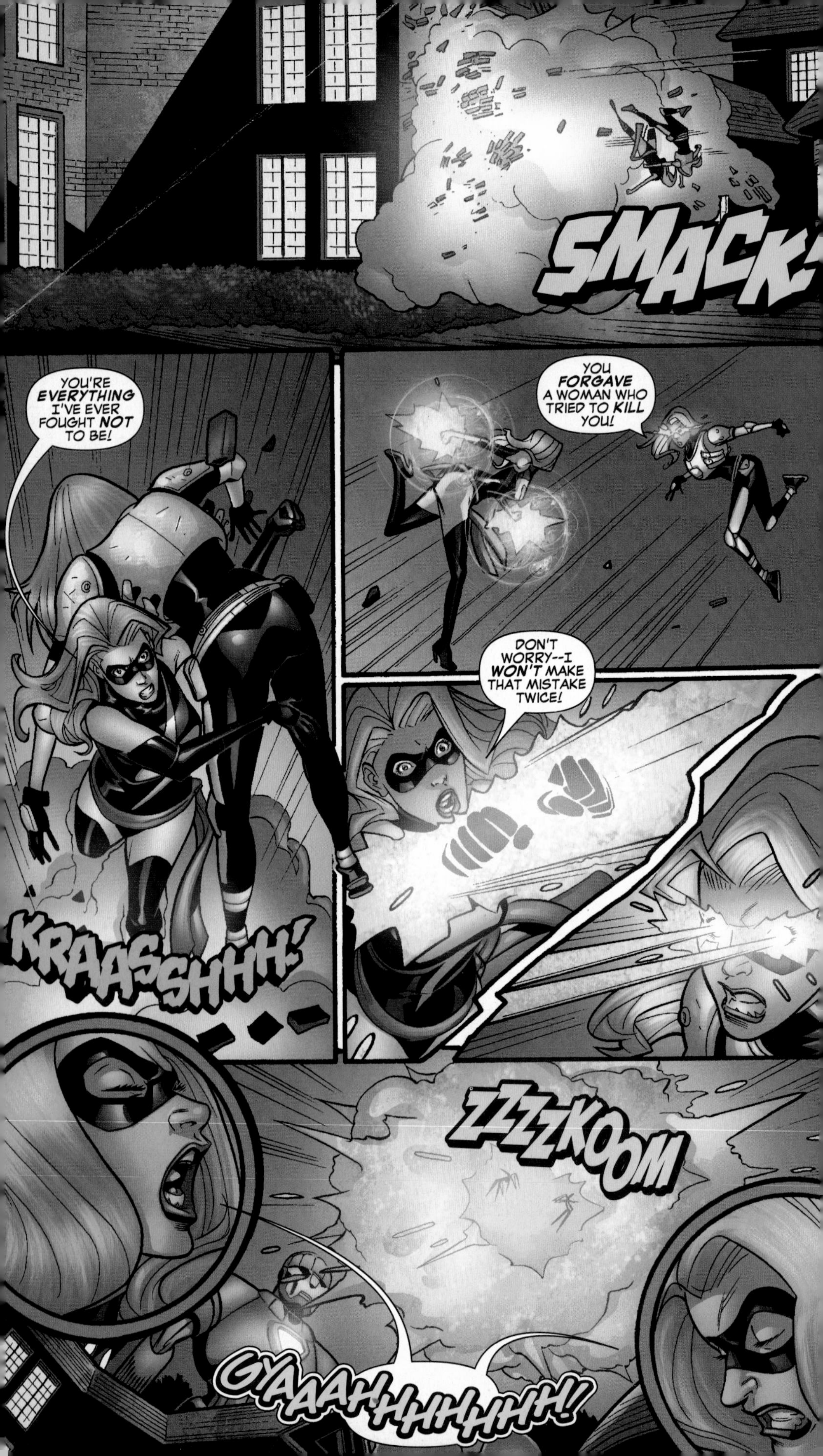
SMACK!
YOU'RE EVERYTHING I'VE EVER FOUGHT NOT TO BE!
KRAASSHHH!
YOU FORGAVE A WOMAN WHO TRIED TO KILL YOU!
DON'T WORRY--I WON'T MAKE THAT MISTAKE TWICE!
ZZZZKOOOM
GYAAAHHHHHHH!

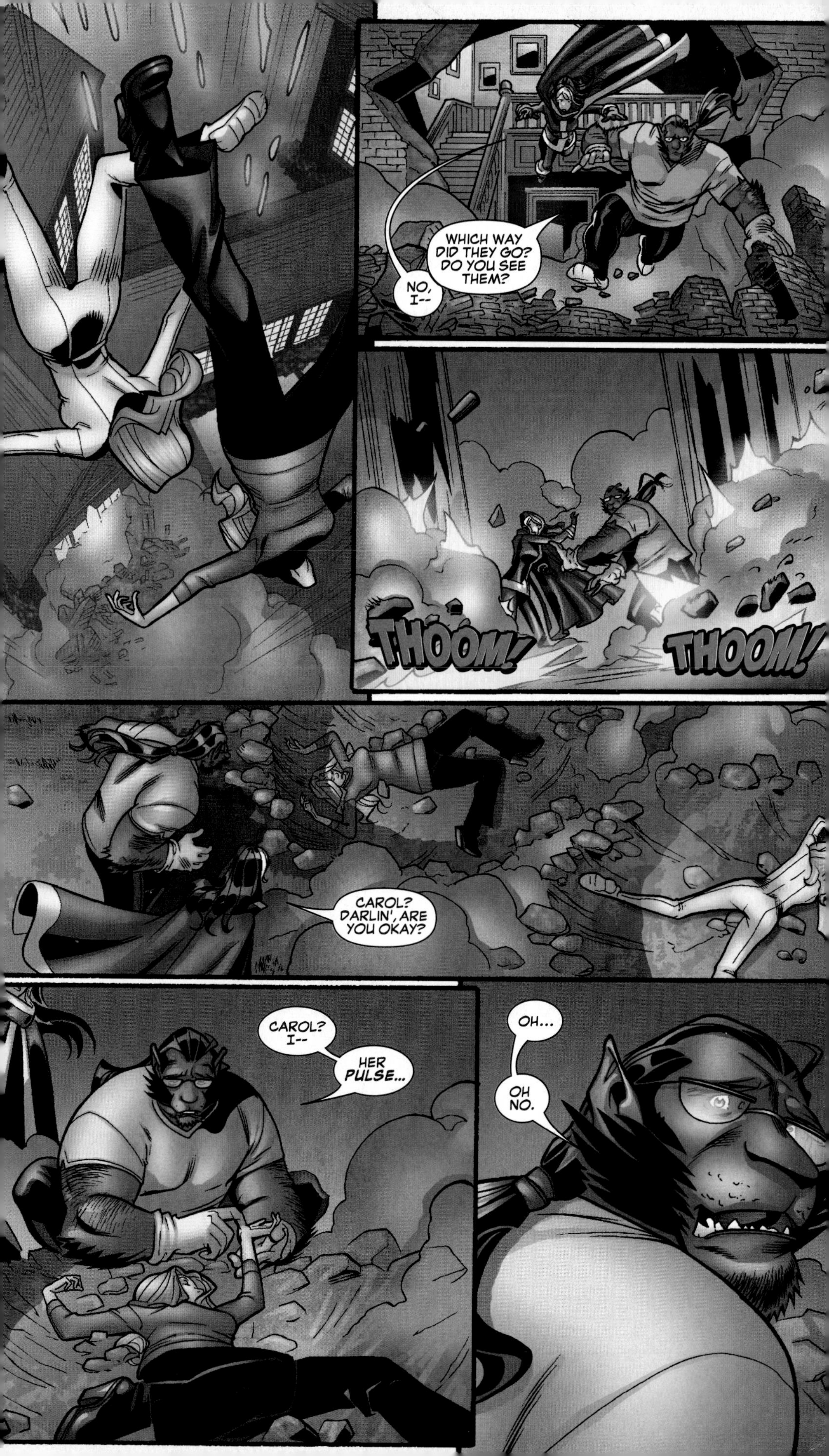
WHICH WAY DID THEY GO? DO YOU SEE THEM?
NO, I--
THOOM!
THOOM!
CAROL? DARLIN', ARE YOU OKAY?
CAROL? I--
HER PULSE...
OH...
OH NO.

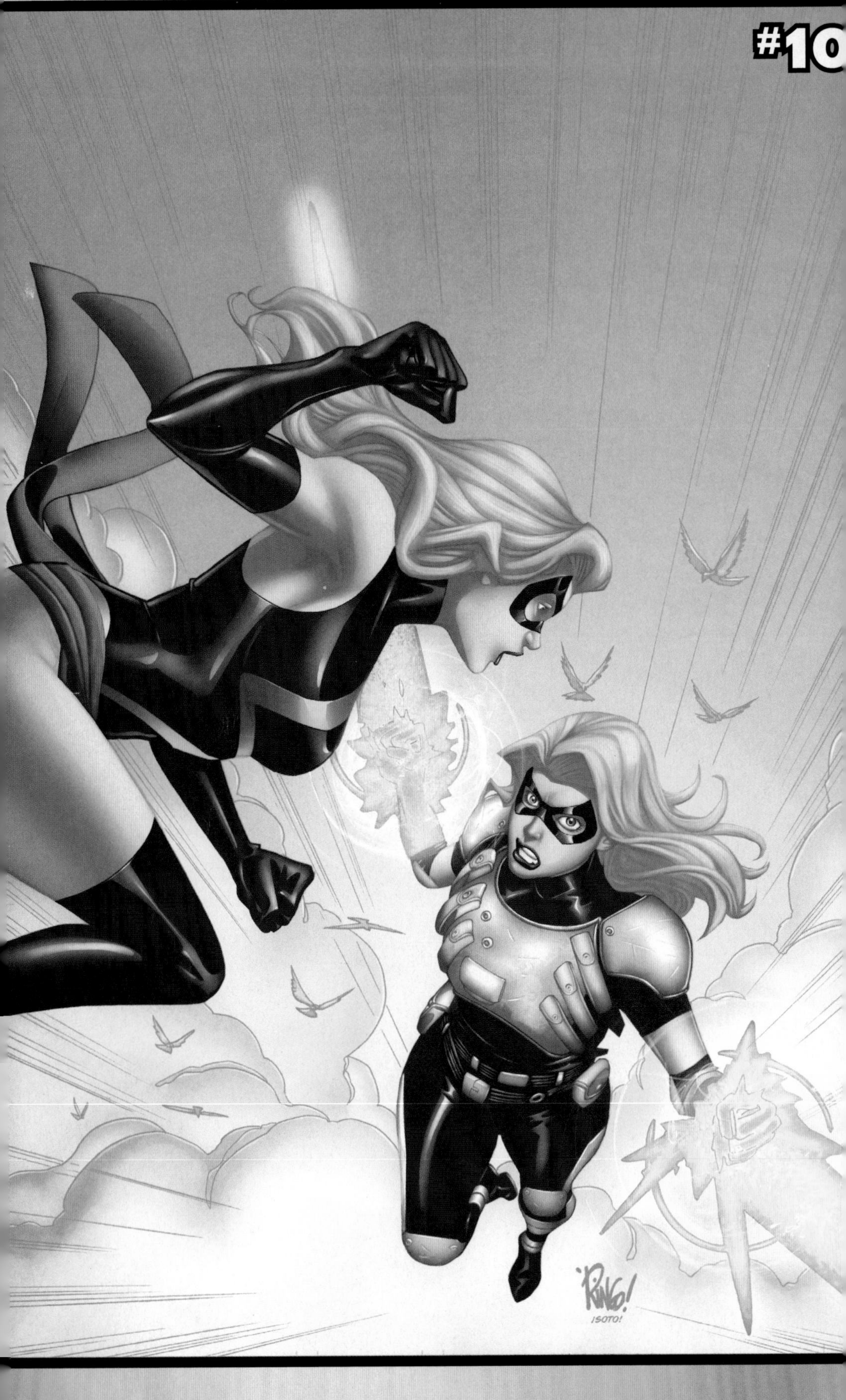
#10
RINGO!
¡SOTO!

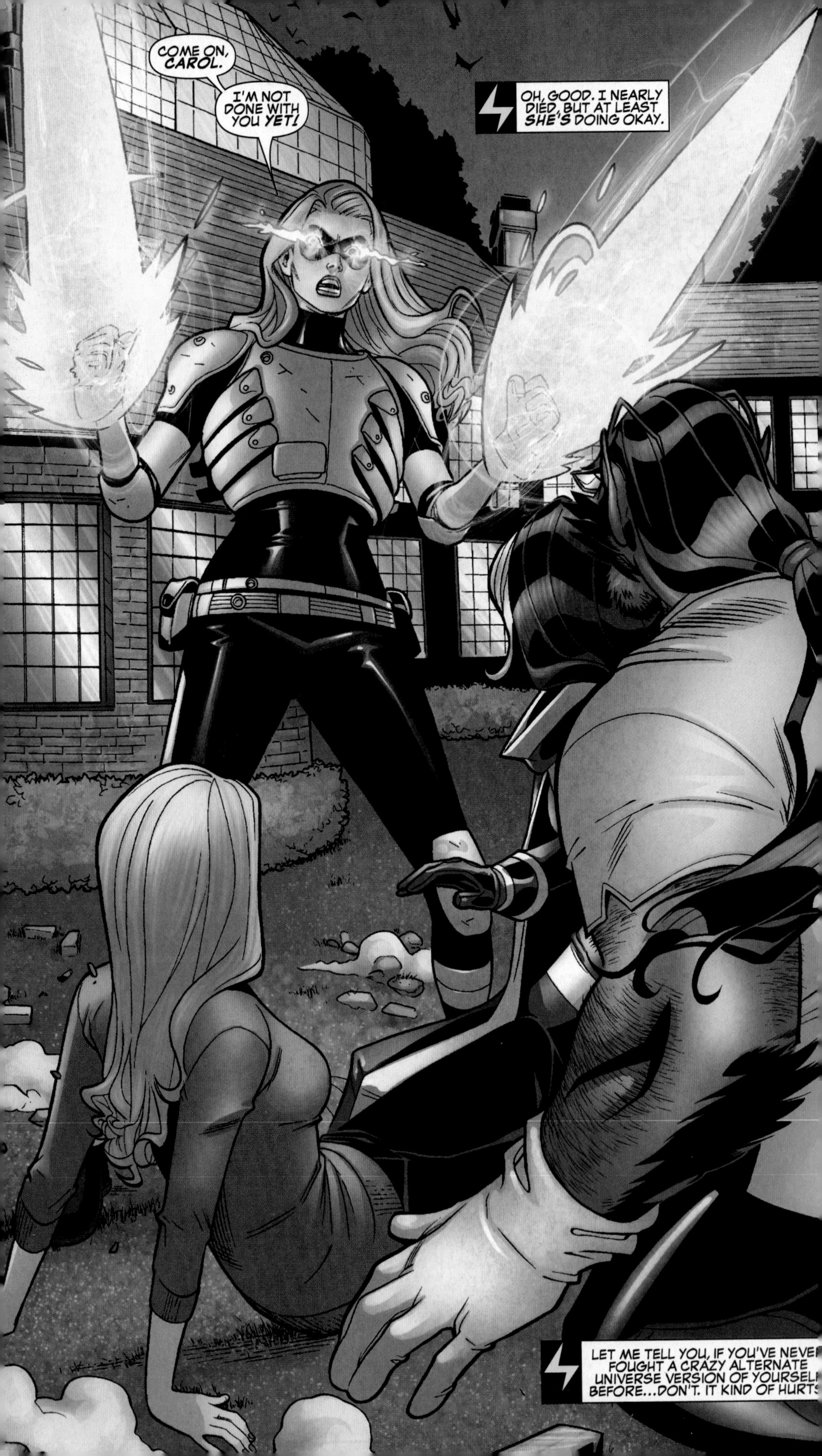
COME ON, CAROL.
I'M NOT DONE WITH YOU YET!
OH, GOOD. I NEARLY DIED, BUT AT LEAST SHE'S DOING OKAY.
LET ME TELL YOU, IF YOU'VE NEVER FOUGHT A CRAZY ALTERNATE UNIVERSE VERSION OF YOURSELF BEFORE...DON'T. IT KIND OF HURTS

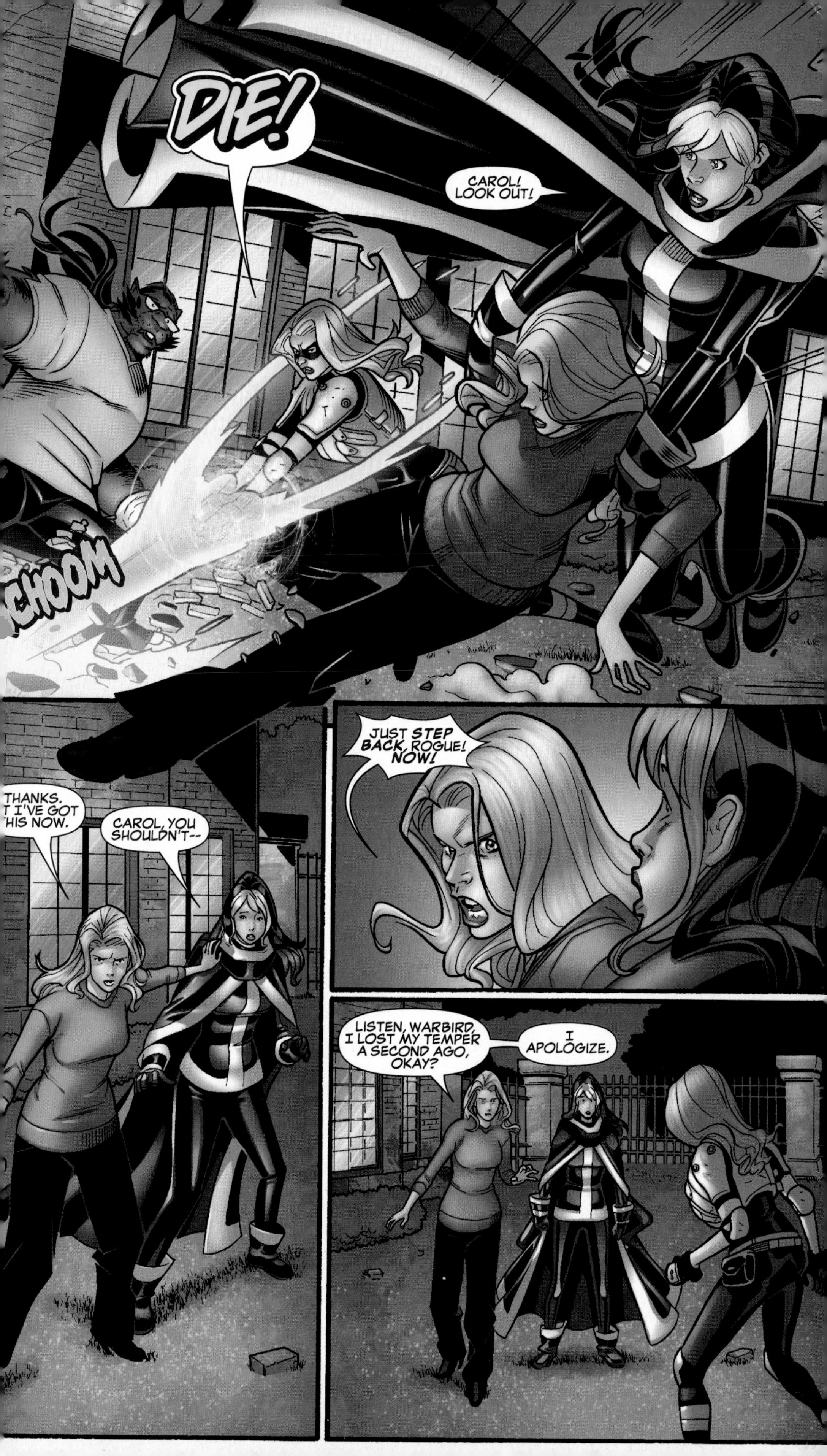

DIE!
CAROL! LOOK OUT!
CHOOM
THANKS. T I'VE GOT HIS NOW.
CAROL, YOU SHOULDN'T--
JUST STEP BACK, ROGUE! NOW!
LISTEN, WARBIRD, I LOST MY TEMPER A SECOND AGO, OKAY?
I APOLOGIZE.

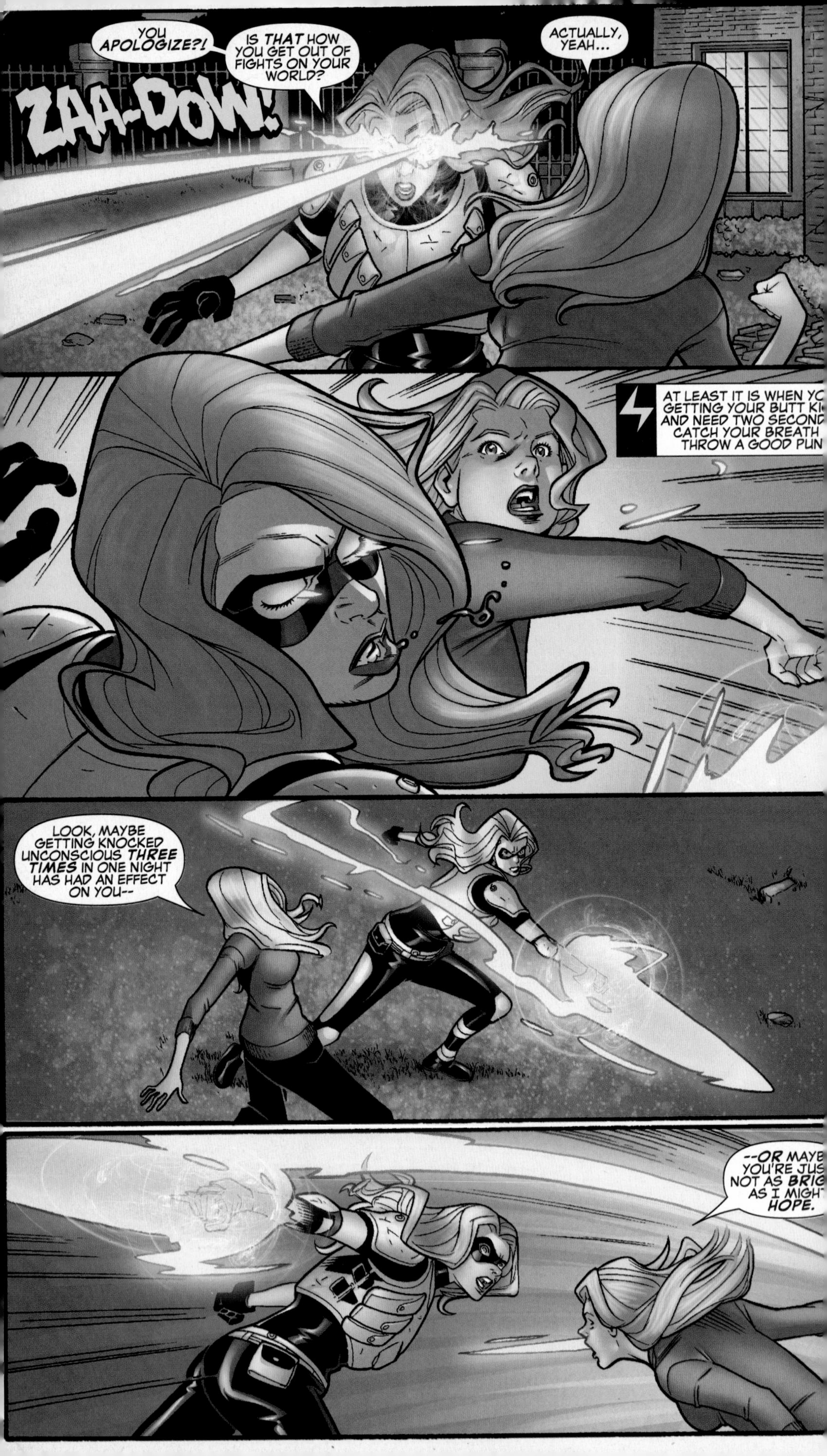

YOU APOLOGIZE?!
IS THAT HOW YOU GET OUT OF FIGHTS ON YOUR WORLD?
ZAA-DOW!
ACTUALLY, YEAH...
AT LEAST IT IS WHEN YO GETTING YOUR BUTT KI AND NEED TWO SECOND CATCH YOUR BREATH THROW A GOOD PUN
LOOK, MAYBE GETTING KNOCKED UNCONSCIOUS THREE TIMES IN ONE NIGHT HAS HAD AN EFFECT ON YOU--
--OR MAYB YOU'RE JUS NOT AS BRIG AS I MIGHT HOPE.

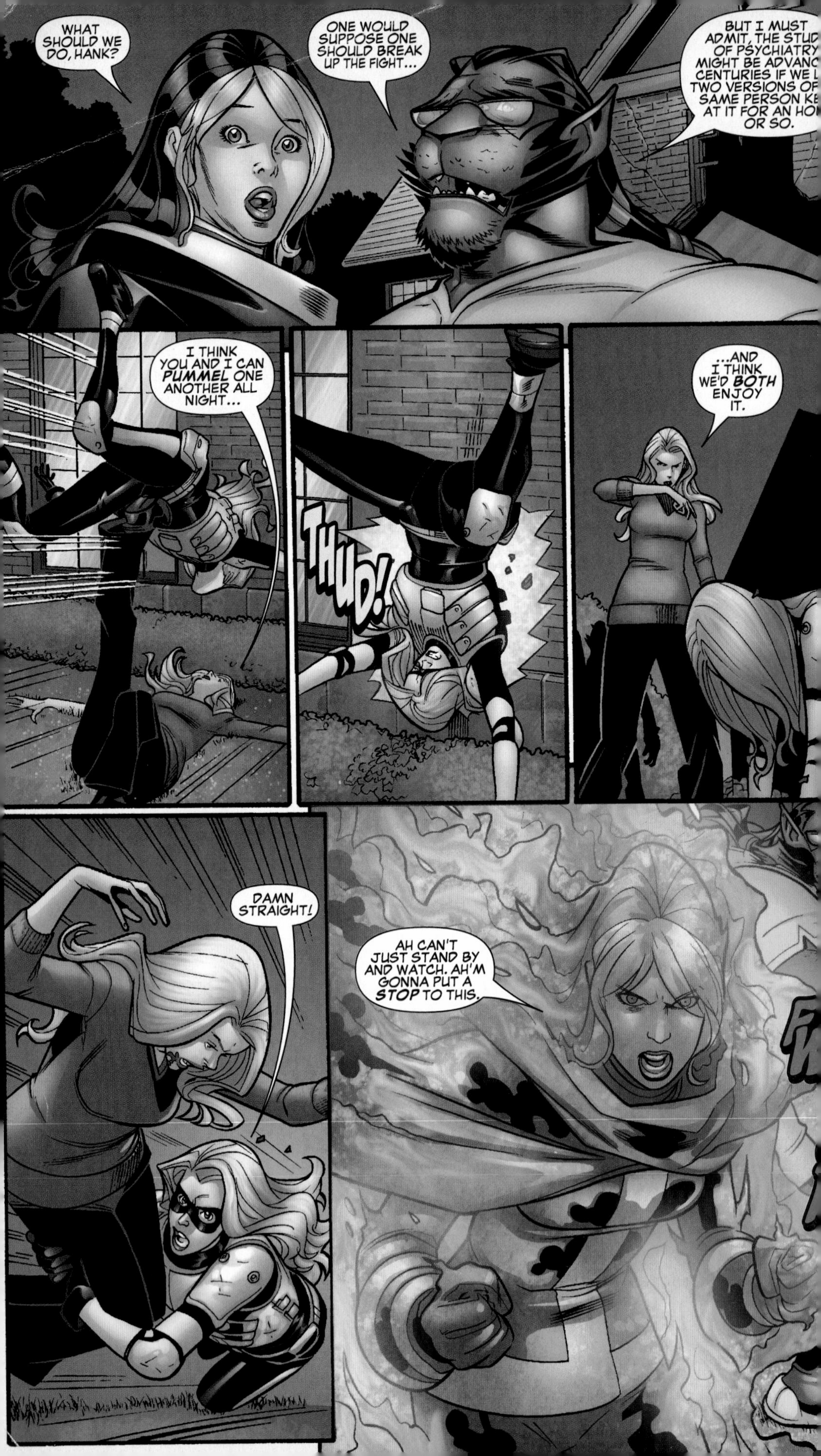
WHAT SHOULD WE DO, HANK?
ONE WOULD SUPPOSE ONE SHOULD BREAK UP THE FIGHT...
BUT I MUST ADMIT, THE STUD OF PSYCHIATRY MIGHT BE ADVANC CENTURIES IF WE L TWO VERSIONS OF SAME PERSON KE AT IT FOR AN HO OR SO.
I THINK YOU AND I CAN PUMMEL ONE ANOTHER ALL NIGHT...
THUD!
...AND I THINK WE'D BOTH ENJOY IT.
DAMN STRAIGHT!
AH CAN'T JUST STAND BY AND WATCH. AH'M GONNA PUT A STOP TO THIS.

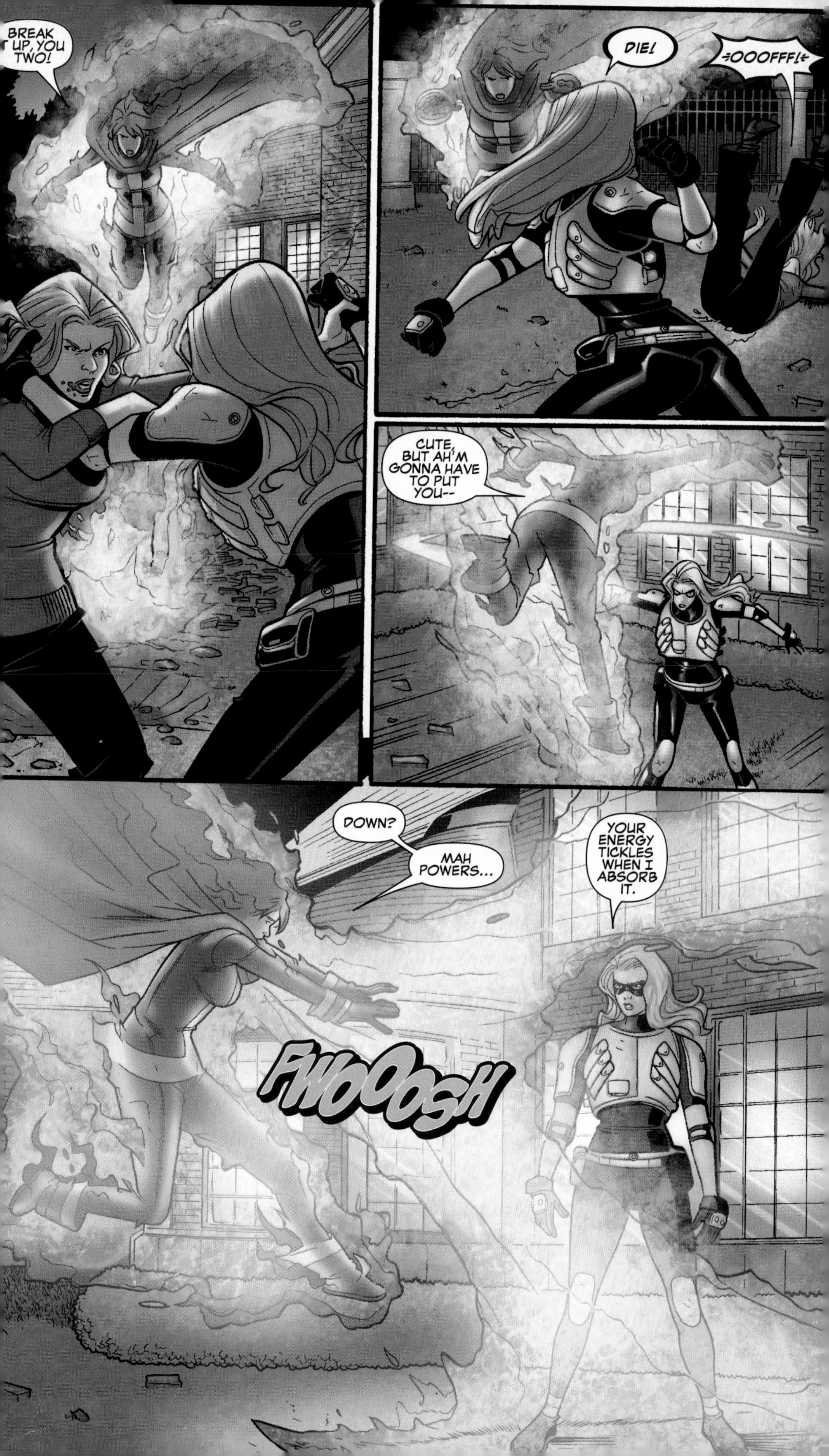
BREAK UP, YOU TWO!
DIE!
OOOFFF!
CUTE, BUT AH'M GONNA HAVE TO PUT YOU--
DOWN?
MAH POWERS...
YOUR ENERGY TICKLES WHEN I ABSORB IT.
FWOOOSH

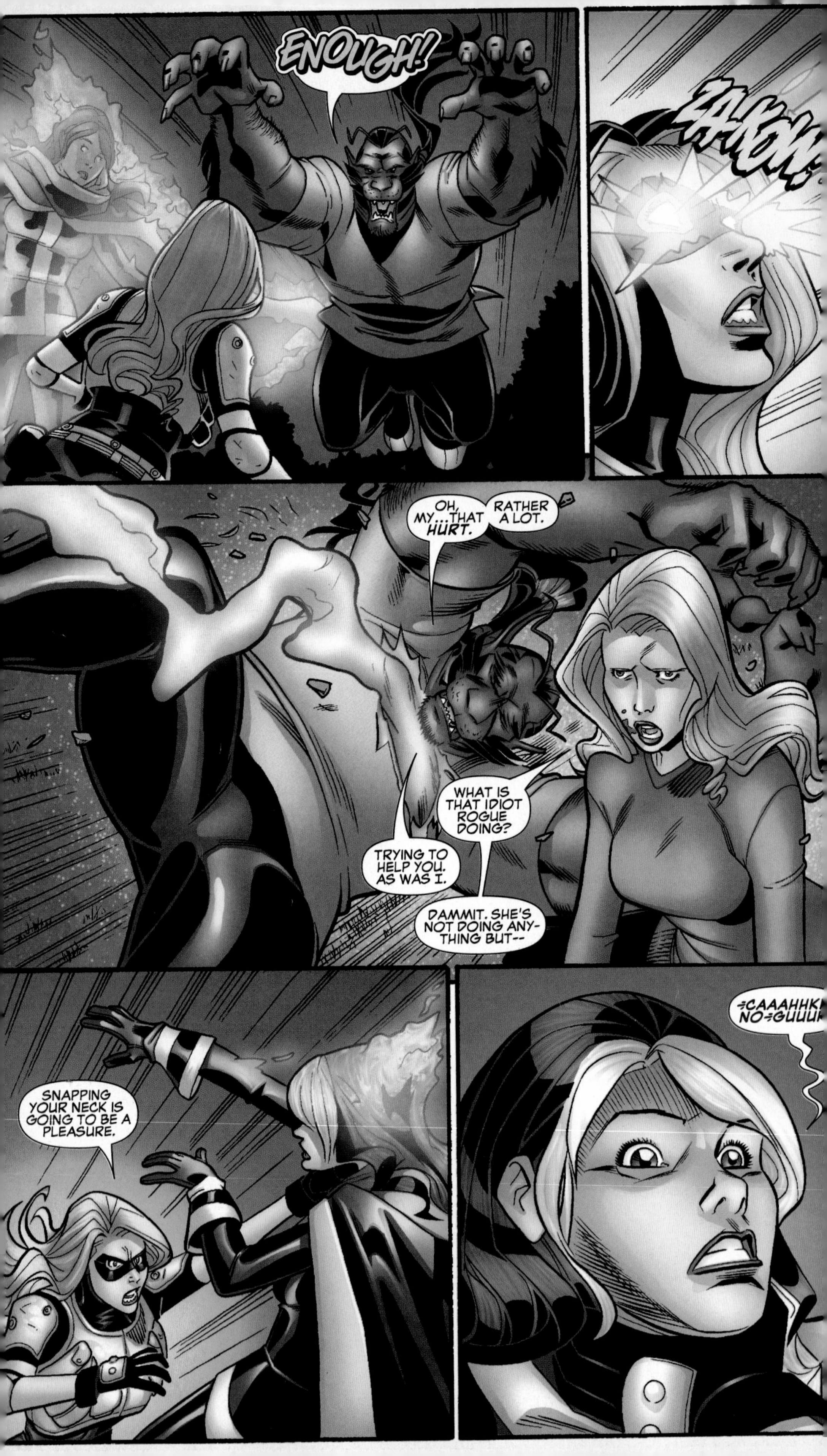
ENOUGH!
ZAKOW!
OH, MY...THAT HURT.
RATHER A LOT.
WHAT IS THAT IDIOT ROGUE DOING?
TRYING TO HELP YOU. AS WAS I.
DAMMIT. SHE'S NOT DOING ANY-THING BUT--
SNAPPING YOUR NECK IS GOING TO BE A PLEASURE.
=CAAAHHK NO=GUUU

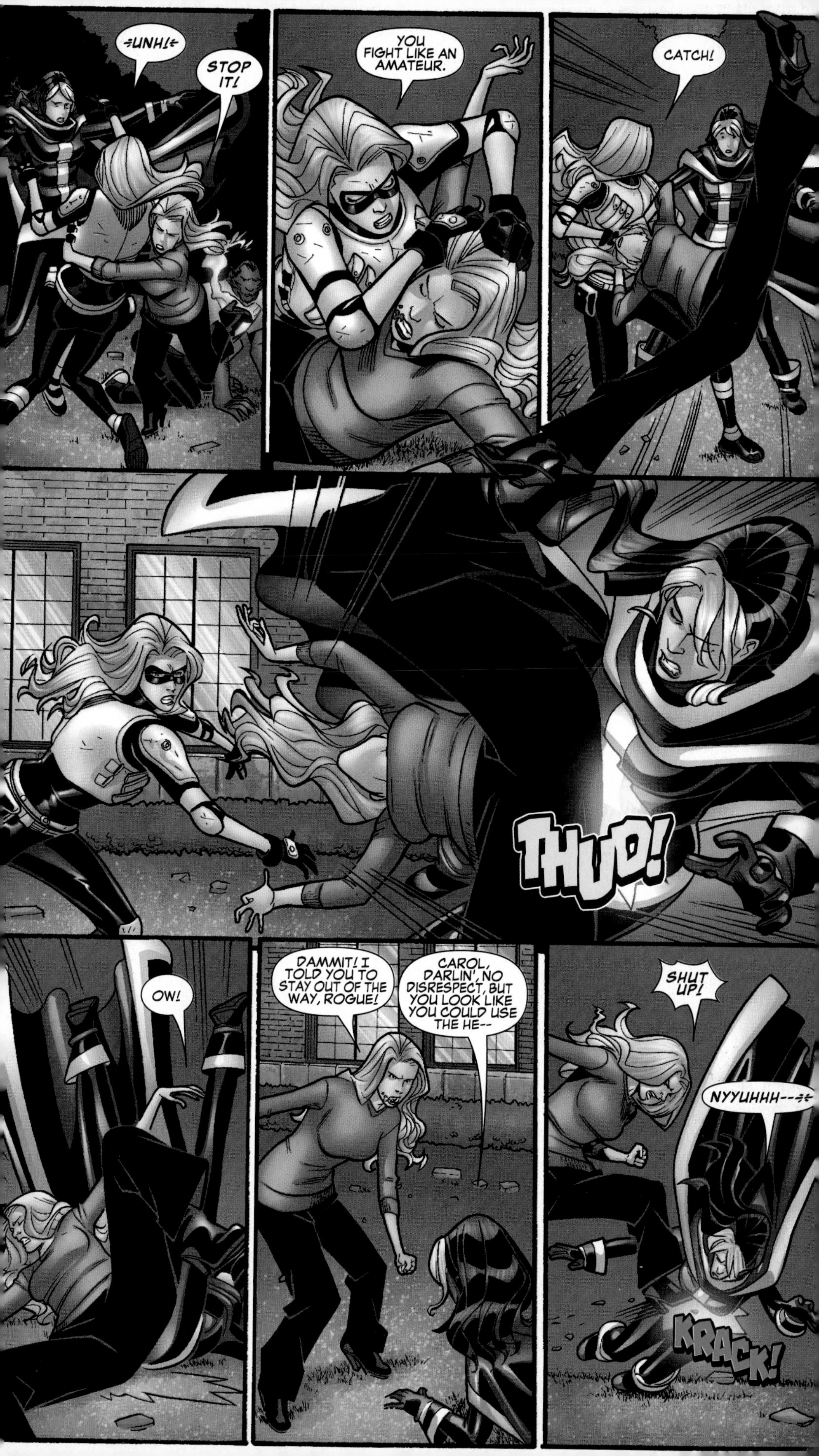
UNH!
STOP IT!
YOU FIGHT LIKE AN AMATEUR.
CATCH!
THUD!
OW!
DAMMIT! I TOLD YOU TO STAY OUT OF THE WAY, ROGUE!
CAROL, DARLIN', NO DISRESPECT, BUT YOU LOOK LIKE YOU COULD USE THE HE--
SHUT UP!
NYYUHHH--
KRACK!

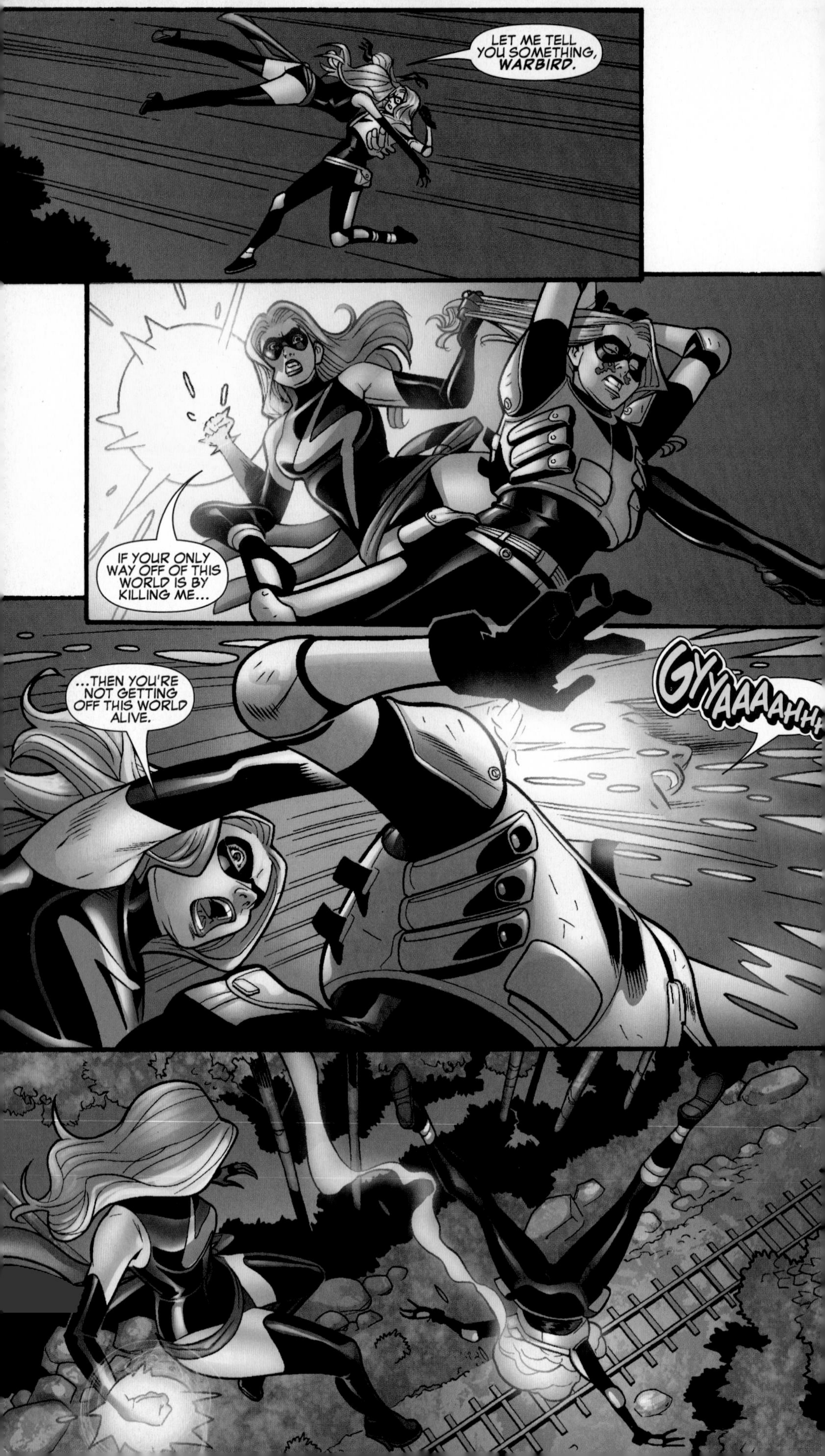
LET ME TELL YOU SOMETHING, WARBIRD.
IF YOUR ONLY WAY OFF OF THIS WORLD IS BY KILLING ME...
...THEN YOU'RE NOT GETTING OFF THIS WORLD ALIVE.
GYYAAAAHH

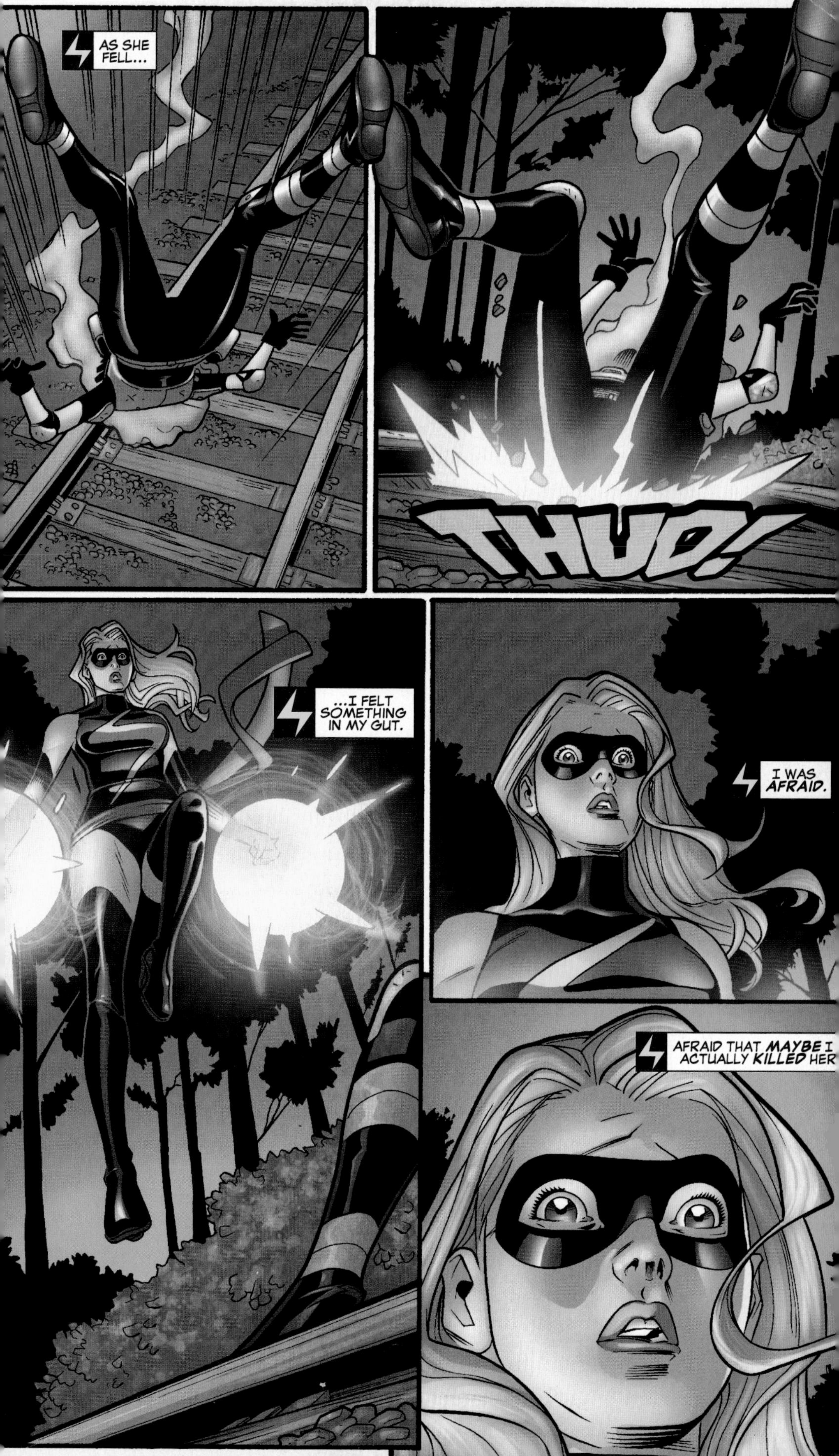

AS SHE FELL...
THUD!
...I FELT SOMETHING IN MY GUT.
I WAS AFRAID.
AFRAID THAT MAYBE I ACTUALLY KILLED HER

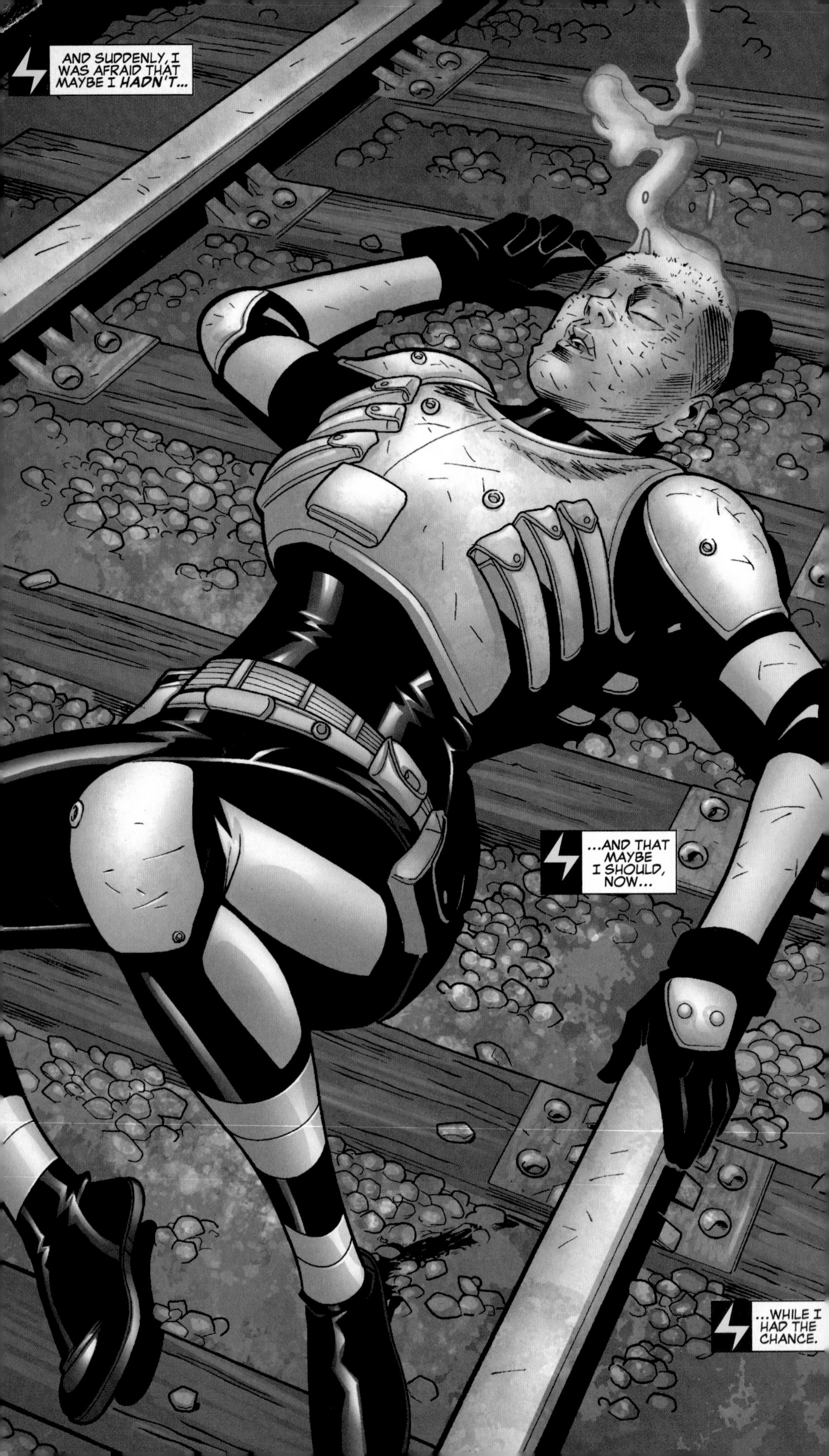
AND SUDDENLY, I WAS AFRAID THAT MAYBE I HADN'T...
...AND THAT MAYBE I SHOULD, NOW...
...WHILE I HAD THE CHANCE.

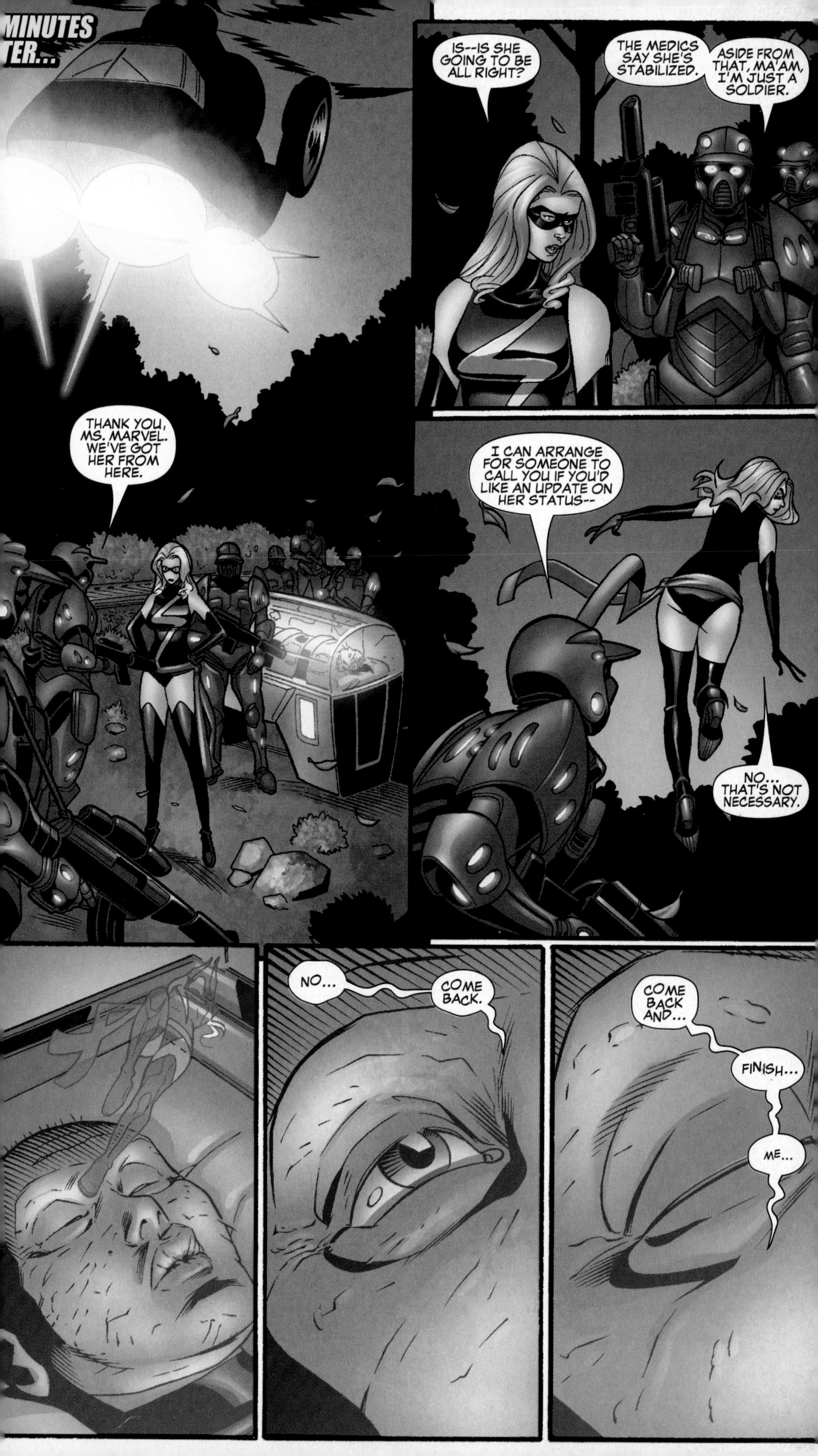
MINUTES
TER...
IS--IS SHE GOING TO BE ALL RIGHT?
THE MEDICS SAY SHE'S STABILIZED.
ASIDE FROM THAT, MA'AM, I'M JUST A SOLDIER.
THANK YOU, MS. MARVEL. WE'VE GOT HER FROM HERE.
I CAN ARRANGE FOR SOMEONE TO CALL YOU IF YOU'D LIKE AN UPDATE ON HER STATUS--
NO... THAT'S NOT NECESSARY.
NO...
COME BACK.
COME BACK AND...
FINISH...
ME...

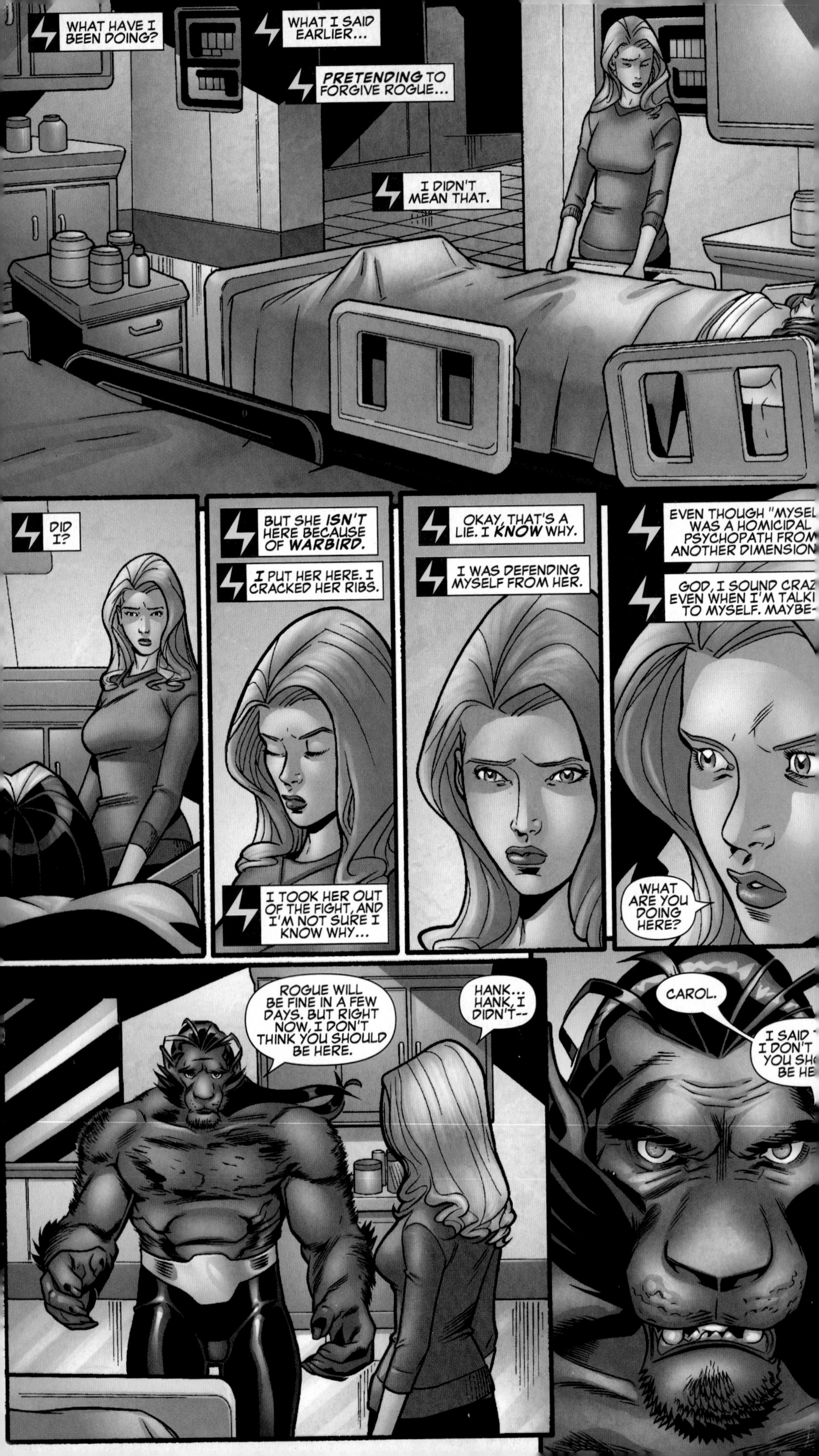
WHAT HAVE I BEEN DOING?
WHAT I SAID EARLIER...
PRETENDING TO FORGIVE ROGUE...
I DIDN'T MEAN THAT.
DID I?
BUT SHE ISN'T HERE BECAUSE OF WARBIRD.
I PUT HER HERE. I CRACKED HER RIBS.
I TOOK HER OUT OF THE FIGHT, AND I'M NOT SURE I KNOW WHY...
OKAY, THAT'S A LIE. I KNOW WHY.
I WAS DEFENDING MYSELF FROM HER.
EVEN THOUGH "MYSEL WAS A HOMICIDAL PSYCHOPATH FROM ANOTHER DIMENSION
GOD, I SOUND CRAZ EVEN WHEN I'M TALKI TO MYSELF. MAYBE-
WHAT ARE YOU DOING HERE?
ROGUE WILL BE FINE IN A FEW DAYS. BUT RIGHT NOW, I DON'T THINK YOU SHOULD BE HERE.
HANK... HANK, I DIDN'T--
CAROL.
I SAID I DON'T YOU SH BE HE

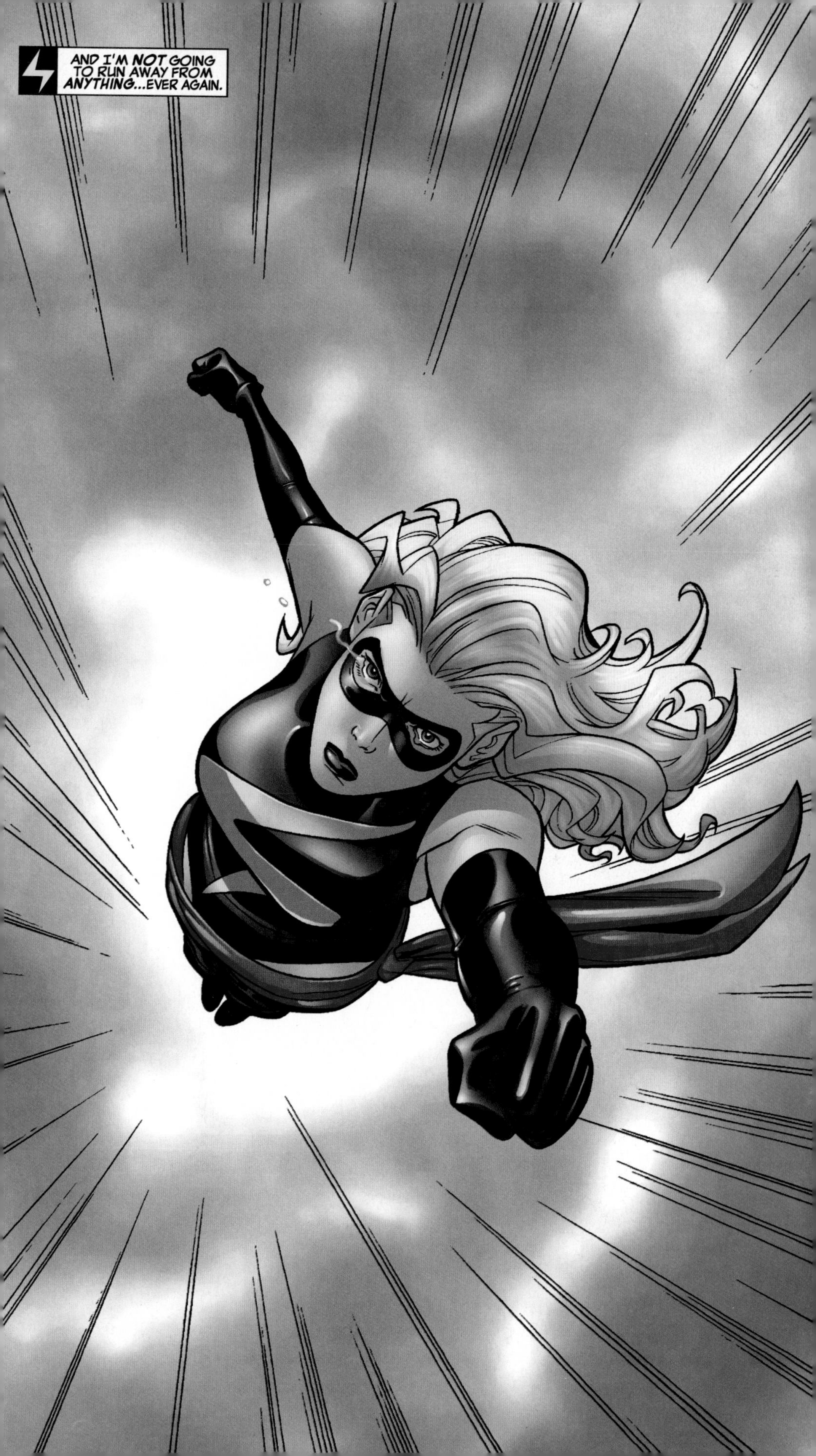
AND I'M NOT GOING TO RUN AWAY FROM ANYTHING...EVER AGAIN.

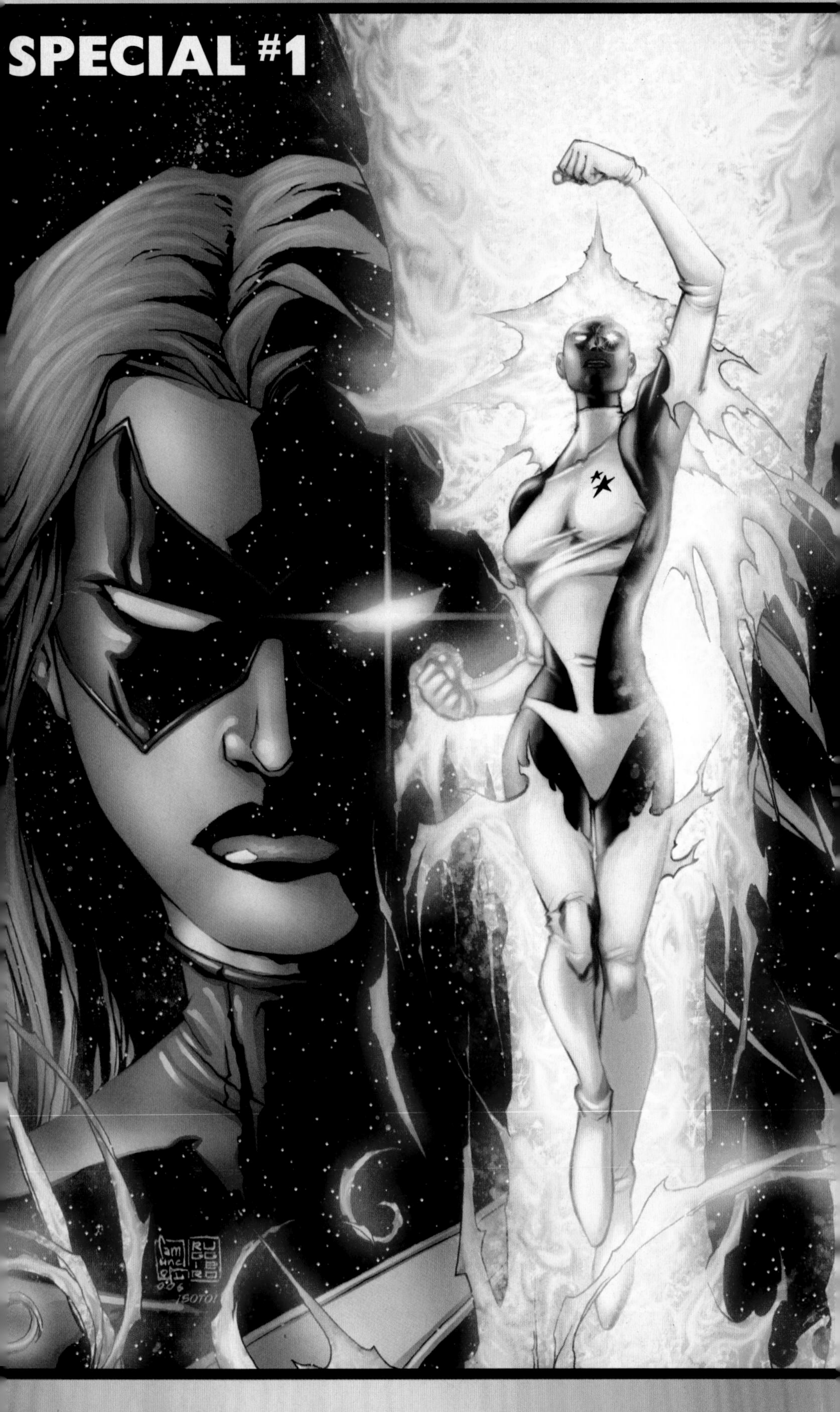
SPECIAL #1

HEY, GAVIN, I THINK I WANNA DO THIS ONE!

CHECK IT OUT.

I DUNNO, RICH. WE DID SCI-FI *YESTERDAY*.

AND I READ THAT BOOK A COUPLE YEARS BACK--

BUT THE GIRL ON THE COVER IS *HAWWT*.

Binary
a novel by
Carol Danvers

FINE. GIVE ME THE BOOK.

I THINK I KNOW A GOOD CHAPTER FOR THIS.

IT LOOKS ALL CLEAR.

IT'S SUNDAY AFTERNOON. PEOPLE HAVE BETTER THINGS TO DO.

NOT ME.

YEAH, WELL...

OKAY. HERE WE GO. NOW, THIS IS IN THE MIDDLE OF THE STORY, SO IT MIGHT NOT MAKE MUCH SENSE AT FIRST, BUT IT'S STILL PRETTY COOL.

THAT'S FINE, MAN. WHATEVER WORKS.

CHAPTER TEN. THE KEEPERS.

IN THE DAYS THAT FOLLOWED HER DEPARTURE FROM THE STAR-JAMMER SHIP...

Chapter 10:
The Keepers

In the days that followed her departure from the Starjammer ship, Binar traveled the galaxy aimlessly, lost in the great void of space and loving ever moment of it. It was a simple matter for her to aim herself at a distant star and find new adventures along the way.

Yet, Binary realized that the moments of the day that made her feel "human" or "normal" were gone. Such routine moments as a simple "hello" to another member of the Starjammer crew, or something as mundane as following a schedule for waking and sleeping... In the depths of space, these things were lost. Time carried little meaning to Binary. Companionship was a thing of the past. The cosmos itself was her home now, and she found a certai comfort in its cold expanse.

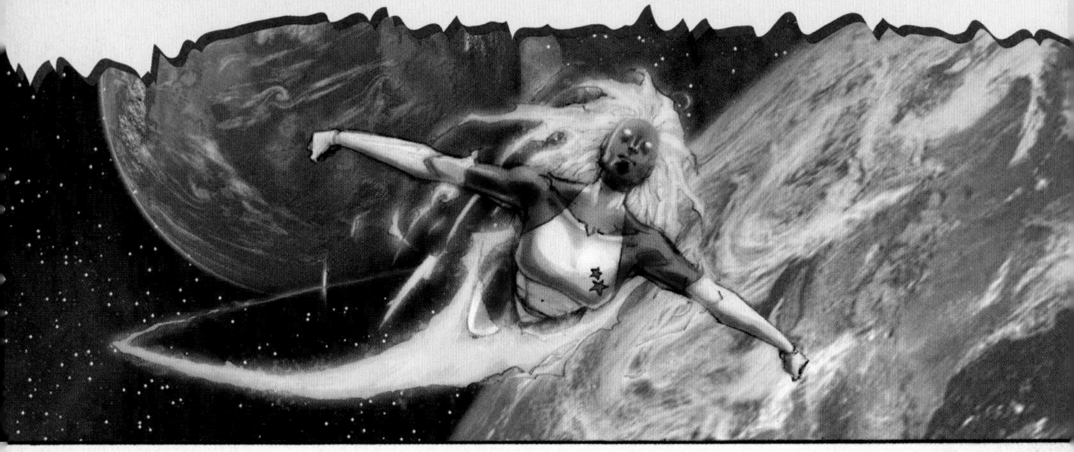

Binary was several months alone in the void before she encountered another living creature. At first, it was a gentle whisper in the back of her consciousness-

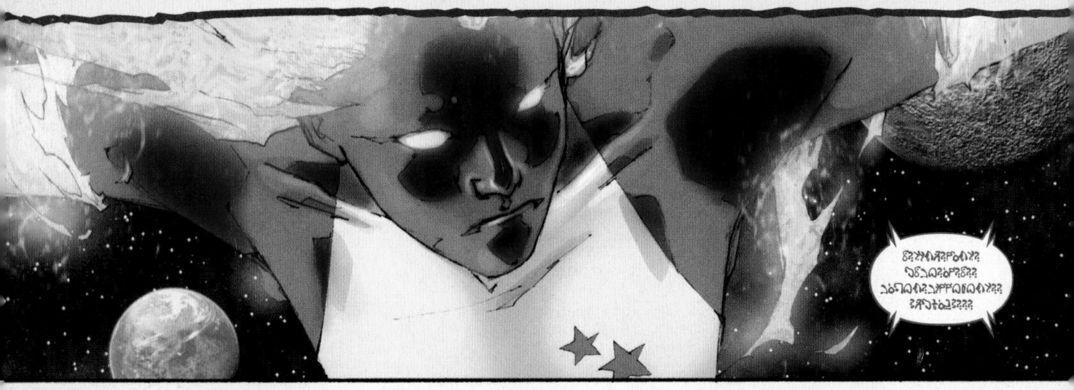

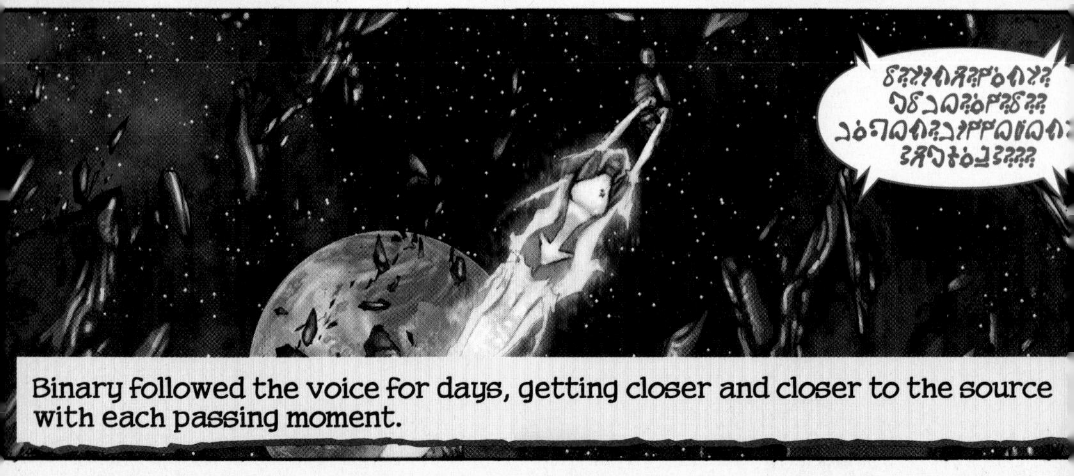
Binary followed the voice for days, getting closer and closer to the source with each passing moment.

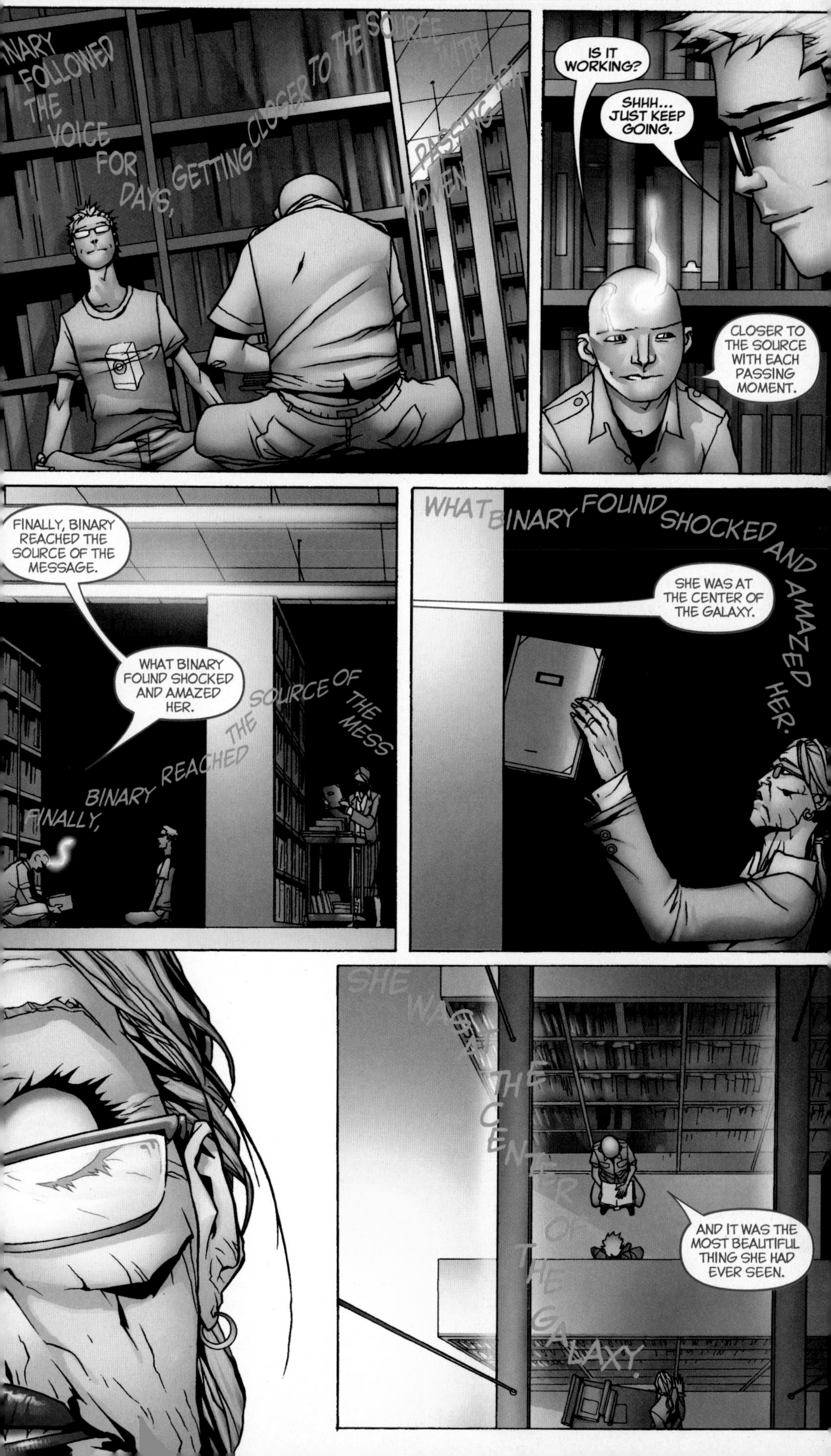
NARY FOLLOWED THE VOICE FOR DAYS, GETTING CLOSER TO THE SOURCE WITH EACH PASSING MOMEN
IS IT WORKING?
SHHH... JUST KEEP GOING.
CLOSER TO THE SOURCE WITH EACH PASSING MOMENT.
FINALLY, BINARY REACHED THE SOURCE OF THE MESSAGE.
WHAT BINARY FOUND SHOCKED AND AMAZED HER.
FINALLY, BINARY REACHED THE SOURCE OF THE MESS
WHAT BINARY FOUND SHOCKED AND AMAZED HER.
SHE WAS AT THE CENTER OF THE GALAXY.
SHE WAS AT THE CENTER OF THE GALAXY.
AND IT WAS THE MOST BEAUTIFUL THING SHE HAD EVER SEEN.

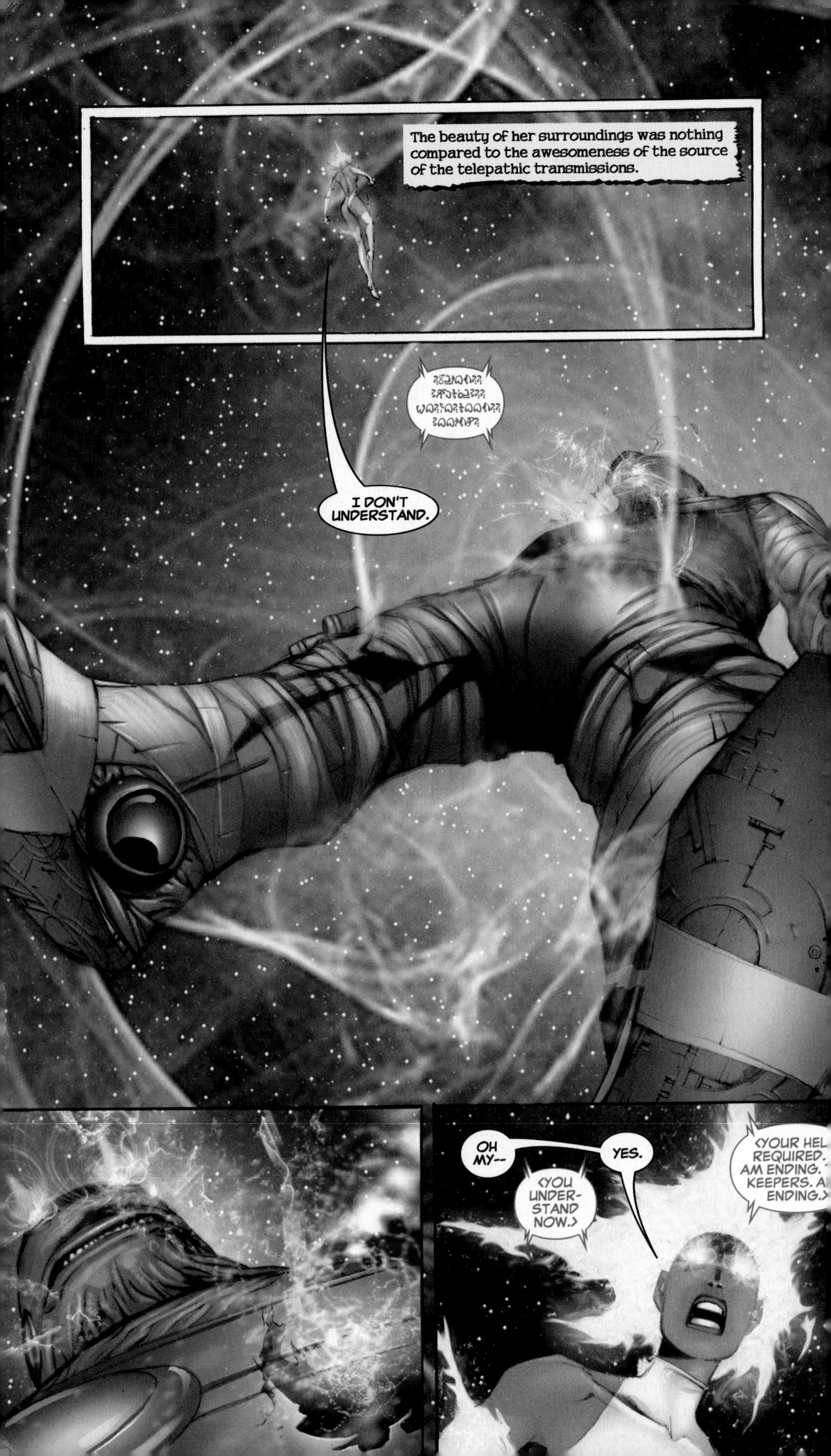

The beauty of her surroundings was nothing compared to the awesomeness of the source of the telepathic transmissions.
I DON'T UNDERSTAND.
OH MY--
<YOU UNDER-STAND NOW.>
YES.
<YOUR HEL REQUIRED. AM ENDING. KEEPERS. A ENDING.>

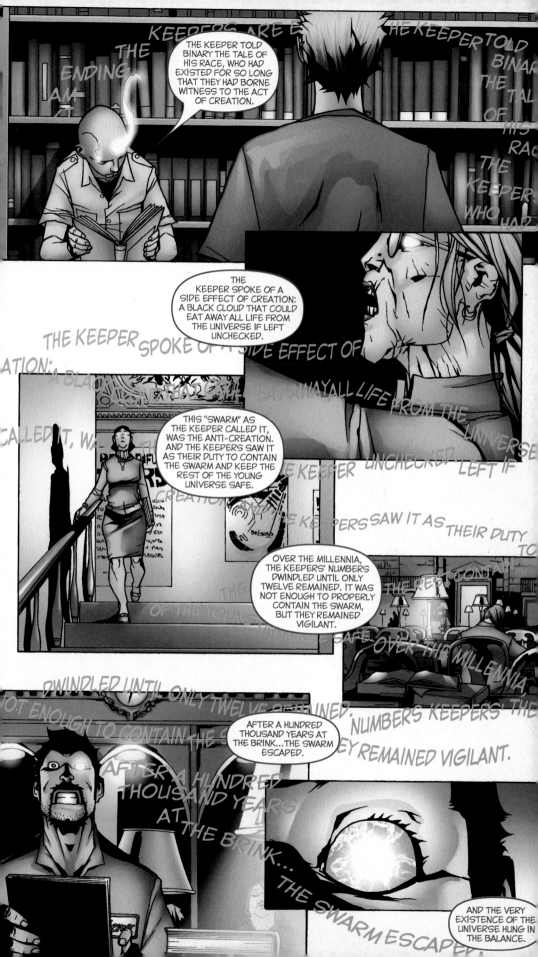

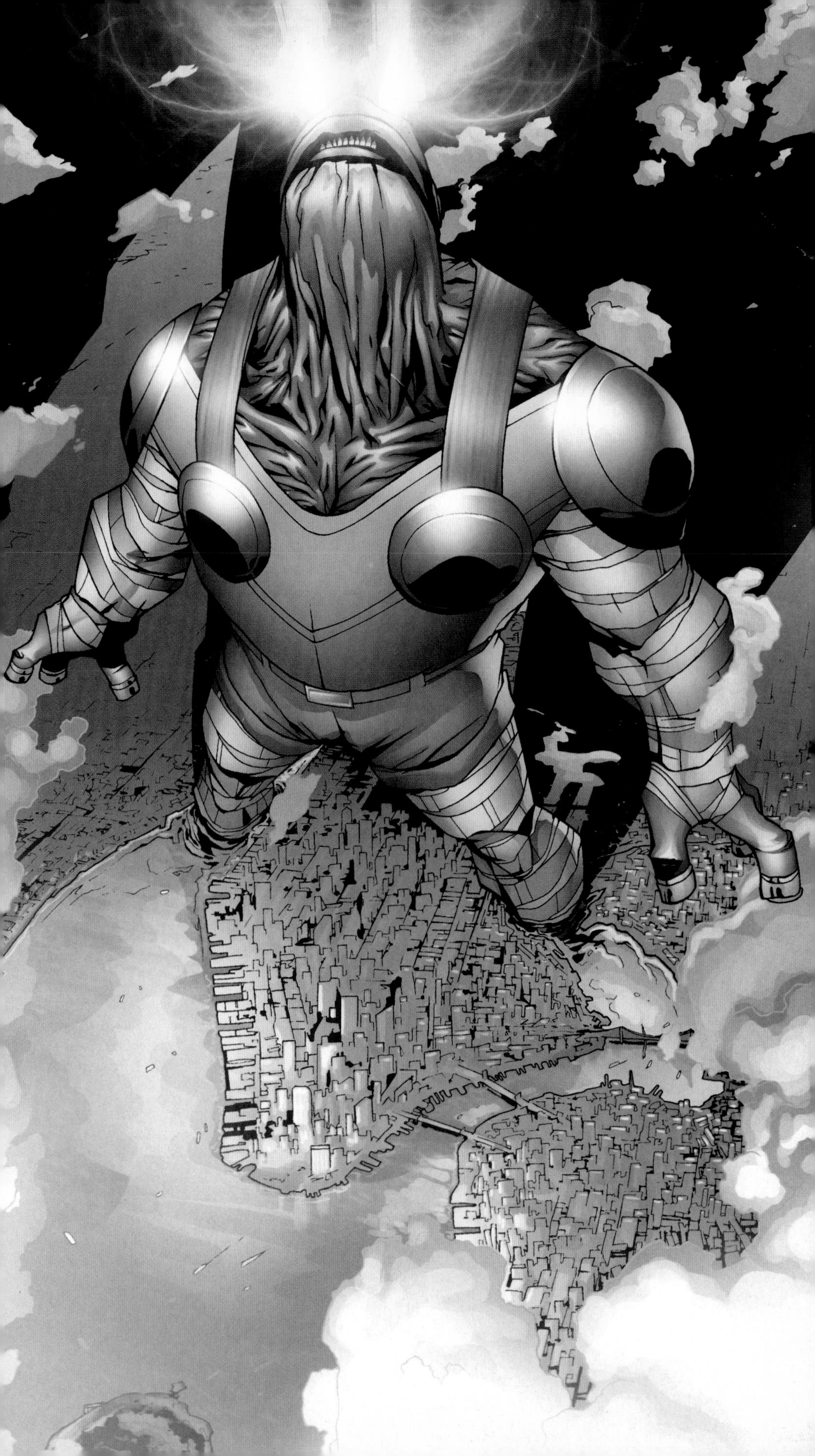

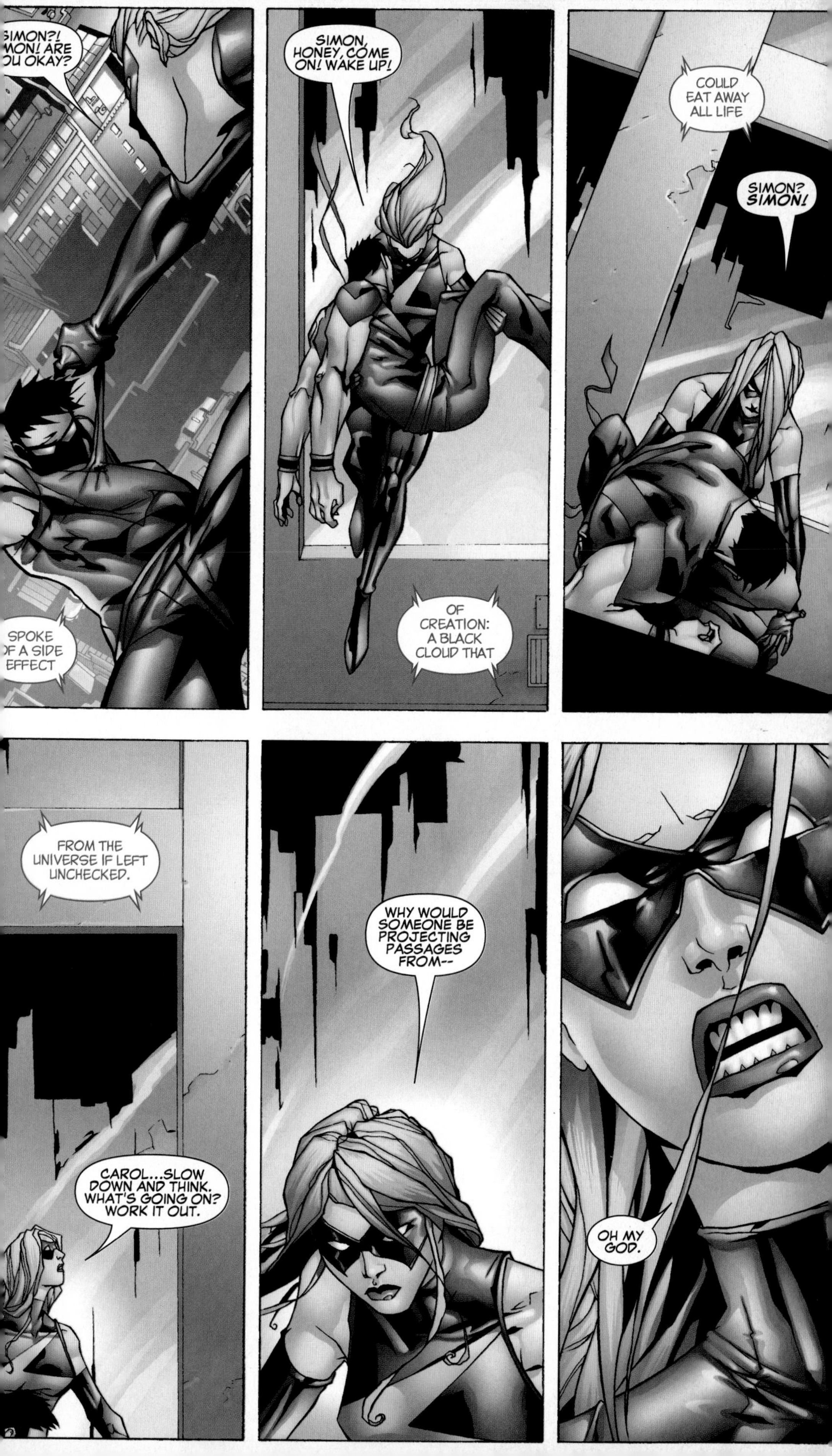
SIMON?! MON! ARE OU OKAY?
SPOKE OF A SIDE EFFECT
SIMON, HONEY, COME ON! WAKE UP!
OF CREATION: A BLACK CLOUD THAT
COULD EAT AWAY ALL LIFE
SIMON? SIMON!
FROM THE UNIVERSE IF LEFT UNCHECKED.
CAROL...SLOW DOWN AND THINK. WHAT'S GOING ON? WORK IT OUT.
WHY WOULD SOMEONE BE PROJECTING PASSAGES FROM--
OH MY GOD.

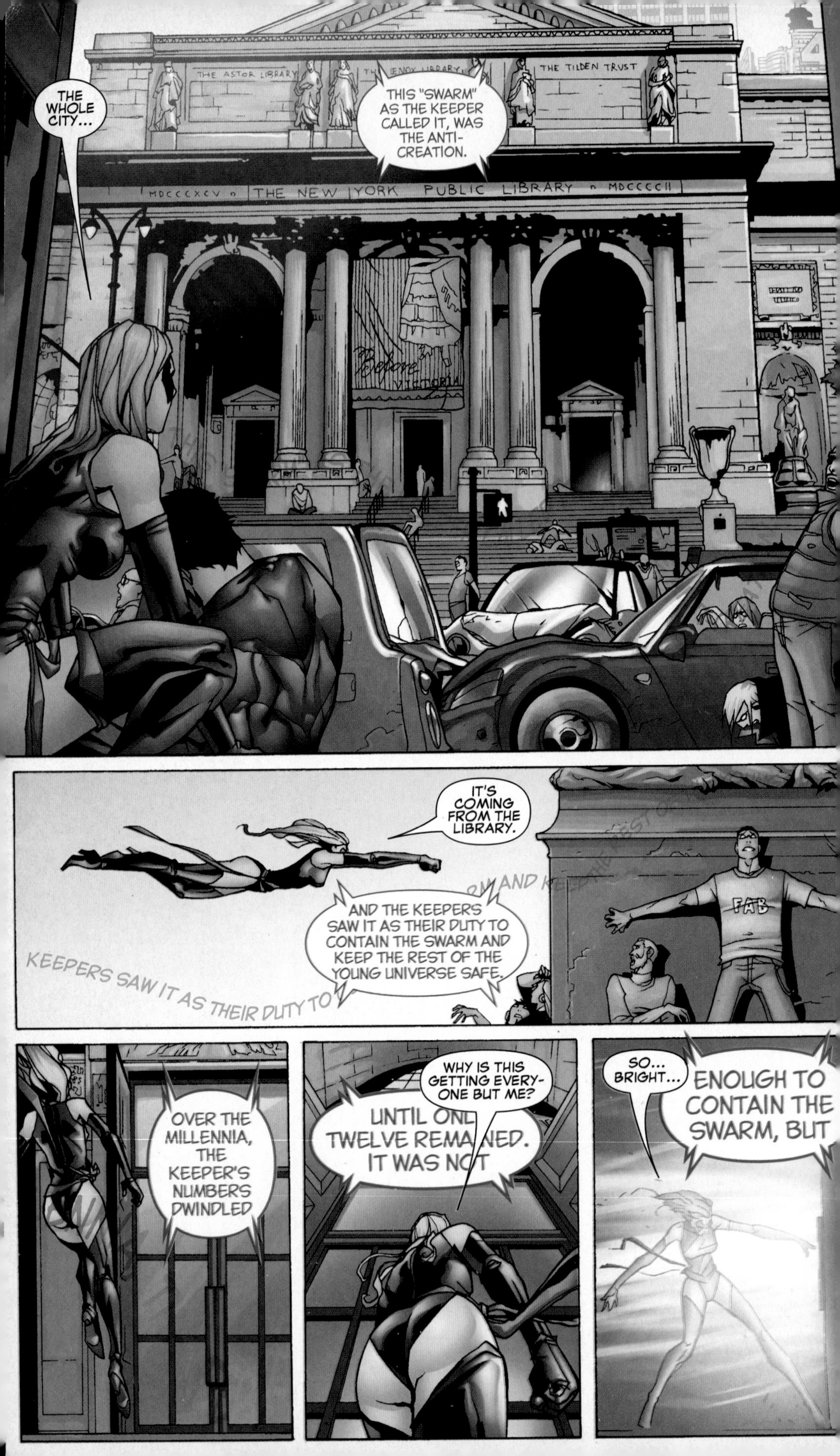
THE ASTOR LIBRARY
THE TILDEN TRUST
MDCCCXCV THE NEW YORK PUBLIC LIBRARY MDCCCCII
THE WHOLE CITY...
THIS "SWARM" AS THE KEEPER CALLED IT, WAS THE ANTI-CREATION.
Before VICTORIA
IT'S COMING FROM THE LIBRARY.
AND THE KEEPERS SAW IT AS THEIR DUTY TO CONTAIN THE SWARM AND KEEP THE REST OF THE YOUNG UNIVERSE SAFE.
FAB
OVER THE MILLENNIA, THE KEEPER'S NUMBERS DWINDLED
UNTIL ONLY TWELVE REMAINED. IT WAS NOT
WHY IS THIS GETTING EVERY-ONE BUT ME?
SO... BRIGHT...
ENOUGH TO CONTAIN THE SWARM, BUT

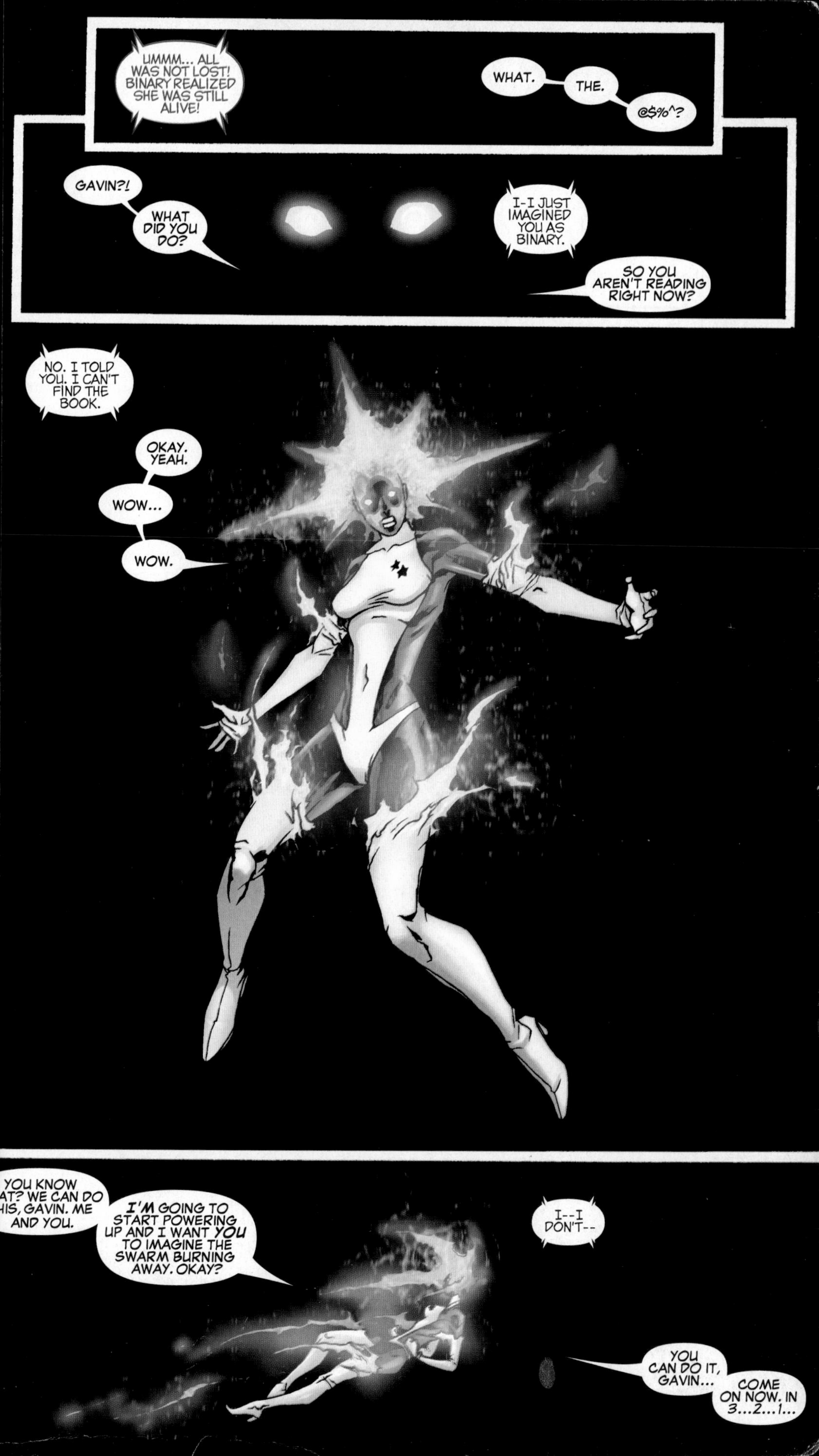
UMMM... ALL WAS NOT LOST! BINARY REALIZED SHE WAS STILL ALIVE!
WHAT.
THE.
@$%^?
GAVIN?!
WHAT DID YOU DO?
I-I JUST IMAGINED YOU AS BINARY.
SO YOU AREN'T READING RIGHT NOW?
NO. I TOLD YOU. I CAN'T FIND THE BOOK.
OKAY. YEAH.
WOW...
WOW.
YOU KNOW AT? WE CAN DO HIS, GAVIN. ME AND YOU.
I'M GOING TO START POWERING UP AND I WANT YOU TO IMAGINE THE SWARM BURNING AWAY. OKAY?
I--I DON'T--
YOU CAN DO IT, GAVIN...
COME ON NOW. IN 3...2...1...

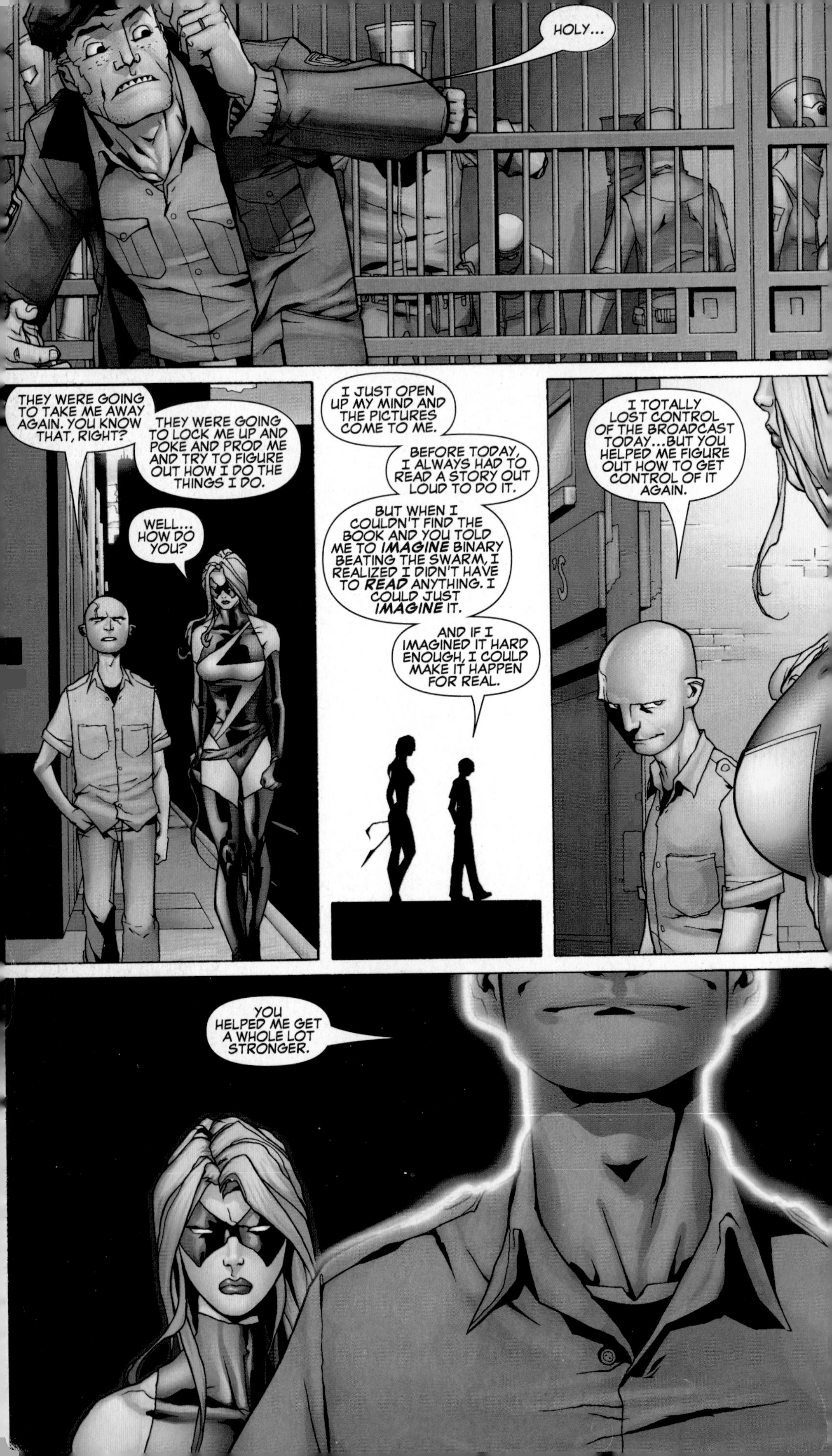

HOLY...
THEY WERE GOING TO TAKE ME AWAY AGAIN. YOU KNOW THAT, RIGHT?
THEY WERE GOING TO LOCK ME UP AND POKE AND PROD ME AND TRY TO FIGURE OUT HOW I DO THE THINGS I DO.
WELL... HOW DO YOU?
I JUST OPEN UP MY MIND AND THE PICTURES COME TO ME.
BEFORE TODAY, I ALWAYS HAD TO READ A STORY OUT LOUD TO DO IT.
BUT WHEN I COULDN'T FIND THE BOOK AND YOU TOLD ME TO *IMAGINE* BINARY BEATING THE SWARM, I REALIZED I DIDN'T HAVE TO *READ* ANYTHING. I COULD JUST *IMAGINE* IT.
AND IF I IMAGINED IT HARD ENOUGH, I COULD MAKE IT HAPPEN FOR REAL.
I TOTALLY LOST CONTROL OF THE BROADCAST TODAY...BUT YOU HELPED ME FIGURE OUT HOW TO GET CONTROL OF IT AGAIN.
YOU HELPED ME GET A WHOLE LOT STRONGER.